Architecture
for Science

Architektur
für Forschung

SCIE
NCE

Christine Nickl-Weller
Hans Nickl

BRAUN

Foreword

In the past two years, the head of a research institute has made unusually frequent appearances in the daily news. The President of the Robert Koch Institute presents his updates to TV cameras on an almost daily basis, accompanied by politicians, who play a supporting role in the strategy to cope with the COVID-19 pandemic.

The image vividly demonstrates how we have transformed into a society of science. Data are the currency of this new society, while sovereignty over such data confers power. Just as once, the agricultural society tilled the land and industrial society strived to generate energy, today's society uses data as a resource to harvest knowledge, progress and ultimately dominance. Thus we are, "on the way to a form of society in which knowledge will enjoy the highest status among all socially significant resources."[1] However, is the status we afford to science and research reflected in the buildings we construct for those fields?

Research and laboratory buildings are not regularly presented on the covers of architecture magazines. They are defined by practical considerations and programmatic constraints. Today's research buildings require a high degree of technical equipment that limits design freedoms. Old photos present Rudolf Virchow, the great pathologist and hygienist, around 120 years ago in a simple room in the Charité, crammed full with all manner of apparatus. Much has changed since Virchow's time, of which the most enduring turn of events is the technological transformation of research. As complex technologies became established in laboratories, research buildings experienced a continuous and ongoing process of specialisation. Virchow's successors now move in a highly installed environment and the emergence of robotics in laboratories will consolidate this trend.

We are also experiencing another revolution: today, knowledge can be generated everywhere and at any time. The classic workplace

Vorwort

Selten wurde der Leiter eines Forschungsinstituts so häufig in den aktuellen Nachrichten des Tages gezeigt, wie in den vergangenen 24 Monaten. Mitunter täglich trat der Präsident des Robert Koch-Instituts vor die Kameras, begleitet von Politikerinnen und Politikern als Nebendarsteller in der Strategie zur Bekämpfung der Corona-Pandemie.

Dieses Bild hält uns deutlich den Wandel unserer Gesellschaft hin zu einer Wissensgesellschaft vor Augen. Daten sind die Währung dieser Gesellschaft, Hoheit über diese Daten verleiht Macht. Wie die Agrargesellschaft den Boden nutzte, die Industriegesellschaft die Erzeugung von Energie, so nutzen wir heute Daten als Ressource, um daraus Wissen, Fortschritt und letztlich Überlegenheit zu ernten. So sind wir „auf dem Weg in eine Gesellschaftsform, in der Wissen den wichtigsten Stellenwert unter all den gesellschaftlich bedeutsamen Ressourcen haben wird".[1] Doch spiegelt sich dieser Stellenwert, den wir Wissenschaft und Forschung beimessen, auch in den Bauten wider, die wir für sie errichten?

Forschungs- und Laborbauten gehören nicht gerade zu den Bauwerken, die regelmäßig auf dem Cover der Architekturmagazine zu finden sind. Es sind Bauten, die von praktischen Überlegungen und programmatischen Zwängen definiert sind. Forschungsgebäude benötigen heute ein hohes Maß an technischer Ausstattung, welche die gestalterischen Spielräume begrenzen. Alte Fotos zeigen Rudolf Virchow, den großen Patholtogen und Hygieniker, vor etwa 120 Jahren in einem einfachen, mit allerlei losen Gerätschaften vollgestopften Zimmer der Charité. Seit Virchows Zeiten hat sich einiges getan. Nachhaltigstes Ereignis: die Technisierung der Forschung. Mit Einzug komplexer Technologien in die Labore erlebten die Forschungsgebäude eine fortschreitende und bis heute anhaltende Spezialisierung. Virchows Nachfolger bewegen sich nun in einer hochinstallierten Umgebung. Der Einzug der Robotik in die Labore wird diesen Trend weiter fortsetzen.

Gleichzeitig erleben wir eine weitere Revolution: Wissen kann heute überall und jederzeit produziert werden. Der klassische Arbeitsplatz existiert nicht mehr. Was bedeutet das für das Forschungsgebäude? Im Kern zunächst einmal nicht viel. Das Herzstück des Forschungsgebäudes – das Modul „Labor" als abstraktes Gebilde – wird zunächst fortbestehen und sich an die digitalisierte Arbeitswelt anpassen. Was sich aber ändern wird, ist das Umfeld, in das dieses Modul eingebettet sein wird. Hier lösen sich die Strukturen auf, setzten sich neu und in locker vernetzter Form wieder zusammen. Der Dokumentationsarbeitsplatz ist kein fest definierter Ort mehr. Freiflächen, Erschließungsflächen, Lounges und Terrassen können zu Orten der Kommunikation und des Austausches umfunktioniert werden. Der gesamte Typ Forschungsgebäude

no longer exists. What does that mean for the research building? Essentially, not much to begin with. The heart of the research building – the abstract structure of the "laboratory" module – will continue to exist and adapt to the digitised working world. What will change is the environment in which this module is embedded. These structures will be broken down, reconfigured and reconnected in a loosely networked form. The documentation workplace is no longer a defined location, while open spaces, connecting walkways, lounges and terraces can be converted into places for communicating and exchanging information. The entire type of a research building surrounding the laboratory module will be able to redefine itself. Equally, the relationship between the research building and nearby urban spaces will change.

     This book presents research buildings together with their internal and external relationships. It reveals the diversity of research and laboratory architecture, ranging from major elements to small details, from the scale of urban environments to typologies and on to façade elements. It scrutinises a colourful array of buildings, including exterior identities and interior configurations. Far from intending to be an exhaustive investigation of research and laboratory buildings, this volume aims to demonstrate aspects that we have found important during the period of more than twenty years in which we have been working on architecture for research. Many articles by experts from various fields complement this personal perspective. Finally, we take a look into the future, picking up on some themes that will fundamentally change research buildings and their architecture.

Christine Nickl-Weller and Hans Nickl
December 2021

1
Bernd Streich:
Stadtplanung in der
Wissensgesellschaft.
VS Verlag für
Sozialwissenschaf-
ten, Wiesbaden
2005 [trans.]

rund um das Labormodul wird sich neu definieren können. Genauso verändert sich die Beziehung zwischen Forschungsgebäude und Stadt.

In diesem Buch werden Forschungsgebäuden mit ihren inneren und äußeren Beziehungen dargestellt. Vom Großen bis ins Kleine, vom urbanen Umfeld über die Typologie bis zum Fassadendetail offenbart sich die Vielfalt der Forschungs- und Laborarchitektur. Ein bunter Blumenstrauß an Gebäuden, deren äußere Identität und innere Ausgestaltung näher unter die Lupe genommen werden. Weit entfernt davon, den Forschungs- und Laborbau erschöpfend aufarbeiten zu wollen, sollen auf den nachfolgenden Seiten vielmehr Aspekte aufgezeigt werden, die uns in den über zwanzig Jahren, die wir uns mit Architektur für Forschung auseinandersetzen, von Bedeutung erschienen. Viele Beiträge von Expertinnen und Experten verschiedener Fachbereiche erweitern diese persönliche Perspektive. Am Schluss blicken wir in die Zukunft und greifen einige Themen auf, welche sowohl das Forschungsgebäude als auch deren Architektur nachhaltig verändern werden.

Christine Nickl-Weller und Hans Nickl
im Dezember 2021

1
Vgl. Bernd Streich: Stadtplanung in der Wissensgesellschaft. VS Verlag für Sozialiwissenschaften, Wiesbaden 2005

Pioneering
architecture for
science:
SC Johnson
Research Tower
by Frank L. Wright,
1950
Wegweisende
Wissenschafts-
architektur:
SC Johnson
Research Tower
von Frank L. Wright,
1950

1 City

Stadt → 10–51

¹ Science cities

Research drives innovation forward. Thus, science and teaching not only contribute to a city or region's reputation and status in the field of research, but also bring growth and prosperity. The political, scientific and social interrelationships between scientific institutions and their urban context are diverse. This book focuses on the structural relationships. What relationships exist between architecture for science and the urban context? And how have these relationships changed with the passing of time? Various examples of major cities demonstrate the trend towards a mixture of research structures and public urban life. Is the closed university and research campus becoming obsolete? The following chapters shed light on these questions from the perspective of planners and users.

Forschung ist der Motor der Innovation. Wissenschaft und Lehre bringen daher einer Stadt oder einer Region nicht nur Ehre und einen Stellenwert in der Forschung ein, sondern auch Wachstum und Prosperität. Die politischen, wirtschaftlichen und gesellschaftlichen Verflechtungen zwischen Einrichtungen der Wissenschaft und ihrem urbanen Kontext sind vielfältig. Hier soll aber der Fokus auf die baulichen Beziehungen gelegt werden. Welche Beziehungen bestehen zwischen „Architecture for Science" und dem städtischen Kontext? Und wie haben diese Beziehungen sich im Laufe der Zeit gewandelt? Am Beispiel verschiedener Metropolen erkennen wir einen Trend zur Durchmischung von Forschungsstrukturen und öffentlichem urbanem Leben. Ist der in sich geschlossene Universitäts- und Forschungscampus ein Auslaufmodell? Die folgenden Kapitel beleuchten diese Fragen aus Perspektive der Planer und der Nutzer.

1.1 Transforming relationship between campus and city

ANOUK KUITENBROUWER

The change narrative

So called disruptions caused by digitisation, big data and the sharing economy are leading to a shift in many areas of human activity: living, working, leisure, education, mobility, manufacturing, trade and logistics are currently undergoing radical changes. While in certain areas we can make an educated guess about the impact on cities and urban life, in other areas, we are at the very start of this process of change.

What these changes seem to have in common is that pairs of opposites, such as private-public or life-work and city-countryside are dissolving. Translated into spatial design, we observe a change towards hybridization and an ever-increasing need for flexibility. Daily life is less and less strictly separated into categories such as working, leisure and learning. Instead, many hybrids of these categories are developing. Similarly, spaces are increasingly used simultaneously for different purposes.

As urban planners and architects, whether we question or accommodate these changes in our practice, we have to look past current trends and think beyond design to create urban environments and buildings that stand the test of time. This text addresses aspects of change in the working world, because this is where the change in urban development is currently most dynamic.

The innovation economy is an urban phenomenon

Preceded by a long history of academic campus typologies, from the 1960s onwards, science and technology parks grew as suburban out-of-town developments across Europe. For sectors that require control and ownership of intellectual property or that have specific conditions in terms of emissions and logistics, these campuses still offer an efficient and necessary location, but as an attractive location for their workers, they are challenging. That is why many existing and emerging sectors that do not have specific suburban needs have turned their focus back to the city.

Because cities bring together a diversity of sectors, international networks and cultural life, they are the 21st-century testing ground for innovation and cross-fertilization.

The innovation economy that spans industries such as advanced manufacturing, life sciences, robotics or

1.1 Campus & Stadt, Beziehung im Wandel

ANOUK KUITENBROUWER

Das Narrativ des Wandels

So genannte Disruptionen, hervorgerufen durch die Digitalisierung, Big Data und die Sharing Economy, führen zu einem Wandel in vielen Bereichen menschlicher Tätigkeitsfelder: Wohnen, Arbeit, Freizeit, Bildungswesen, Mobilität, Produktion und Fertigung, Handel und Logistik erleben derzeit radikale Veränderungen. Während wir für bestimmte Bereiche auf Kenntnis gestützte Vermutungen bezüglich der Auswirkung auf Städte und urbanes Leben treffen können, befinden sich andere Bereiche gerade erst ganz am Anfang dieses Prozesses.

Diese Umwälzungen haben allem Anschein nach gemeinsam, dass sich Gegensätze wie privat-öffentlich, Life-Work oder Stadt-Land auflösen. Übertragen auf die Raumgestaltung beobachten wir einen Wandel hin zur Hybridisierung und ein stetig wachsendes Bedürfnis nach Flexibilität. Das alltägliche Leben ist immer weniger streng in Kategorien wie Arbeit, Freizeit und Bildung unterteilt, sondern vielmehr entwickeln sich etliche Hybride dieser Kategorien. Gleichermaßen werden Räume zunehmend simultan für verschiedenste Zwecke genutzt.

Als Stadtplaner und Architekten müssen wir, ob wir diesen Wandel in unserer Praxis nun hinterfragen oder aufnehmen, auch jenseits aktueller Trends suchen und Design weiterdenken, um urbane Umgebungen und Gebäude zu schaffen, die die Zeit auch überdauern. Dieser Text beleuchtet Aspekte des Wandels in der Arbeitswelt, weil der Wandel im Städtebau hier zur Zeit am dynamischsten ist.

Die Innovationswirtschaft ist ein urbanes Phänomen

Von einer langen Geschichte akademischer Campustypologien vorausgegangen, wuchsen ab den 1960er Jahren in ganz Europa Wissenschafts- und Technologieparks als suburbane, vorstädtische Entwicklungen. Für Branchen, die Kontrolle und Schutz des geistigen Eigentums verlangen, oder in Bezug auf Emissionen und Logistik besondere Voraussetzungen haben, können derartige Campusse nach wie vor einen effektiven und auch notwendigen Standort darstellen, doch als ein für ihre Arbeiterschaft attraktiver Standort sind sie eher als Herausforderung anzusehen. Hierin ist dann auch der Grund zu finden, weshalb viele bereits existierende und auch im Entstehen begriffene Branchen ohne diese vorstädtischen Bedürfnisse ihren Fokus wieder zurück auf die Stadt gerichtet haben.

Weil Städte eine Vielfalt an Branchen, internationale Netzwerke und kulturelles Leben zusammenbringen, sind sie im 21. Jahrhundert zum Versuchsfeld für Innovation und gegenseitige Befruchtung

001
ETH Science City
Zurich, KCAP,
since 2005
Science City,
ETH Zürich, KCAP,
seit 2005

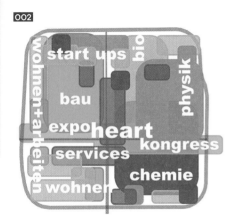

002–004
ETH Science
City Zurich, KCAP,
since 2005
Science City,
ETH Zürich, KCAP,
seit 2005

clean energy has rediscovered these urban qualities; people are more closely connected and markets, finance and other enablers are better accessible. From isolated innovation to open innovation, the new model of innovation districts shows its high appreciation of "cityness" as defined by Saskia Sassen[1] – complexity, density, diversity of people and cultures, as well as a layering of the old and the new. Innovation will no longer just happen in separated laboratories, in isolated buildings and in the middle of nowhere. Instead, it will happen on streets, squares, shared spaces, cafes and common areas in mixed-use buildings.

Today, innovation areas take many different forms. Some are campuses located at the edge of cities or along transport routes, benefiting from an exclusive environment, good access and links to universities. Others are designated districts that benefit from government policy and investment programmes. Some are intended to achieve success in one specific sector while others are designed to accommodate a functional mix.

Both, the campus and the district, are distinct urban typologies that have their own design challenges. Because the urban models seem to be a better answer to changing demands by innovative companies and knowledge workers, Jacques van Dinteren and Paul Jansen in "The 4th industrial revolution: considerations for science parks to remain competitive"[2] suggest there could be competition between science and technology parks and innovation districts. But the science and technology park concept can develop further and keeps its own position among innovation area typologies, provided that they adjust to the new era. We see opportunities for new types of co-existence and sometimes hybridisation between functions that create attractive living, working and leisure environments, as well as successfully accommodating the innovation economy, both in campus typologies and urban innovation districts. It is important to consider both types as focus points that co-exist within an innovative region.

The urbanised campus: the challenge of science and technology parks

However attractive the original campus concepts might have been, more than half a century after their widespread implementation, it is clear that most science and technology park concepts did not lead to attractive environments for their users. They are hampered by their isolated location, their mono-functional disposition and their remoteness from mixed urban structures. At the same time, in many cases, the city caught up with the campus and eventually integrated it into the urban spatial structure. When the Science City

geworden. Die Innovationswirtschaft, die Wirtschaftszweige wie fortgeschrittene Fertigungstechnologie, Biowissenschaft, Robotik oder saubere Energie umfasst, hat diese urbanen Qualitäten wiederentdeckt; Menschen sind enger vernetzt und Märkte, das Finanzwesen und andere Enabler sind einfacher zugänglich. Von isolierter Innovation zu offener Innovation zeigt das neue Modell von Innovationsbezirken in hohem Grad seine Wertschätzung für den von Saskia Sassen[1] geprägten Begriff der „Cityness" – Vielschichtigkeit, Dichte, Vielfalt von Menschen und Kulturen und eine Schichtung von Altem und Neuem. Innovation würde nicht länger nur in separaten Laboren in isolierten Gebäuden mitten im Nirgendwo stattfinden. Stattdessen wird sie sich auf Straßen und Plätzen, in gemeinsamen Räumen (sog. shared spaces), in Cafés und Gemeinschaftsflächen in gemischt genutzten Gebäuden abspielen.

Heutzutage können Innovationsräume viele unterschiedliche Formen annehmen. Manche sind am Stadtrand oder entlang von Transportrouten gelegene Campusse, die von einer exklusiven Umgebung und gutem Zugang und Verbindungen zu Universitäten profitieren. Weitere sind ausgewiesene Distrikte, die von der Regierungspolitik und Investitionsprogrammen profitieren. Andere sind auf den Erfolg einer spezifischen Branche angelegt, während wieder andere für die Beherbergung einer Funktionsmischung konzipiert sind.

Beide, sowohl der Campus als auch der Distrikt, sind verschiedene städtebauliche Typologien mit ganz eigenen Herausforderungen an das Design. Da die urbanen Modelle allem Anschein nach die bessere Antwort für die sich wandelnden Anforderungen durch die Innovationswirtschaft und Wissensarbeiter bereit halten, vermuten Jacques van Dinteren und Paul Jansen in „The 4th industrial revolution: considerations for science parks to remain competitive"[2], dass es zum Wettbewerb zwischen Wissenschafts- und Technologieparks und Innovationsdistrikten kommen könnte. Doch das Konzept des Wissenschafts- und Technologieparks kann sich weiterentwickeln und seine Stellung innerhalb der Innovationsraumtypologien behalten, sofern es an die neue Zeit angepasst wird. Wir sehen sowohl in der Campustypologie als auch in urbanen Innovationsdistrikten Möglichkeiten für neue Formen der Koexistenz und bisweilen der Hybridisierung von Funktionen, die attraktives Wohnen, Arbeiten und Freizeitumfelder schaffen und die Innovationswirtschaft gut beherbergen. Es ist wichtig beide Typen als koexistierende Schwerpunkte innerhalb einer innovativen Region zu begreifen.

Der urbanisierte Campus: die Herausforderung für Wissenschafts- und Technologieparks

So attraktiv die originalen Campuskonzepte auch gewesen sein mögen, über ein halbes Jahrhundert nach ihrer weitverbreiteten Realisierung ist klar,

Masterplan for the ETH Zurich was developed by KCAP Architects & Planners in 2004, the aim of the project was to integrate the city and university, both on the campus and in terms of reconciliation with its context. This approach to integrate features of an urban environment within the exclusive conditions of the campus (as described by Bruce Katz and Julie Wagner in 2014 in "The Rise of Innovation Districts. A New Geography of Innovation in America"[3] with respect to urbanised science parks) has been a continuing narrative through a generation of campus masterplans by KCAP. In the case of the Science City for ETH Zurich, more than 10 years later, we can confirm that a gradual development towards a more attractive environment has been established. → 001–004

At Munich Airport the 2017 LabCampus Masterplan for a new type of innovation campus went one step further in creating a "simulation of urbanity" by integrating urban features in order to create more attractive conditions for the future working community. LabCampus distinguishes itself from other classic business parks through its mix of classic offices with light industrial uses such as prototyping, testing and showrooms accompanied with entertainment, lifestyle and sport. The intention was to create a balanced mix of single and multi-tenant buildings for diverse companies that tap into Bavaria's industrial strengths with strong global players and a superb mobility/advanced manufacturing/robotics sector and the proximity to the airport with an Asian network. This programmatic strategy is supported by urban design guidelines to steer variation in typology, height and floor-area-ratio, and to stimulate architectural variation, mixing high-end with more generic architecture and even temporary structures. Time will tell whether the development can resist the pressure to maximize value through office mono-functionality and whether a programmatic diversification that requires strong management will be pursued. → 005–007

Drawing from these masterplanning experiences, we have learned that for the creation of attractive innovation environments, urban design must go hand in hand with programmatic strategies. Attracting and combining multiple target groups beyond corporate and academic users increases the robustness of the development. Enhancing the functional mix, especially with housing, is positive for the liveliness of the urban environment and helps establish attractive service levels and accessibility. These specific environments have a strong need for area management, so an emphasis on community management and amenities is necessary. While as masterplanners, we can prepare the ground for high-quality spatial design, the success of a development will depend to a large extent on intelligent long-term programmatic and area management strategies.

18

dass Wissenschafts- und Technologieparkkonzepte meist eher nicht zu attraktiven Umfeldern für ihre Nutzer geführt haben. Ihre isolierte Lage, ihre mono-funktionale Ausrichtung und ihre Distanz zu gemischtwirtschaftlichen urbanen Strukturen stellen eine klare Beeinträchtigung dar. Gleichzeitig hat die Stadt in vielen Fällen zum Campus aufgeschlossen und ihn schlussendlich in das urbane Raumgefüge integriert. Als 2004 der Science City Masterplan für die ETH Zürich durch KCAP Architects & Planners ausgearbeitet wurde, war das Ziel des Projekts sowohl auf dem Campus als auch in Stimmigkeit mit dem Kontext, die Integration von Stadt und Universität. Dieser von Bruce Katz und Julie Wagner in „The Rise of Innovation Districs. A New Geography of Innovation in Amercia"[3] 2014 „urbanisierter Wissenschaftspark" genannte Ansatz, der die Integration von Elementen urbaner Umgebungen innerhalb der exklusiven Gegebenheiten des Campus vorsieht, ist ein anhaltendendes Narrativ innerhalb einer von KCAP erarbeiteten Generation an Campus-Masterplänen. Im Falle der Science City für die ETH Zürich können wir, mehr als zehn Jahre später, bestätigen, dass eine schrittweise Entwicklung hin zu einem attraktiveren Umfeld stattgefunden hat. → 001–004

Am Münchener Flughafen ging der LabCampus Masterplan von 2017 für einen neuen Typus von Innovationscampus mit der Erzeugung einer „Simulation von Urbanität", durch die Integration von urbaner Funktionalität für die Erschaffung attraktiverer Konditionen für die zukünftige Working Community, einen Schritt weiter. LabCampus zeichnet sich, im Vergleich mit anderen klassischen Business Parks, durch den Mix von klassischen Büros und der Nutzung durch Leichtindustrie, darunter Prototypenentwicklung, Erprobung und Showrooms, sowie Entertainment, Lifestyle und Sport aus. Es war die Absicht, eine ausgewogene Mischung aus Single- und Multitenantobjekten für diverse Unternehmen zu schaffen, die so Bayerns industrielle Stärke mit seinen großen Global Playern und hervorragenden Sektoren in den Bereichen Mobility, fortgeschrittene Fertigungstechnik und Robotik anzapfen können, während die Nähe zum Flughafen sie mit asiatischen Netzwerken verbindet. Diese programmatische Strategie wird durch städtebauliche Richtlinien derart unterstützt, dass diese Richtlinien für Variation in Typologie, Höhe und Geschossflächenzahl sorgen und somit architektonische Vielfalt, einen Mix aus High-End und eher generischer Architektur, sogar temporären Strukturen, anregen. Die Zeit wird zeigen, ob die Planung dem Druck der Wertschöpfung und -maximierung durch vornehmlich Büroflächen und resultierender Monofunktionalität standhalten kann, und ob die programmatische Vielfalt, die ein starkes Management erfordert, weiter verfolgt werden wird. → 005–007

Anhand der Erfahrungen aus diesen Masterplanungsverfahren haben wir gelernt, dass Städteplanung und programmatische Strategien für die Errichtung attraktiver Innovationsräume Hand in Hand

005

005
LabCampus,
Munich Airport,
KCAP, since 2018
LabCampus,
Flughafen München,
KCAP, seit 2018

19

The adaptive re-use area:
Opportunities for innovation districts

As part of a broader process of re-urbanisation and densification, areas or neighbourhoods are being transformed to attract the innovation economy. This development is mostly concentrated in former industrial areas, near established business, financial and creative industry districts and around areas with good public transport. In his book "City as a Loft",[4] Kees Christiaanse has called these processes "adaptive re-use", while Bruce Katz and Julie Wagner defined them as "re-imagined urban areas" in the above mentioned article. Prior to the rise of the innovation economy, these transformation strategies where practiced by other sectors such as the creative industry.

Some innovation districts, like the 22@Barcelona, are heavily planned and scripted, while others like Harvard University have grown organically. →008 In innovation districts, companies of different sizes typically cluster and connect with other start-ups, incubators and accelerators. If centred around existing major institutions, Katz and Wagner call them the "anchor plus models", which can apply to adaptive re-use areas as well as to the urbanised campus. Although there are overlaps between high-tech sector environments and traditional urban working developments, there are also some distinct needs that real estate and urban development have to respond to. Specific needs, such as flexible and diverse space offerings and contracts, shared and collaborative spaces with stimulating office design, professional support for start-ups, and networking and socialising opportunities, often explain the explosion of co-working facilities. Therefore, innovation districts are probably more characterised by their economic and networking assets than by their specific urban typology.

As Kees Christiaanse puts it in "Campus to City: Urban Design for Universities",[5] when he compares how inner-city university campuses like the TU Berlin or the London School of Economics are integrated in the city, "the formidable urban qualities of such an unplanned university raise the question as to whether we should actually design universities at all or perhaps rather allow them to infiltrate and transform a city district through improvisation and embroidering existing structures." Projected onto innovation districts, it seems that what works for creating attractive urban areas also works for innovation districts. The creation of a functional mix of residential and other urban functions, the quality of public transport access and the walkability and ground floor activity are all important for creating attractive and comfortable urban environments. The specificity of innovation districts lies more in the above-mentioned assets and

gehen müssen. Gewinnung und Einbindung vielfältiger Zielgruppen, neben Firmen und akademischen Nutzern, erhöhen die Robustheit derartiger Entwicklungen. Die Erweiterung der funktionalen Mischung, insbesondere durch Wohnraum, wirkt sich positiv auf die Lebendigkeit der urbanen Umgebung aus und hilft bei der Etablierung attraktiver Dienstumfänge und der Zugänglichkeit.

Diese konkreten Umgebungen haben ein ausgeprägtes Bedürfnis eines Gebietsmanagements, eine hohe Gewichtung von Quartiersmanagement und öffentlichen Einrichtungen ist daher erforderlich. Während wir als Masterplaner den Grundstein für eine hochqualitative Raumgestaltung legen können, hängt der Erfolg einer solchen Entwicklung jedoch zu einem großen Teil an langfristigen, intelligenten programmatischen und Gebietsmanagementstrategien.

Die adaptive re-use area:
die Chancen von Innovationsdistrikten

Als Teil eines umfassenden Prozesses von Reurbanisierung und Nutzungsverdichtung werden Gegenden oder Viertel umgestaltet, um die Innovationswirtschaft anzuziehen. Diese Entwicklung findet vornehmlich in ehemaligen Industriegebieten, in der Nähe zu etablierten Unternehmen, Finanzvierteln und der Kreativwirtschaft, sowie in vom Personennahverkehr erschlossenen Gegenden, statt. Im Buch „City as a Loft"[4] bezeichnet Kees Christiaanse diesen Prozess als „Adaptive Re-use", während Bruce Katz und Julie Wagner im oben genannten Artikel von „re-imagined urban areas" sprechen. Vor dem Aufkommen der Innovativwirtschaft wurden diese Transformationsstrategien unter anderem von der Kreativwirtschaft umgesetzt.

Einige dieser Innovationsdistrikte, etwa 22@Barcelona, sind erheblich geplant und gelenkt worden, während andere, wie z. B. die Harvard Universität, eher organisch und natürlich gewachsen sind. →008 In Innovationsdistrikten finden sich typischerweise Firmen unterschiedlicher Größe, die sich mit anderen Start-Ups, Inkubatoren und Acceleratoren vernetzen. Zentrieren sich diese Distrikte um existierende, bedeutende Institutionen, sprechen Katz und Wagner vom „Anchor Plus model", welches sowohl auf adaptive re-use areas als auch den urbanisierten Campus angewendet werden kann. Wenngleich diverse Überschneidungspunkte zwischen Umgebungen des High-Tech Sektors und traditionellen urbanen Arbeitervierteln existieren, gibt es dennoch einige sehr spezifische Anforderungen, denen Liegenschaften und Stadtplanung Sorge tragen müssen. Spezifische Anforderungen wie flexible und vielfältige Raumangebote und Verträge, geteilte und gemeinschaftlich genutzte Räume mit animierendem Bürodesign, professioneller Support für Start-Ups, sowie Networkingmöglichkeiten und Gelegenheiten zum Sozialisieren und Zusammenkommen erklären oftmals ein explosionsartiges Aufkommen von Coworking Spaces. Daher sind Innovationsdistrikte wohl eher durch ihre wirtschaftlichen und

006–007
**Science Lab
Campus,
Munich Airport,
KCAP, since 2018**
Science Lab
Campus, Flughafen
München, KCAP,
seit 2018

008
Harvard University's
history dates back
to the 17th century.
SOM developed
a future-oriented
framework for
the organically
grown campus.
Harvard University
North Campus,
Cambridge,
SOM, 2002–12

Die Geschichte der
Havard University
reicht bis ins 17. Jhr.
zurück. SOM ent-
wickelte einen zu-
kunftsoffenen
Rahmenplan für den
organisch gewach-
senen Campus.
Harvard University
North Campus,
Cambridge,
SOM, 2002-12

the successful stakeholder management to create an eco-system of diverse user groups and regulations that enable, rather than limit development.

Nowadays, innovation is everywhere. All metropolitan areas and even mid-size cities are developing their innovation campuses, districts or incubators. This is why the positioning of a development, based on thorough context analysis, is essential: to carefully consider what makes a specific location unique, which specific sectors are already driving regional innovation, which companies or organisations can become an anchor within a development and how the development will tap on or create an attractive urban environment for the working population. Those aspects are all key when setting out for the challenge.

Networkingmöglichkeiten charakterisiert als durch ihre spezifische städtebauliche Typologie.

Wie Kees Christiaanse es in „Campus to City: Urban Design for Universities"[5] sagt, wo er anhand der TU Berlin und der London School of Economics vergleicht, wie innerstädtische Universitätscampusse in die Stadt integriert sind: „die beachtlichen urbanen Qualitäten einer solchen ungeplanten Universität werfen die Frage auf, ob wir Universitäten eigentlich überhaupt planen sollten, oder ihr erlauben sollten sich selbst in einen städtischen Bezirk und bestehende Strukturen einzuweben und diese so zu infiltrieren und durch Improvisation letztlich zu transformieren." Bezogen auf Innovationsdistrikte scheint es, dass was bei der Erschaffung attraktiver urbaner Areale erfolgreich ist, ebenfalls für Innovationsdistrikte funktioniert. Die Etablierung einer funktionalen Mischung aus Wohnraum und anderen urbanen Funktionen, die Qualität des Zugangs zu öffentlichen Verkehrsmitteln, Walkability und Aktivität auf Straßenlevel sind alle wichtig für die Gestaltung einer attraktiven und angenehmen urbanen Umgebung. Die Besonderheit von Innovationsdistrikten liegt eher in den oben genannten Schwerpunkten und einem erfolgreichen Stakeholder Management, um ein Ökosystem verschiedenster Nutzergruppen mit einem befähigenden, anstatt limitierenden Regularium zu schaffen.

Innovation ist heutzutage allgegenwärtig. Alle Metropolregionen und sogar mittelgroße Städte entwickeln ihren Innovationscampus, -distrikte oder -inkubatoren. Deswegen ist die Positionierung einer Bebauung auf Basis einer gründlichen Analyse des Kontexts essentiell. Sorgfältige Betrachtung was einen konkreten Standort besonders macht, welche konkreten Branchen bereits treibende Kräfte der regionalen Innovation sind, welche Unternehmen und Organisationen Anker innerhalb einer Erschließung darstellen könnten und wie das Projekt entweder eine attraktive urbane Umgebung für die Erwerbstätigen schaffen oder erschließen kann – all diese Aspekte sind Schlüsselmerkmale, wenn man sich einer solchen Herausforderung annehmen will.

Sources:

1
Sassen, S.: "Cityness in the urban age" in Urban Age, Bulletin No. 2, Autumn 2005

2
Dinteren, J. van, (Zjak Consult / Innovation Area Development Partnership (IADP)) and Jansen, P., (Arup / Innovation Area Development Partnership (IADP)): "The 4th industrial revolution: considerations for science parks to remain competitive", Discussion paper for 36th IASP World Conference, Nantes 24–27 September 2019

3
Katz, B. and Wagner, J.: "The Rise of Innovation Districts: A New Geography of Innovation in America" in Brookings I May 2014

4
Baum, M., Christiaanse, K. [Eds.]: City as Loft. Adaptive Reuse as a Resource for Sustainable Urban Development, gta Verlag, 2012

5
Christiaanse, K.: "Campus to City: Urban Design for Universities", in Hoeger, K. and Christiaanse, K.: Campus and the City, gta Verlag, 2017

Quellen:

1
Sassen, S.: "Cityness in the urban age" in Urban Age, Bulletin No. 2, Autumn 2005

2
Dinteren, J. van, (Zjak Consult / Innovation Area Development Partnership (IADP)) and Jansen, P., (Arup / Innovation Area Development Partnership (IADP)): "The 4th industrial revolution: conside-rations for science parks to remain competitive", Discussion paper for 36th IASP World Conference, Nantes 24–27 September 2019

3
Katz, B. and Wagner, J.: "The Rise of Innovation Districts: A New Geography of Innovation in America" in Brookings I May 2014

4
Baum, M., Christiaanse, K. [Eds.]: City as Loft. Adaptive Reuse as a Resource for Sustainable Urban Development, gta Verlag, 2012

5
Christiaanse, K.: "Campus to City: Urban Design for Universities", in Hoeger, K. and Christiaanse, K.: Campus and the City, gta Verlag, 2017

1.2 Open campus – Open house

MAGNUS NICKL

The idea of creating a breeding ground for research and innovation, a meeting place for new ideas in the previously introverted, secluded world of life sciences, can probably be traced back to the publication of a master plan for the Novartis Campus in 2002 and its implementation in stages in the subsequent decades. Conceived by an international planning team led by the renowned urban historian Vittorio Magnago Lampugnani, who evolved into a designing architect, it entailed a far-reaching transformation process. The ambitious plan was to convert the production site of the multinational pharmaceutical and chemical corporation Novartis, a merger between several venerable Swiss companies, into a place of elite research. The planners realised early on that future success depended not on the most efficient production and best manufacturing lines, but on the most ambitious, forward-looking ideas, and that these would probably not emerge from dark, isolated offices and small laboratories. In the words of the Chairman of the Administrative Board, Daniel Vasellas, the master plan, "offers a highly modern, extremely functional and beautiful, aesthetic environment for intensive communication and work."

The campus

Thus, an urban ground plan was developed with passages, squares and courtyards, providing places for people to gather and exchange ideas, while also strengthening the location's identity. Instead of major volumes and construction sites, the existing network of small plots was preserved, thereby avoiding architectural monotony and enabling identity-building architecture that reflects the diverse requirements, while ensuring the future flexibility of its development. It thereby manifests the inherent qualities of architectural sustainability in a strategic plan, integrating ecological, economic and socio-cultural factors. The targeted inclusion of green spaces, as envisaged by the American landscape architect Peter Walker, was an essential premise from the outset. In doing so, the project went beyond an introverted perspective by conceiving the campus as an element of the large-scale urban context, taking other major projects in Basel as well as the general public into account from the outset with a publicly accessible promenade along the River Rhine. → 009

1.2 Offener Campus – Offenes Haus

MAGNUS NICKL

Die Idee, einen Hort der Forschung und Innovation, ein Begegnungspunkt neuer Ideen in der vormals introvertierten und verborgenen Welt der Biowissenschaften, oder Life-Science genannt, zu schaffen, lässt sich vermutlich auf die Publikation des Masterplans des neuen Novartis Campus im Jahr 2002 und dessen etappenweise Realisierung in den zwei darauffolgenden Jahrzehnten zurückverfolgen. Verfasst von einem internationalen Planungsteam, angeführt durch den bekannten Stadthistoriker Vittorio Magnago Lampugnani, der zu einem Entwurfsarchitekt mutierte, sollte dieser weitreichende Transformationen mit sich bringen. Der kühne Plan war es, die Produktion des Pharma- und Chemiemultis Novartis, eines Fusionsprodukts altehrwürdiger Schweizer Firmen, in einen Ort der Spitzenforschung zu transformieren. Früh wurde hier erkannt, dass zukünftige Erfolge nicht von der effizientesten Produktion, der besten Fabrikstraße abhängen würden, sondern von den kühnsten, zukunftsweisenden Ideen und dass diese vermutlich nicht in dunklen Einzelbüros und kleinen Laboren geschaffen werden. In den Worten des damaligen Verwaltungsratsvorsitzenden Daniel Vasellas ein Masterplan, „der ein hochmodernes und äußerst funktionales, aber auch ein schönes und ästhetisches Umfeld für intensive Kommunikation und Arbeit bietet".

Der Campus

Also wurde ein Stadtgrundriss geschaffen, mit Gassen, Plätzen und Höfen, die Orte des Verweilens, des Austausches und der Identität darstellen. Statt grosser Volumen und Baufelder wurde das bestehende Netz an kleineren Parzellen erhalten, wodurch ein architektonischer Einheitsbrei verhindert und eine identitätsstiftende Architektur ermöglicht wird, welche die differierten Anforderungen abbildet und zukünftige Flexibilität der Entwicklung sicherstellt. Es werden somit die Inbegriffe der architektonischen Nachhaltigkeit, die Integration ökologischer, ökonomischer und sozio-kultureller Faktoren in einen strategischen Plan manifestiert. Der gezielte Einbezug von Grünräumen, getrieben durch den amerikanischen Landschaftsarchitekten Peter Walker, stellt von Anfang an eine essenzielle Prämisse dar. Dabei wurde aber nicht nur ein introvertierter Blick gewagt, sondern der Campus wurde, unter Einbezug der anderen Großprojekte in Basel, als Bestandteil eines großräumlichen, städtischen Kontextes gedacht und die Öffentlichkeit von Anbeginn durch eine öffentlich zugängliche Uferpromenade am Rhein eingebunden. → 009

All diese Ideen, die Reise, die im Jahr 2002 begann, kumulieren im Jahr 2022, dem Jahr, in dem die letzten Zäune durchlässig werden und das gesamte

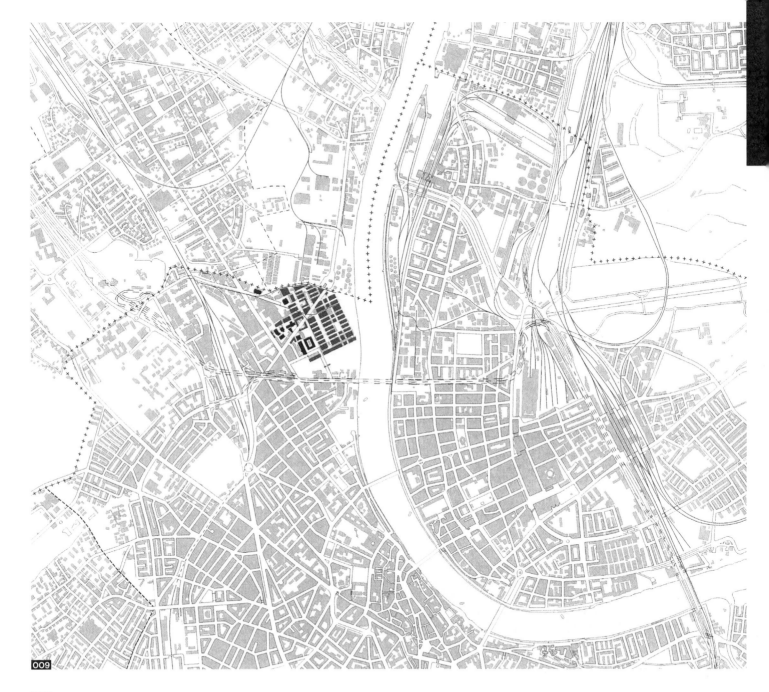

009
Novartis Campus in
Basel's St. Johann
district, master plan
by Vittorio Magnago
Lampugnani, 2002
Novartis Campus
auf dem St. Johann-
Areal in Basel,
Masterplan von
Vittorio Magnago
Lampugnani, 2002

All the ideas conceived on the journey that began in 2002 have come together in 2022, as the last barriers have become permeable, making the entire campus, including the newly created visitor pavilion, publicly accessible. The forbidden city has become a public city.

Generally, the history of life sciences in Basel is the story of transformation, innovation and change. With its origins in the textile industry, the evolution of the chemical industry and its major 20th-century production sites has seen a stronger focus on specialist chemistry and pharmaceuticals since the turn of the millennium. This is precisely where many young, innovative companies play an essential role, operating at innovation hotspots emerging from the symbiosis of powerful universities and an ideal environment for start-ups and growth. The result is a biotope of new ideas and developments. The COVID-19 pandemic has highlighted how essential networked, cooperative thinking and activities are, and the power that such networks can generate.

Precisely this development supports another Basel transformation project: the new Life Science Campus on the Schällemätteli site. In four steps, a new location for university research in the field of medicine and life science is to be created opposite the University Hospital, which in the long term will strengthen the strategically unique situation of the city of Basel in the two sectors and deepen the interlinking of university research and industry. → `010-011`

The concept of the open house

The head-end building of this new campus will be the future building of the Department of Biosystems Science and Engineering (D-BSSE) of the Swiss Federal Institute of Technology (ETH) Zurich, which will be constructed by Nickl & Partner Schweiz in mid-2022 following its success in the project competition. The BSSE Department is dedicated to research and teaching on complex processes in cells and organisms using experimental, theoretical and data-analytical methods.

At an extremely concise urban-planning location, the building assumes the task of creating a visual highlight for the new area, while also providing a pedestrian entrance to the campus buildings behind it. Furthermore, the diversified use requirements and a desire for maximum flexibility demand a complex spatial programme. This is precisely where the design's approach is effective: instead of a highrise development, a head-end building with a staggered height was conceived to integrate it into the surrounding

Areal, inklusive eines neu geschaffenen Besucherpavilions, der Öffentlichkeit zugänglich gemacht wird. Die Verbotene Stadt wird zu einer Öffentlichen Stadt.

Allgemein ist die Geschichte der Life Sciences in Basel eine Geschichte der konstanten Transformation, Innovation und des Wandels. Geboren in der Textilindustrie, erfolgte der Wandel zu chemischen Industrie und deren großen Produktionsstandorten des 20. Jahrhunderts, gefolgt seit der Jahrtausendwende von einer verstärkten Fokussierung auf Spezialchemie und Pharmazie. Gerade hier spielten viele junge, innovative Firmen eine essenzielle Rolle, die an Hotspots der Innovation, die aus einer Symbiose von starken Hochschulen und einem idealen Umfeld für Gründungen und Wachstum entstanden. Ein Biotop an neuen Ideen und Entwicklungen wurde somit geschaffen. Gerade die Corona-Pandemie hat noch einmal unterstrichen, wie essenziell das vernetzte und kooperative Denken und Handeln ist und welche Leistungsfähigkeit innerhalb eines solchen Netzwerkes geschaffen werden kann.

Genau diese Entwicklung unterstützt ein weiteres Basler Transformationsprojekt: der neue Life-Science-Campus auf dem Schällemätteli-Areal. In vier Schritten soll gegenüber des Universitätsspitals ein neuer Ort der universitären Forschung im Bereich der Medizin und Life Science geschaffen werden, welcher langfristig die strategisch einmalige Situation der Stadt Basel in den beiden Sektoren stärken und die Verzahnung von universitärer Forschung und Industrie vertiefen soll. → `010-011`

Das Konzept des Open House

Als Kopfbau des neuen Areals dient das zukünftige Gebäude des Departements Biosysteme (D-BSSE) der Eidgenössischen Technischen Hochschule (ETH) Zürich, welches durch Nickl & Partner Schweiz nach gewonnenem Projektwettbewerb bis Mitte 2022 errichtet wird. Das Department BSSE widmet sich der Erforschung und der Vermittlung komplexer Prozesse in Zellen und Organismen auf experimentelle, theoretische und datenanalytische Weise.

In einer städtebaulich äusserst prägnanten Lage kommt dem Gebäude die Aufgabe zuteil, einerseits ein visuelles Ausrufezeichen für das neue Gebiet zu setzten und zugleich einen Zugang des fußläufigen Verkehrs zu den dahinter liegenden Bauten des Campus zu schaffen. Zudem implizieren die breit gefächerten Nutzungsanforderungen sowie der Wunsch nach höchster Flexibilität ein komplexes Raumprogramm. Genau an diesem Punkt setzt der Entwurf an: Anstelle eines Hochhauses wurde ein, in seiner Höhenentwicklung an die umgebende Bebauung angepasster, Kopfbau geschaffen, der eine Verbindung zwischen der zentralen Straßengabelung und dem dahinter liegenden Campus herstellt.

Aerial view of the Schällemätteli district in Basel, where the new Life Science Campus is being developed near the University Clinic.
Luftbild des Schällemätteli-Areals in Basel, wo ein neuer Life Science Campus nahe des Universitätsklinikums entsteht.

011
Figure-ground diagram of the Schällemätteli campus with the new research building of the Biosystems Department, ETH Zurich
Schwarzplan des Schällemätteli-Areals mit dem neuen Forschungsgebäude des Departments für Biosysteme der ETH Zürich

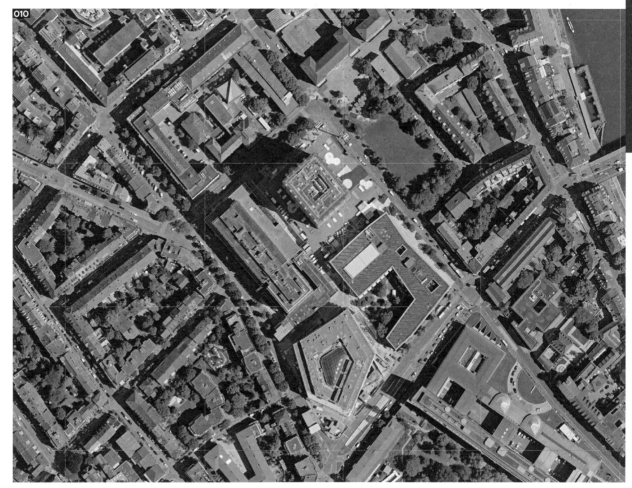

27

O12

O12
BSS research
building,
ETH Zurich in Basel,
Nickl & Partner
Architekten, building
site in January 2022
BSS-Forschungs-
gebäude der
ETH Zürich in Basel,
Nickl & Partner
Architekten, Baustelle
im Januar 2022

O13
The ground floor
serves as a public
passage.
Das Erdgeschoss
dient als öffentlicher
Durchgangsraum.

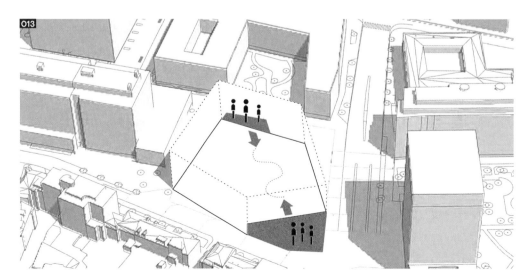

O13

structures, while also creating a connection between the central fork in the road and the campus behind it.

The polygonal volumetric development creates five different façades that react differently to their respective environments and each offer different qualities, as well as inward and outward views.

The strategy of interweaving the urban development is continued inside the building, where a large-scale diagonal, which bridges the different street levels and is framed by a large atrium, creates a public connection between the street space and the campus. → `012-013` Instead of hiding the diverse uses behind corridors, as is standard in conventional buildings, they are arranged and made visible around this atrium, which provides zenithal light to the lower floors. Science thereby becomes visible and tangible to the general public. Like an urban ground plan with streets, passages and squares, the varying spatial layers and access areas offer a multifaceted spatial experience: the communal gathering areas, different walkway connections and changing corridor widths serve to encourage communication. While student uses are focused on the ground floor, where they have an enlivening effect, the laboratories, including short-cut stairs to encourage exchange between researchers, are located on the upper levels. The science lounge overlooks them all with its spacious seminar and catering opportunities, as well as a rooftop terrace affording a marvellous view of the city. → `014-018`

The two above-described development projects, namely the Novartis Campus and the Life Science Campus with its new head-end building for the future BSSE Department of the ETH Zurich, are exemplary in demonstrating how strongly the typology of research buildings has changed in recent decades. Starting with a typology of isolation, this transformation has moved towards openness, flexibility, urbanity and mutual exchange, without undermining the high demands of security and hazard prevention. In the following years, innovative planning ideas will continue to drive this transformation forward and enhance public awareness of the researchers' essential activities.

Die volumetrische Ausbildung als Polygonal schafft fünf verschiedene Fassaden, die unterschiedlich auf ihr entsprechendes Umfeld reagieren und jeweils verschiedene Qualitäten und Ein- und Ausblicke bieten.

Die städtebauliche Verschränkungsstrategie setzt sich im Inneren des Gebäudes fort, wo eine großformatige, die unterschiedlichen Straßenniveaus überbrückende Diagonale, umrahmt von einem großen Atrium, eine öffentliche Verbindung zwischen Straßenraum und Campus schafft. → `012-013` Entlang dieses Atriums, welches die Untergeschosse zudem mit zenitalem Licht versorgt, werden die vielfältigen Nutzungen angeordnet und sichtbar gemacht, statt sie, wie bei konventionellen Bauten, hinter Korridoren zu verstecken. Die Wissenschaft wird also erlebbar und wahrnehmbar für eine breite Öffentlichkeit. In Analogie an einen Stadtgrundriss mit seinen Straßen, Gassen und Plätzen, bieten die variierenden Raumschichten und Erschließungsflächen ein vielfältiges Raumerleben: der Kommunikation dienende Aufenthaltsräume, unterschiedliche Wegverbindungen sowie wechselnde Korridorbreiten. Während studentische Nutzungen sich insbesondere im Erdgeschoss befinden und dieses beleben, sind die Labore, inklusive eigener Short Cut Treppen, die den Austausch zwischen den Forscherinnen und Forschern fördern sollen, in den Obergeschossen zu finden. Darüber thront die Science Lounge mit ihren großzügigen Seminar- und Verpflegungsmöglichkeiten sowie einer Dachterrasse, die einen wunderbaren Blick über die Stadt freigibt. → `014-018`

Die beiden hier erläuterten Projekte, die Entwicklung des Novartis Campus und die Arealentwicklung des Life-Science Campus mit dem neuen Kopfbau des zukünftigen BSSE Departements der ETH Zürich, veranschaulichen beispielhaft, wie stark sich die Typologie des Forschungsbaus in den letzten Jahrzehnten gewandelt hat. Ausgehend von einer Typologie der Abschottung erfolgte die Transformation in eine Typologie der Offenheit, der Flexibilität, der Urbanität und des Austausches, ohne dass weiterhin sehr hohe Anforderungen an Sicherheit und Gefahrenprävention vernachlässigt werden. Innovative Planungsideen werden diesen Wandel in den kommenden Jahren weiter fortschreiben und das öffentliche Bewusstsein für die essenziellen Tätigkeiten der Forscherinnen und Forscher schärfen.

014
Foyer of the BSS
research building
in Basel,
Nickl & Partner
Architekten,
building site in
January 2022
Foyer der
Forschungsge-
bäudes BSS in Basel,
Nickl & Partner
Architekten, Baustelle
im Januar 2022

015 – 018
BSS research
building, Basel,
sectional view
and floor plans:
–1, 0 and +1
Forschungsge-
bäude BSS, Basel,
Querschnitt und
Grundrisse der
Geschosse -1,
0 und +1

019
View of one of the
laboratory areas
around the foyer
Blick in einen der
Laborbereiche rund
um das Foyer

016

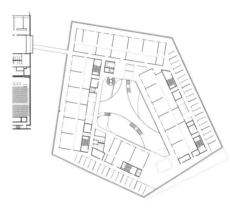

015

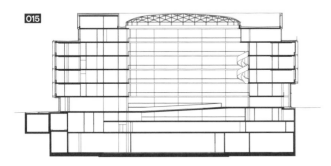

017

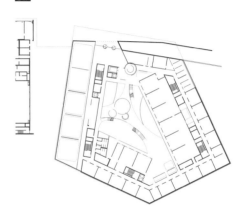

018

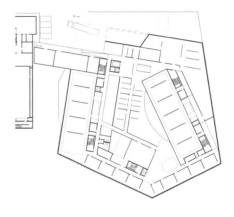

019

1.3 Identity through unity – The university campus

The university campus has a special place in the canon of buildings for science and research. Education and research facilities have generally grown over a period of several decades and centuries, and their existing structures date from a wide variety of eras and are located in scattered places. Thus, an entire university campus planned at a single stroke is rather a rare phenomenon. The respective demands of research and teaching at the time are crystallised in the architecture (→ see 1.4 Learning environments). The prestige and status afforded by society to teachers and students is perpetuated in the design of a university campus, as well as the prevailing social, political and technical values.

This excursus briefly describes a few impressive examples of the iconographic architecture of the university campus.

In many European major cities, educational institutions were initially accommodated in structures that were not purpose-built. For instance the Humboldt-Universität zu Berlin, which was founded in 1810, first moved into the palais of Prince Henry of Prussia, which had been constructed for him by Frederick William III. It took until the mid-19th century for an "educational culture" to develop, including buildings for science in prestigious buildings that were inspired by baroque palaces.[1]

As the disciplines of natural sciences, engineering and medicine became increasingly differentiated, demands grew with respect to their spatial conditions, particularly their lighting, ventilation, room dimensions and shock-proof qualities. To begin with, prestigious new buildings were planned for technical and scientific faculties, reflecting their growing confidence.

In the late 19th and early 20th centuries, as student numbers increased, the ideal of an educational campus according to US role models became increasingly attractive, for instance in Princeton for New Jersey College, which had been founded in 1746, or the University of Virginia in Charlottesville. The latter, which was constructed in the early 1800s according to plans by the US President and Palladio-admirer Thomas Jefferson, is the archetypal university campus per se and has served as a role model for numerous North American universities. The grounds have a strictly hierarchical structure. The central element is a generous green space, around which all university buildings are grouped.

The rotunda dominates at the head end, serving both as the centre of knowledge in the form of a library,

1.3 Identität durch Einheit – Der Universitätscampus

Der Universitätscampus nimmt eine Sonderstellung im Kanon der Bauten für Wissenschaft und Forschung ein. Während Bildungs- und Forschungseinrichtungen in der Regel über viele Jahrzehnte und Jahrhunderte gewachsen sind und sich ihr baulicher Bestand aus verschiedensten Epochen an verstreut liegenden Standorten zusammensetzt, ist der aus einem Guss geplante Universitätscampus eher ein seltenes Phänomen. In seinen Architekturen kristallisieren sich die jeweilig geltenden Anforderungen an Forschung und Lehre heraus. (→ siehe 1.4 Lernwelten) Prestige und Stellenwert, der den Lehrenden und den Studierenden in der Gesellschaft eingeräumt wurde, ist in der Ausgestaltung eines Universitätscampus verewigt, genauso wie die jeweils zur Entstehungszeit geltenden sozialen, politischen und technischen Leitbilder.

In diesem Exkurs soll daher kurz auf einige prägnante Beispiele einer ikonografischen Architektur des Universitätscampus eingegangen werden.

In vielen Metropolen Europas wohnten Bildungsstätten zunächst in fremden Gehäusen, so bezog zum Beispiel die 1810 gegründete Humboldt-Universität zu Berlin das ehemalige Palais des Prinzen Heinrich von Preußen, welches ihr von Friedrich Wilhelm III. gestiftet wurde. Erst etwa Mitte des 19. Jahrhunderts etablierte sich eine „Bildungsarchitektur", ein Bauen für die Wissenschaft in repräsentativen Gebäuden, inspiriert vom barocken Schlossbauschema.

Mit fortschreitender Spezifizierung der Disziplinen in Naturwissenschaften, Technik und Medizin wuchsen jedoch die Anforderungen an die räumlichen Gegebenheiten hinsichtlich Belichtung und Belüftung, Raummaße und Erschütterungsfreiheit. Einhergehend mit einem erstarkenden Selbstbewusstsein gerade der technischen und naturwissenschaftlichen Fachbereiche, wurden zunächst vor allem diesen Disziplinen repräsentative Neubauten gewidmet.

Im späten 19. und frühen 20. Jahrhundert und mit steigenden Studierendenzahlen gewann das Ideal eines Bildungscampus nach US-amerikanischem Prinzip an Attraktivität, wie es zum Beispiel in Princeton mit dem New Jersey College, gegründet im Jahr 1746, oder auf dem Campus der University of Virginia in Charlottesville umgesetzt wurde. Dieser Campus, der nach Plänen des US-Präsidenten und Palladio-Verehrers Thomas Jefferson in den frühen 1800er Jahren errichtet wurde, ist der Prototyp eines Universitätscampus schlechthin und diente als Vorbild zahlreicher nordamerikanischer Universitäten. Die Anlage ist streng hierarchisch aufgebaut. Zentrales Element ist die weitläufige Grünfläche, um die sich alle Universitätsgebäude gruppieren. Am Kopf erhebt sich die Rotunde, gleichsam als Zentrum des Wissens dient sie als Bibliothek und Veranstaltungsort. Zwei Reihen von Studierendenunterkünften durchbrochen von Pavillons

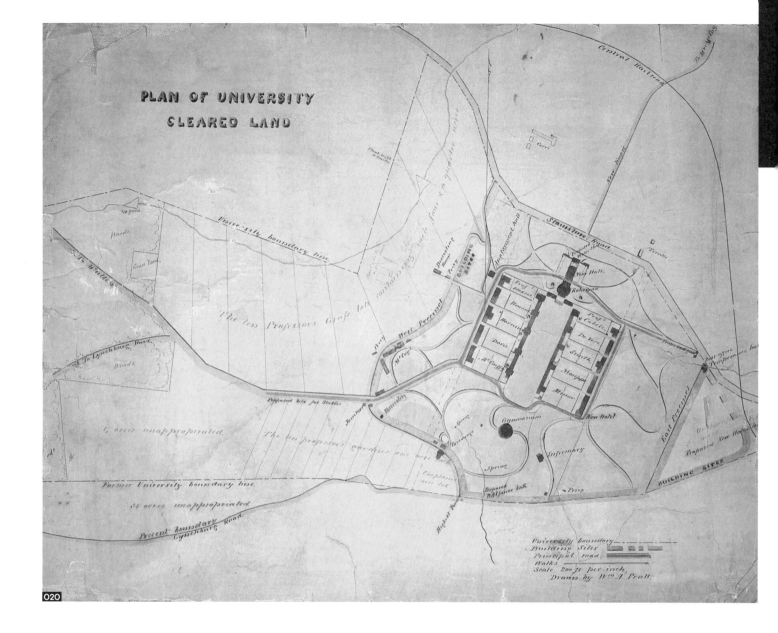

PLAN OF UNIVERSITY
CLEARED LAND

020
Ideal campus plan.
The University of
Virginia, conceived
by US President
Thomas Jefferson,
was developed
around 1825.
Idealbild des Campus.
Die University of
Virginia entstand
nach den Plänen des
US-Präsidenten
Thomas Jefferson,
um 1825

and as an event location. Two rows of student accommodation, which are intersected by pavilions, line the two sides of the campus-green rotunda, their rooms opening up directly towards the green area, while being mutually connected by a long colonnade. The pavilions were used as accommodation for teachers and for teaching. Service facilities and canteen services were accommodated in the so-called hotels in the two outer rows. The design thereby represents a model of an ideal world, in which science and teaching were central, while also highlighting the image of communal, democratic learning. → 020

The idea of homogeneous campus architecture also reflects the dream of the unity of science.[2] In the 19th century, the notion of a universally educated person was gradually replaced by increasing specialisation. Both in terms of content and design, the campus can provide the framework for the diversification of disciplines and their resulting splits into individual buildings. However, in the early 20th century, the concept of an educational campus in green surroundings also reflected the difficulty of finding suitable land to develop in the rapidly growing major cities, making locations outside the cities more attractive.

During the 1930s, under National Socialist rule, the concept was driven to the extreme, reflecting the megalomania of the times, as can for instance be seen in the design of an enormous university city as the "Gateway to the Reich Capital Germania".[3]

After the war, the search began in Europe for a countermodel to this authoritarian and prestigious educational architecture. The revolutionary design for the Dahlem campus of the Freie Universität Berlin, which was founded in 1948, is a symbolic example. The young Parisian architects Georges Candilis, Alexis Josic and Shadrach Woods won the architectural competition in 1963.

Their design is "anti-authority architecture": instead of visual axes and prestige buildings, they developed a cluster-like, two-storey spatial fabric that is permeated by a public network of walkways and open spaces. It was designed as a flexible, modular system that could react to future developments at the university, expressing equal rights and democracy.

The influence of Le Corbusier and his 1964 Ospedale di Venezia can be seen in the modular fabric, which strongly recalls an urban plan, with walkways, main streets and squares. Woods and Candilis had previously worked for Le Corbusier. In keeping with the buildings' intended ability to adapt and expand, the engineer Jean Prouvé developed a modular building nicknamed the "Rostlaube" (trans.: "rusty arbour"). → 021-025

rahmen zu beiden Seiten der Rotunde das Campusgrün, die Zimmer öffneten sich direkt zur Grünfläche hin und sind mit einem langen Säulengang miteinander verbunden. Die Pavillons dienten den Lehrenden zur Unterkunft und als Ort der Wissensvermittlung. Serviceeinrichtungen und Speisenversorgung sind in sogenannten Hotels in den beiden äußeren Reihen untergebracht. So entstand das Modell einer inszenierten Idealwelt, in der Wissenschaft und Wissensvermittlung in den Mittelpunkt gestellt und gleichzeitig das Bild gemeinschaftlichen, demokratischen Lernens hochgehalten wird. → 020

Hinter dem Gedanken einer homogenen Campusarchitektur verbirgt sich auch der Traum der Einheit der Wissenschaft.[2] An die Stelle des Universalgelehrten rückte im 19. Jahrhundert die zunehmende fachliche Spezifizierung. Für die Vielfalt der Disziplinen und die daraus folgende räumliche Aufsplitterung in einzelne Gebäude kann der Campus als inhaltlicher wie gestalterischer Rahmen dienen. Das Konzept des Bildungscampus im Grünen trug im beginnenden 20. Jahrhundert aber auch der zunehmenden Schwierigkeit Rechnung, innerhalb der rasant wachsenden Metropolen geeignete Bauflächen zu finden, so gewannen die den Städten vorgelagerten Standorte an Attraktivität.

Im Nationalsozialismus der 30er Jahre fand dieser Gedanke eine, dem Hang zum Größenwahn dieser Ära entsprechende, Maßlosigkeit, wie sie sich zum Beispiel im Entwurf einer ganzen Hochschulstadt gigantischer Ausmaße als „Tor zur Reichshauptstadt Germania" manifestiert.[3]

Nach dem Krieg begann in Europa die Suche nach dem Gegenmodell einer autoritäts- und prestigeverhafteten Bildungsarchitektur. Symbolhaft sei hier der revolutionäre Entwurf für den Campus der 1948 gegründeten Freien Universität Berlin in Dahlem genannt. Aus dem Architekturwettbewerb 1963 gingen die jungen Pariser Architekten Georges Candilis, Alexis Josic und Shadrach Woods hervor. Ihr Entwurf ist eine „Anti-Autoritätsarchitektur", nicht Sichtachsen und Prachtbauten, sondern ein Cluster-ähnliches, zweigeschossiges Raumgefüge, durchzogen von einem öffentlichen Netz aus Fußwegen und Freiräumen. Es sollte als flexibles, modulares System auf künftige Entwicklungen der Hochschule reagieren können – eine Gleichberechtigung und Demokratie wiederspiegelnde Architektur. In dem modularen Gefüge, welches stark an einen Stadtgrundriss mit Wegen, Hauptstraßen und Plätzen erinnert, lässt sich die Handschrift Le Corbusiers für das Ospedale di Venezia von 1964 wiedererkennen. Woods und Candilis hatten für Le Corbusier gearbeitet. Entsprechend der vorgesehenen Wandel- und Erweiterbarkeit der Gebäude entwickelte der Ingenieur Jean Prouvé ein modulares Fassadensystem aus dem damals neuen Corten-Stahl. Die typische und beabsichtigte Rostbildung hat dem Gebäude den Spitznamen „Rostlaube" eingebracht. → 021-025

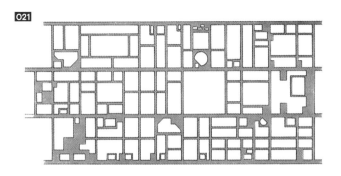

O21

O22

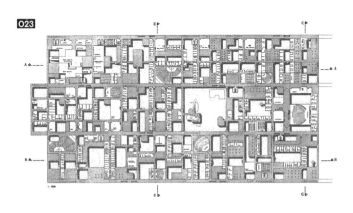

O23

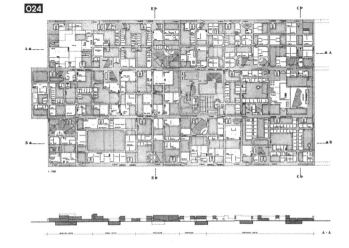

O24

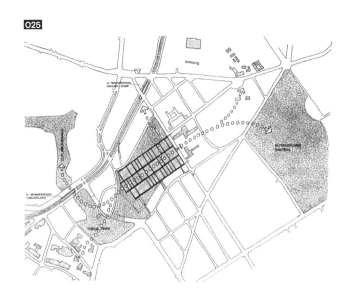

O25

O21–O25
Freie Universität
Berlin, design
by Candilis, Josic,
Woods, 1963
Freie Universität
Berlin, Entwurf
von Candilis,
Josic, Woods, 1963

O26–O27
Indian Institute of
Management,
Ahmedebad, India,
Louis Kahn,
1962–1974
Indian Institute of
Management,
Ahmedabad Indien,
Louis Kahn,
1962–1974

A similar atmosphere of social togetherness pervades the campus of the Indian Institute of Management, which Louis Kahn designed in the 1960s, but never saw completed. He explicitly regarded the entire campus as a place of learning. Not just the lecture theatres and seminar rooms, with their intrinsic hierarchies between the teachers and students, but also the campus grounds, with its walkways, open spaces, squares and passages, were aimed at encouraging the free exchange of ideas and interdisciplinary discussion. As if shaped in a single mould, the archaic red brickwork forms, circles and round arches define the location's appearance. → `026–027`

In the LabCity on the Paris-Saclay science and university campus, around 30 kilometres south of the French capital, the thought of a homogeneous campus experience has been replanted in a university building. OMA (Office for Metropolitan Architecture) organise the laboratory and seminar rooms of the engineering school CentraleSupélec as an internal urban landscape. The functional modules, described by OMA as "discreet parcels", are positioned within a strict orthogonal grid. They form islands of work and concentration in a loose structure of bright passages and gathering areas. Only one diagonal intersects the grids and serves as a semi-public connecting axis between the future science campus, for which OMA also designed the master plan, and a railway station. A translucent roof spans the entire two-storey learning landscape. From balconies and bridges, one can also observe all the activity from above – communal discussions, learning, relaxation and working – in the passages of the LabCity. Is it still a building or already a city? The transitions are deliberately fluent. → `028–030`

The approach was developed more radically in the Masdar City project near Abu Dhabi. Masdar City is a city, a science campus and a research project in one. Commissioned by the authorities of Abu Dhabi, the plan was to create an energy-optimised ideal city of the future, providing a mix of housing, commerce, cultural venues and service facilities in a single structure fabric. For their campus design, Foster + Partners were inspired by traditional building forms of the Arab Emirates, planning a highly densified city; its in-situ, fibre-glass reinforced concrete with red sand appears to have emerged directly from the surrounding desert. The entire city was to be based on maximum walkable distances, as narrow passages offer shady walkways in the extreme heat. No vehicles using fossil fuels are permitted. The facilities of the Masdar Institute are seamlessly integrated into the urban space and also use the city as a research object to investigate sustainable forms of housing and energy. The section constructed between 2007 and

Einen ähnlichen Geist sozialen Miteinanders durchweht den Campus des Indian Institutes of Management, welchen Louis Kahn in den 1960er-Jahren entwarf, dessen Fertigstellung er aber nicht mehr miterlebte. Explizit sah er den gesamten Campus als einen Lernort. Nicht nur Hörsaal und Seminarraum, mit ihrer immanenten Hierarchie zwischen Lehrenden und Studierenden, sondern das Campusgelände mit seinen Fluren, Freiräumen, Plätzen und Gassen sollte dem freien Austausch und der interdisziplinären Diskussion zur Verfügung stehen. Wie aus einem Guss geformt, prägen der rote Backstein, archaische Formen, Kreise und Rundbögen das Erscheinungsbild. → `026–027`

In der LabCity auf dem Wissenschafts- und Universitätscampus Paris-Saclay, rund 30 Kilometer südlich der französischen Hauptstadt, wird der Gedanke einer homogenen Campuserfahrung zurückimplantiert in ein Universitätsgebäude. OMA (Office for Metropolitan Architecture) organisieren die Labore und Seminarräume der Ingenieursschule CentraleSupélec als eine interne Stadtlandschaft. Die Funktionsbausteine, von OMA als „diskrete Pakete" (discreet parcels) deklariert, werden innerhalb eines strengen orthogonalen Rasters positioniert. Sie bilden Inseln der Arbeit und Konzentration in einem lockeren Gefüge von lichten Gassen und Aufenthaltsflächen. Allein eine Diagonale durchkreuzt das Raster und dient als semiöffentliche Verbindungsachse zwischen künftigem Wissenschaftscampus, für den OMA ebenfalls den Masterplan zeichnet, und einer Bahnstation. Ein transluzentes Dach überspannt die gesamte, zweigeschossige Lernlandschaft. Von Balkonen und Brücken aus lässt sich das Geschehen, das gemeinsame Diskutieren, Lernen, Entspannen und Arbeiten in den Gassen der LabCity auch von oben betrachten. Ist dies noch Gebäude oder bereits Stadt? Die Übergänge sind hier bewusst fließend. → `028–030`

Noch weiter auf die Spitze getrieben hat diesen Ansatz das Projekt Masdar City bei Abu Dhabi. Masdar City ist Stadt, Wissenschaftscampus und Forschungsprojekt in einem. Im Auftrag der Autoritäten von Abu Dhabi sollte hier eine energieoptimierte Idealstadt der Zukunft entstehen, die einen Mix aus Wohnen, Kommerz, Wissenschaft und Bildung, Kultur- und Serviceeinrichtungen innerhalb eines baulichen Gefüges anbietet. Foster + Partners orientierten sich für den Campus an traditionellen Bauformen der Arabischen Emirate und planten eine hochgradig verdichtete Stadt, deren mit örtlichem, rotem Sand eingefärbter, glasfaserverstärkter Beton direkt aus dem umgebenden Wüstenboden gewachsen zu sein scheint. Die gesamte Stadt sollte maximal auf fußläufige Verbindungen ausgelegt werden, daher bieten die engen Gassen in dem extremen Klima schattige Wege. Es wird vollständig auf Fahrzeuge mit fossilen Energieträgern verzichtet. Die Einrichtungen des Masdar Institute sind nahtlos in diesen städtischen Raum integriert und nutzen die Stadt zugleich als Forschungsobjekt zur Erkundung nachhaltiger Wohn-

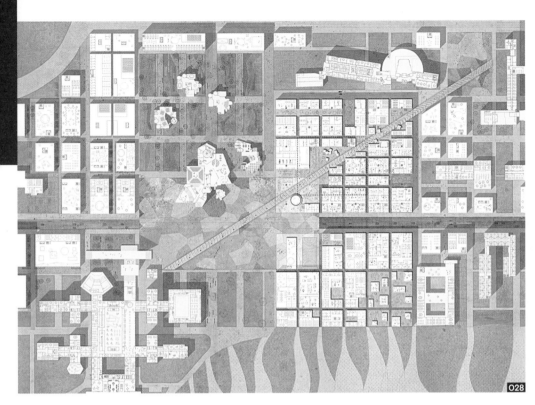

028–030
**Lab City
CentraleSupélec,
Paris Saclay,
OMA, 2013–2017**
Lab City
CentraleSupélec,
Paris Saclay,
OMA, 2013–2017

028

029

031

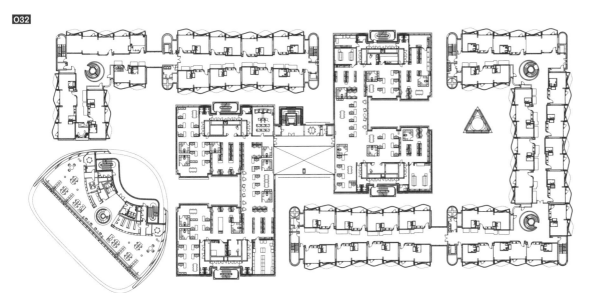

032

2015 will serve as the germ for further developments in this prototypical science city. To do so, Foster+Partners developed a forward-looking master plan, surrounded by enormous photovoltaic farms. →`031–032`

The two latter examples provide a glimpse of the features of future campus architecture in the field of research and education. They represent a vision of a mixed urban landscape in which public life, learning and research, as well as housing and industry, are all mixed together. Retreating into a temple of education is no longer an option. Instead, these university science cities of tomorrow have become a field of experimentation for forward-looking urban life and work.

1
Metzler, Gabriele, Schirrmacher, Arne (Ed.), Architekturen der Wissenschaft. Die Architekturen Berlins in europäischer Perspektive (exhibition documentation, Humboldt-Universität Berlin), Berlin 2019.

2
Ibid.

3
Ibid.

und Energieformen. Der 2007 bis 2015 zunächst entstandene Abschnitt soll als Keimzelle weiterer Entwicklungen dieser prototypischen Wissensstadt dienen. Foster + Partners zeichneten dafür einen zukunftsoffenen Masterplan, umgeben von enormen Photovoltaik-Farmen. →`031–032`

Die beiden letztgenannten Beispiele zeichnen ein Bild dessen, was künftige Campusarchitektur im Forschungs- und Bildungswesen ausmachen wird. Es entsteht die Vision einer durchmischten Stadtlandschaft, in der sich öffentliches Leben, Lernen und Forschen genauso wie Arbeiten, Wohnen und Industrie durchmischen. Der Rückzug in einen Bildungstempel ist passé. Vielmehr sind diese universitären Wissensstädte von morgen ein Experimentierraum für zukunftsfähiges urbanes Leben und Arbeiten geworden.

1
Metzler, Gabriele, Schirrmacher, Arne (Hrsg.), Architekturen der Wissenschaft. Die Architekturen Berlins in europäischer Perspektive (Ausstellungs-Dok. Humboldt-Universität Berlin), Berlin 2019.

2
Ebd.

3
Ebd.

O33

Learning
worlds

BRIGITTE GRASS + NICKL & PARTNER ARCHITEKTEN

Lernwelten

In today's well-developed European science landscape, the task of designing a uniform university campus is an extremely rare and fortunate opportunity. Much more often, architects find themselves in the situation of being commissioned to contribute a single element of a master plan. In 2008, the Hochschule Düsseldorf, formerly known as the Fachhochschule Düsseldorf, began planning a new university campus in the district of Derendorf. The infrastructure of the university of applied sciences had previously been divided over two locations in the city. Its buildings, some of which dated back to the Seventies and Eighties, required urgent refurbishment and extension. The Building and Real Estate Enterprise of the Federal State of NRW (North Rhine-Westphalia) therefore decided in favour of a new building on an 85,000-square metre former industrial estate to the north of the centre.

How can a university campus meet today's requirements for teaching and research? What does a modern "place of education" look like? An interview with the former President of the Düsseldorf University of Applied Sciences, Brigitte Grass, about changed expectations of students and teachers for campus life.

In der gut entwickelten europäischen Wissenschaftslandschaft von heute ist die Aufgabe, einen einheitlichen Universitätscampus zu entwerfen, für den Architekten ein äußerst seltener Glücksfall. Sehr viel häufiger findet er sich in der Situation wieder, einen einzelnen Baustein zum Masterplan eines Campus beisteuern zu dürfen. Die Hochschule Düsseldorf, ehemals Fachhochschule Düsseldorf, konnte im Jahr 2008 mit den Planungen eines neuen Uni-Campus im Stadtteil Derendorf beginnen. Die universitäre Infrastruktur der Fachhochschule hatte sich bisher auf zwei Standorte im Stadtgebiet verteilt. Diese Gebäude, teils aus den siebziger und achtziger Jahren, bedurften dringend der Sanierung und Erweiterung. Der Bau- und Liegenschaftsbetrieb NRW entschloss sich daher zum Neubau auf einem 85.000 Quadratmeter großen ehemaligen Industriegelände nördlich der Stadtmitte.

Wie kann ein Universitätscampus den heutigen Anforderungen an Lehre und Forschung gerecht werden? Wie sieht ein zeitgemäßer „Ort der Bildung" aus? Ein Gespräch mit der ehemaligen Präsidentin der Hochschule Düsseldorf, Brigitte Grass, über veränderte Erwartungen von Studierenden und Lehrenden an das Campusleben.

033
Main lecture theatre, Hochschule Düsseldorf Audimax, Hochschule Düsseldorf

In the winter semester of 2018/2019, the last departments of the Hochschule Düsseldorf moved onto the new campus. By pooling the formerly widely distributed university, the intension was to strengthen interaction between students and employees, encourage interdisciplinary in research and teaching, simplify administrative processes and, not least, present a new, contemporary image. The new "address" was introduced together with the transformation from a university of applied sciences to a full university, with 11,000 students, making it one of the large universities in North Rhine-Westphalia.

Nickl & Partner: With the move to a newly designed campus, Düsseldorf University of Applied Sciences was given the rare opportunity to create a completely new teaching and research environment tailored to their needs. What special expectations were attached to the relocation and conception of the campus?

Brigitte Grass: Today, students and teachers prefer colleges in the city or near the city, which, in addition to their studies and work, offer many advantages and leisure opportunities. This also leads to massive housing bottlenecks in these cities. The central location in Düsseldorf-Derendorf makes this campus, which is directly connected to the S-Bahn, attractive for students and teachers. The railway station and airport are also nearby and can be reached quickly by S-Bahn. The motorway connection to the north is excellent. Until 2002, the Schlösser brewery and the old livestock and slaughterhouse were located on this Derendorfer site. The remaining old buildings of the large cattle hall and the horse slaughterhouse were integrated into the campus. Today, it houses the campus IT, the library and the learning and study centre. Furthermore, a place of remembrance was attached to the old large cattle hall, which recalls the Jewish citizens deported between 1941 and 1944 and retraces

Im Wintersemester 2018/2019 bezogen die letzten Fachbereiche der Hochschule Düsseldorf ihren neuen Campus. Mit der Zusammenlegung der ehemals auf mehrere Standorte verteilten Hochschule erhoffte man sich mehr interne Interaktion zwischen Studierenden und Mitarbeitenden, mehr Interdisziplinarität in Forschung und Lehre, vereinfachte Verwaltungsabläufe und nicht zuletzt ein neues, zeitgemäßes Image. Eine „Adresse", die einherging mit der Wandlung von Fachhochschule zu Hochschule, mit heute rund 11.000 Studierenden eine der großen Hochschulen in NRW.

Nickl & Partner: Mit dem Umzug auf einen neu konzipierten Campus bekam die Hochschule Düsseldorf die seltene Gelegenheit, sich eine ganz neue und auf ihre Bedürfnisse zugeschnittene Lehr- und Forschungsumwelt zu schaffen. Welche besonderen Erwartungen waren an die Verlegung des Standortes und die Konzeption des Campus geknüpft?

Brigitte Grass: Studierende und Lehrende bevorzugen heutzutage Hochschulen in Stadtlage oder Stadtnähe, die neben dem Studium und der Arbeit noch vielfältige Vorteile und auch Freizeitmöglichkeiten bieten. Dies führt in diesen Städten auch zu massiven Wohnraumengpässen. Die zentrale Lage in Düsseldorf-Derendorf macht diesen Campus, der unmittelbar an die S-Bahn angeschlossen ist, für Studierende und Lehrende attraktiv. Bahnhof und Flughafen liegen ebenfalls in der Nähe und sind mit der S-Bahn schnell erreichbar. Auch die Autobahnanbindung nach Norden ist hervorragend. Bis 2002 standen auf diesem Derendorfer Gelände die Schlösser-Brauerei und der alte Vieh- und Schlachthof. Die noch vorhandenen alten Gebäude der Großviehhalle und die Pferdeschlachthalle wurden in den Campus integriert. Heute sind dort die Campus IT, die Bibliothek und das Lern- und Studierendenzentrum untergebracht. Weiterhin wurde der Erinnerungsort an die alte Großviehhalle angegliedert, der auf die zwischen 1941 und 1944 deportierten jüdischen Bürgerinnen und Bürger hinweist und das Geschehene in Form eines Museums aufarbeitet. Die Gebäude am Campus Derendorf sind so angeordnet, dass der von der Stadt geforderte Grünzug mitten durch den Campus führt. Dabei sind die Flucht- und Sichtachsen der bebauten Umgebung so angelegt, dass sie auf

034 – 035
Hochschule
Düsseldorf campus,
Derendorf district,
Nickl & Partner
Architekten,
2012 – 2018
Campus der
Hochschule
Düsseldorf im
Stadtteil
Derendorf,
Nickl & Partner
Architekten,
2012 – 2018

O36

O36
**Interior, Building 6,
Architecture
and Design Faculty,
Hochschule
Düsseldorf**
Innenansicht
Gebäude 6,
Fachbereich
Architektur und
Design,
Hochschule
Düsseldorf

O37
**Campus,
Hochschule
Düsseldorf**
Campusansicht,
Hochschule
Düsseldorf

O37

the events in the form of a museum. The buildings on the Derendorf campus are arranged in such a way that the green space demanded by the city passes right through the campus. The escape and visual axes of the built environment are designed so that they lead to the central focus on the campus. The campus centre can be reached from many sides of the city. The exits of the individual buildings are aligned with buildings facing the centre. The only exit to Münsterstrasse is in Building 4, which houses the main lecture theatre and also provides a clear address for the university.

N & P: On entering the campus, you find yourself in a homogeneous ensemble. Aluminum and glass façades envelop all buildings and contrast with the soft green of the meadows. How do you experience the ensemble from the centre of the campus?

BG: The uniform external façade of the new components follows the leitmotif: unity despite diversity. What is hidden behind the exterior façade is usually not revealed to the outsider – such as an auditorium, a laboratory, or an office. The only exception are large openings in the aluminum façade, which indicate foyers and lounges. The corporate design developed by the university also pursues the leitmotif of unity despite diversity through its own font, which allows different acronyms for the departments. However, "unity and identity" are not abandoned. The clear arrangement of the buildings towards the centre with the clearly visible head buildings and entrances allows an easy orientation.

N & P: These buildings are accentuated by large-format figures, which illuminate the visitor in bold colours.

BG: The colour concept, which was developed in the colour design of students of the university, supports orientation on the campus, in the buildings and also in the underground car park with 1,100 parking spaces. The buildings developed for all members of the university are decorated in four shades of red. Red is also the university colour used since 1971. Building 6 for the Departments of Architecture and Design is yellow in the basic colour, combined with grey or black. The humanists have been assigned the color green in four shades (Building 3). The technical departments are in four shades of blue (Building 5 and the two upper floors of Building 4). The colour scheme is stringently maintained (e.g. stairs, toilets, kitchen colour, chair colour in seminar and lecture rooms, parking markings in the underground car park). Similar to the colour system, the consistently bilingual steles and orientation boards are also used in the outdoor area, the buildings and the underground car park. The building numbers are taken up here orientation is aided by the simple coding (building number, floor, room number).

dem Campus zum zentralen Mittelpunkt führen. Die Campusmitte ist von vielen Seiten der Stadt aus zu erreichen. Die Ausgänge der einzelnen Gebäude sind durch Kopfbauten zum Zentrum hin ausgerichtet. Lediglich in Gebäude 4, in dem sich das Audimax befindet, gibt es einen Ausgang zur Münsterstraße, der auch die klare Adressbildung der Hochschule ermöglicht.

N & P: Wer den Campus betritt, findet sich in einem homogen gestalteten Ensemble wieder. Aluminium- und Glasfassaden umhüllen alle Gebäude und kontrastieren mit dem weichen Grün der Wiesen. Wie erleben Sie das Ensemble, wenn Sie in der Mitte des Campus stehen?

BG: Die einheitliche Außenfassade der neuen Bauteile folgt dem Leitmotiv: Einheit trotz Vielfalt. Was sich hinter der Außenfassade verbirgt, erschließt sich dem Außenstehenden in der Regel nicht – etwa ein Hörsaal, ein Labor, ein Büro. Die einzige Ausnahme bilden großflächige Öffnungen der Aluminiumfassade, die auf Foyers und Aufenthaltsräume hinweisen. Das von der Hochschule entwickelte Corporate Design verfolgt ebenfalls das Leitmotiv Einheit trotz Vielfalt durch eine eigene Schrift, die unterschiedliche Akronyme für die Fachbereiche zulässt. Die Einheit und Identität wird dadurch aber nicht aufgegeben.

Die klare Anordnung der Gebäude zum Zentrum hin mit den gut sichtbaren Kopfbauten und Eingängen ermöglicht eine einfache Orientierung.

N & P: Diese Kopfbauten werden von großformatigen Zahlen akzentuiert, die dem Besucher in kräftigen Farben entgegenleuchten.

BG: Das Farbkonzept, das in der Farbgestaltung von Studierenden der Hochschule entwickelt wurde, unterstützt die Orientierung auf dem Campus, in den Gebäuden und auch in der Tiefgarage mit 1100 Parkplätzen. Die für alle Hochschulangehörigen konzipierten Gebäude sind in roten Farbtönen in vier Ausprägungen gehalten. Rot ist auch die seit 1971 verwendete Hochschulfarbe. Das Gebäude 6 für die gestalterischen Fachbereiche Architektur und Design ist mit der Grundfarbe gelb, kombiniert mit grau oder schwarz versehen. Die Geisteswissenschaftler haben die Farbe Grün in vier Schattierungen zugeordnet bekommen (Gebäude 3). Die technischen Fachbereiche sind in vier Blautönen gehalten (Gebäude 5 und die beiden Obergeschosse von Gebäude 4). Das Farbkonzept wird stringent durchgehalten (z.B. Treppen, Toiletten, Küchenfarbe, Stuhlfarbe in Seminar- und Vorlesungsräumen, Parkplatzmarkierung in der Tiefgarage). An das Farbsystem angelehnt sind auch die durchgängig zweisprachig angelegten Stelen und Orientierungstafeln im Außengelände, den Gebäuden und der Tiefgarage. Die Gebäudezahlen werden hier aufgegriffen und die Orientierung durch die einfache Codierung (Gebäudenummer, Etage, Zimmernummer) vereinfacht.

N & P: How do the students accept the new campus?
BG: The demands of students are different today compared to twenty years ago. Nowadays, students also stay on campus outside of the event times and work on projects and tasks alone or in groups. For this purpose, premises and work surfaces are to be created. These are available on the Derendorf campus in open spaces, on wide corridors, in the library with group workspaces and in the interior of the library area in various qualities, as well as in the Student Support Centre. A student project investigated the design of these areas and conceived very different concepts. Today, students wish to spend time on campus to take advantage of various additional amenities, including sports. They also require areas where they can get together and learn. Such facilities are very diverse on the Derendorf campus, even though such a development could not have been foreseen in 2008.

N & P: Did the behaviour of teachers and researchers change in addition to their studies?
BG: In research and teaching, the university increasingly works in an interdisciplinary manner (also between faculties) and transdisciplinarily (with external partners). The head-end structures in the buildings, the foyer in Building 4 and the large outdoor area will be used as public spaces for exhibitions, presentations and events. The library also hosts exhibitions on specific topics or lecture series. These premises are very important for promoting internal and external communication. But they also serve as spaces for encounters in order to cultivate a multifaceted relationship. The partially interlinked arrangement of the faculties in Building 6 enables interdisciplinary communication on each floor, ensuring ad-hoc meetings and communication. The many glass elements (glass walls, doors, partitions) create transparency and openness, thereby overcoming boundaries, inspiring mutual curiosity.

Various projects and the Studium Integrale offer inter-faculty events. The open architecture reflects its practical use in a particularly impressive way.

Over a period of 18 months, the many workshops with various user groups to discover their requirements were certainly demanding. However, the resulting architecture has managed to support and visualise the users' behaviour.

N & P: What trends do you see for the future and how is HSD preparing itself for further changes in the research world of tomorrow?
BG: Digitisation is also introducing new teaching and learning concepts that were not yet foreseeable to that extent when planning new buildings. Among other aspects, laying of a modern fibre-optic network between all buildings

N & P: Wie nehmen die Studierenden den neuen Campus an?
BG: Die Anforderungen der Studierenden sind heute andere als noch vor zwanzig Jahren. Heutzutage halten sich die Studierenden auch außerhalb der Veranstaltungszeiten auf dem Campus auf und arbeiten alleine oder in Gruppen an Projekten und Aufgabenstellungen. Hierfür sind Räumlichkeiten und Arbeitsflächen zu schaffen. Diese sind auf dem Campus Derendorf in freien Flächen, auf breiten Fluren, in der Bibliothek mit Gruppenarbeitsräumen und im inneren der Bibliotheksfläche in unterschiedlichen Qualitäten vorhanden, weiterhin im Studierendensupport-Center. Ein studentisches Projekt hat sich mit der Ausgestaltung dieser Flächen beschäftigt und sehr unterschiedliche Konzepte entworfen. Studierende haben aktuell den Anspruch, sich auf dem Campus aufzuhalten, diverse zusätzliche Angebote, auch Sportangebote, nutzen zu können und dort auch Aufenthaltsflächen und Lernflächen zur Verfügung gestellt zu bekommen. Diese sind auf dem Campus Derendorf sehr vielfältig vorhanden, obwohl 2008 diese Entwicklung noch nicht so abgesehen werden konnte.

N & P: Hat sich neben dem Studium auch das Verhalten der Lehrenden und Forschenden verändert?
BG: In Forschung und Lehre wird an der Hochschule verstärkt interdisziplinär (auch über die Fachbereichsgrenzen hinweg) und transdisziplinär (mit externen Partnern) gearbeitet. Die Kopfbauten in den Gebäuden, das Foyer in Gebäude 4, die große Außenfläche werden als öffentlicher Raum für Ausstellungen, Präsentationen und Veranstaltungen genutzt. Auch in der Bibliothek finden Ausstellungen zu bestimmten Themen oder Vortragsreihen statt. Diese Räumlichkeiten sind sehr wichtig zur Förderung interner und externer Kommunikation. Sie dienen aber auch als Räume für Begegnungen, um ein facettenreiches Miteinander zu kultivieren. Die teilweise verzahnte Anordnung der Fachbereiche in Gebäude 6 ermöglicht fachbereichsübergreifende Kommunikation auf jeder Etage, gewährleistet Begegnungen und Kommunikation ohne anlassbezogen zu sein. Die vielen Glaselemente (gläserne Wände, Türen, Abtrennungen) schaffen Transparenz und Offenheit und überwinden damit Grenzen, machen neugierig für das Andere.

Mit verschiedenen Projekten oder dem ‚Studium Integrale' werden auch Veranstaltungen fachbereichsübergreifend angeboten. Die offene Architektur spiegelt hierbei die gelebte Praxis in besonders beeindruckender Weise wider.

Die vielen Workshops, die mit den unterschiedlichen Nutzergruppen in einem anderthalbjährigen Prozess durchgeführt wurden und die die Nutzeransprüche angesprochen haben, waren sicherlich nicht einfach. Es ist aber gelungen, das Nutzerverhalten durch die Architektur zu unterstützen und zu visualisieren.

O38
Library, Hochschule Düsseldorf, former livestock hall built in 1899
Bibliothek der Hochschule Düsseldorf in der ehemaligen Großviehhalle von 1899

039
Institute building
foyer, Hochschule
Düsseldorf,
Nickl & Partner
Architekten,
2012 – 2018
Foyer in einem
der Institutsgebäude
der Hochschule
Düsseldorf,
Nickl & Partner
Architekten,
2012 – 2018

and the equipment of modern technology in the media centres make it possible to hold online courses, network the lecture theatres and record events. A university is a place where changes occur very quickly, also in the world of research, which then have to be implemented. That's why it's important to have robust materials that can be changed, that can be repaired years later, and that are not expensive. Even decades later, the same quality paint can be reapplied, without needing to replace tiles or granite. The centrepiece of a university is important, since it houses many technical faculties. Thus it is important to invest in information, communication and media technology, while also prioritising laboratory equipment, life-cycle assessment and operative cost-effectiveness. The architecture of the University of Applied Sciences Düsseldorf fulfills these diverse requirements in an impressive way. It is also perceived as aesthetically pleasing and praised by many guests and their users.

N & P: Welche Trends zeichnen sich für die Zukunft ab und wie stellt sich die HSD auf weitere zukünftige Veränderungen der Forschungswelt ein?
BG: Mit der Digitalisierung werden auch neue Lehr- und Lernkonzepte eingesetzt, die bei der Neubauplanung noch nicht in dem Maße absehbar waren. Durch die Verlegung eines modernen Glasfasernetzes zwischen allen Gebäuden und die Ausstattungsmöglichkeit der modernen Technik in den Medienzentralen lassen sich u.a. Online-Kurse, Vernetzung von Hörsälen und Aufnahmen von Veranstaltungen realisieren. Eine Hochschule ist eben ein Ort, an dem sich sehr schnell Veränderungen auch in der Forschungswelt ergeben, die dann umzusetzen sind. Daher kommt es auf robuste, veränderungsfähige Materialien an, die auch nach Jahren ausgebessert werden können, die nicht teuer sind. Farbe kann auch nach Jahrzehnten in der gleichen Qualität aufgetragen werden, Fliesen bzw. Granit sind nicht mehr bzw. nicht zu ersetzen. Wichtig ist das Herzstück einer Hochschule, die viele technische Fachbereiche beherbergt. Auf die Informations-, Kommunikations- und Medientechnik sollte investiert werden, in die Ausstattung der Labore, in die Umweltbilanz und die Effizienz der Betreiberkosten sollte Wert gelegt werden. Die Architektur der Hochschule Düsseldorf erfüllt diese vielfältigen Anforderungen in beeindruckender Weise. Sie wird darüber hinaus noch als ästhetisch empfunden und von vielen Gästen und ihren Nutzerinnen und Nutzern sehr gelobt.

2 Building
Gebäude → 52–105

The laboratory, writing workplace, auxiliary room and corridor – these "modules" and their mutual structural relationships form the basic order of a research building. The number of possible module combinations is limited, so that certain types can be demonstrated despite the diversity of laboratory buildings. Among all research buildings, the tower type is a special form that has produced remarkable buildings, of which a number of interesting examples are presented in this chapter.

Structure and order have also defined the building's internal processes for decades. The dynamism of research and rapid innovation processes demand highly adaptable scientific work on new processes and techniques. Thus, the question how flexibly a research building can react to such dynamism plays a key role in the design process. The flexibility of spatial structures, as well as laboratory modules and their technical equipment, is therefore investigated in detail in this section.

² Struktur & Ordnung

Labor, Schreibarbeitsplatz, Nebenraum, Flur – diese „Bausteine" und ihre strukturelle Beziehung zueinander bilden die Grundordnung eines Forschungsgebäudes. Die Kombinationsmöglichkeiten dieser Bausteine sind begrenzt, so dass sich trotz aller Vielfalt der Laborbauten bestimmte Typen herauskristallisieren lassen. Unter allen Forschungsgebäuden ist der Typ des Turms eine Sonderform, die bemerkenswerte Bauwerke hervorgebracht hat. Einige interessante Beispiele werden hier vorgestellt.

Struktur und Ordnung legen auch die inneren Prozesse in einem Gebäude für Jahrzehnte fest. Die Dynamik der Forschung und rasante Innovationsprozesse verlangen ein hohes Maß der Anpassbarkeit wissenschaftlichen Arbeitens an neue Prozesse und Techniken. Somit spielt die Frage, wie flexibel ein Forschungsgebäude auf diese Dynamik reagieren kann, eine zentrale Rolle für den Entwurf. Flexibilität der räumlichen Strukturen, aber auch der Labormodule und deren technische Ausstattungen werden daher in diesem Teil näher betrachtet.

2.1 The typology of research buildings – Systematics, the basis of design

PETER PFAB

To this day, the Salk Institute in San Diego, designed by the architect Louis Kahn in the 1960s, remains an exemplary, innovative research building that ideally combines urban planning, architecture and functional aspects. Jonas Salk, who discovered and developed the vaccine against polio, worked on the project together with the architect Louis Kahn, both of whom shared a bond of mutual respect. Louis Kahn admired Jonas Salk for his scientific work, while Jonas Salk expressed his great respect for Louis Kahn during a memorial convocation at the University of Pennsylvania on April 2, 1974.

Out of the mind of a tiny whimsical man
who happened by chance,
great forms have come,
great structures, great spaces that function.
Some house the essence of the past,
Others the creators, the discoverers and leaders
of an emerging future.
The wonder surrounding it all
Is in the mystery
of his existence
and in his creations,
a mystery that will endure.[1]

That mutual admiration and trust formed the basis of the historic building. Despite fundamental changes in the research landscape over the past 50 years, the two laboratory buildings of the Salk Institute, with their expressive office wings in front of them, continue to provide a functional and creative working environment, as demonstrated by the six Nobel Prize winners among the past and present researchers at the facility. → 040–045

Research buildings are living and working environments, places of communication and exchanging knowledge that are always orientated towards the future, since they need to enable the as yet unplanned and unknown. They require variable structures that can react to changing demands and conditions.

The foundation for a successful project is laid when developers, users and planners comprehensively and openly discuss and formulate the aims and demands of the planned research building.

2.1 Typologie von Forschungsgebäuden – Systematik als Grundlage für den Entwurf

PETER PFAB

Das Salk Institute in San Diego, entworfen in den 60er Jahren vom Architekten Louis Kahn, ist noch heute Vorbild für ein innovatives Forschungsgebäude, das Städtebau, Architektur und Funktion in idealer Weise verbindet. Jonas Salk, der Entdecker und Entwickler des Impfstoffes gegen Polio, hat gemeinsam mit dem Architekten Louis Kahn, beide verbunden durch gegenseitigen größten Respekt, dieses Projekt verwirklicht. Louis Kahn bewunderte Jonas Salk für seine wissenschaftliche Arbeit, Jonas Salk brachte Louis Kahn seinen großen Respekt mit eindrucksvollen Worten bei einer Gedenkfeier an der Universität von Pennsylvania am 2. April 1974 zum Ausdruck.

Dem Geist eines kleinen, wunderlichen Mannes,
den es zufällig gab,
entsprangen großartige Formen,
großartige Konstruktionen und Räume, die funktionierten.
Einige sind Heim für Vergangenes,
andere für Schöpfer, Entdecker und Führer
einer werdenden Zukunft.
Das Wunder, das all dies umfasst,
liegt im Geheimnis
seines Daseins
und in seinem Werk;
und dieses Geheimnis wird Bestand haben.[1]

Die gegenseitige Hochachtung und das Vertrauen waren die Basis für das Jahrhundertbauwerk. Trotz grundlegender Veränderungen in der Forschungslandschaft in den letzten 50 Jahren bieten die beiden Laborbauten des Salk Institute mit ihren vorgelagerten expressiven Bürotrakten weiterhin ein funktionales und kreatives Arbeitsumfeld. Hiervon zeugen unter anderem sechs Nobelpreisträger, die hier forschten bzw. noch forschen. → 040–045

Forschungsbauten sind Lebensraum, Arbeitswelt, Ort der Kommunikation und des Wissensaustausches. Forschungsbauten sind immer in die Zukunft gerichtet und müssen das noch nicht Geplante und das Unbekannte ermöglichen. Sie benötigen variable Strukturen, die auf sich ändernde Anforderungen und Bedingungen reagieren können.

Der Grundstein für ein erfolgreiches Projekt wird gelegt, wenn Bauherren, Nutzer und Planer umfassend und offen die Ziele und Anforderungen für den zu errichtenden Forschungsbau diskutieren und formulieren.

Die Einflussmöglichkeiten auf ein Projekt sind in der Anfangsphase bei der Wahl des Grundstücks, bei der Definition der funktionellen Anforderungen bzw. deren Umsetzung und schließlich bei der Erstellung des Raumprogramms am größten.

040
Salk Institute for
Biological Studies,
La Jolla (USA),
Louis I. Kahn,
completed in 1963
Salk Institute for
Biological Studies,
La Jolla (USA),
Louis I. Kahn,
fertiggestellt 1963

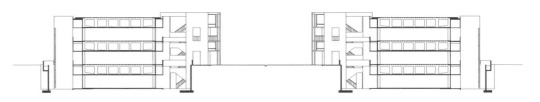

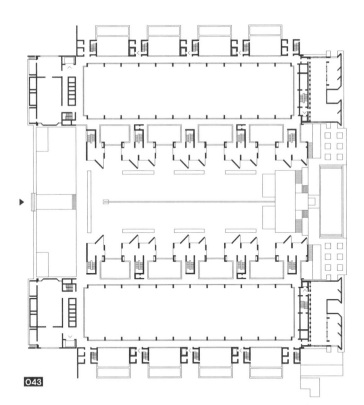

043

044

Initially, the greatest potential to influence a project lies in the choice of location, a definition of the functional demands and their implementation, as well as the development of a spatial programme.

The architect is an inquirer and moderator, investigating the requirements of science and documenting them for the office project. The scientist's task is to describe working methods and formulate expectations with respect to the working environment, communication and creating a representative location.

Initial feasibility studies sound out the possibilities and scope of a building measure. At that stage, which entails the lowest proportion of the overall building costs, the right course is set for a future-proof building.

The budget framework is also defined on this initial design and decision-making level. Only marginal amendments to the cost structure are possible at a later stage. The first reliable cost estimates, based on guideline values and taking special additional costs into account, provide insight on whether the budget ideas are feasible. If not, the project figures should not be "massaged". Instead, either the scope of the building measure should be reduced or the budget should be increased.

After assessing the fundamentals, the next step is to find the best design concept, generally using alternative planning processes, such as announcing an architectural competition. All aspects of the relevant measure should be assessed in an open dialogue between the building client, users, architects, funding bodies and authorities. Also in this context, the better and more intensively the competition process is prepared, the more successful the result will be. The spatial programme should be organised according to the use areas and their mutual relationships, while the specifications with respect to technical equipment and structural requirements must be defined.

So-called laboratory landscapes should also be discussed in this respect. What can these large spatial structures achieve, and what research tasks and fields would benefit from smaller units. It should be discussed whether the two design approaches are feasible in parallel and whether laboratory landscapes can also be subdivided into smaller units at a later date. Such flexibility is always advantageous because marginal conditions can change unpredictably. The COVID-19 pandemic will also provide new insight in this respect.

Engagement with building typologies for research facilities is helpful for such investigations and discussion. → 046–052

Der Architekt ist Fragesteller und Moderator, um die Erfordernisse der Wissenschaft zu eruieren und für das Bauprojekt zu dokumentieren. Von Seiten der Wissenschaft werden die Arbeitsweisen erläutert und die Erwartungen an das Arbeitsumfeld, an die Kommunikation und die Adressbildung formuliert.

Erste Machbarkeitsstudien loten Möglichkeiten und Umfang einer Baumaßnahme aus. In dieser Phase, die den geringsten Mittelaufwand in Bezug auf die Gesamtbaukosten erfordert, werden die Weichen gestellt für ein zukunftsfestes Gebäude.

In dieser ersten Entwurfs- und Entscheidungsebene wird auch der Kostenrahmen definiert. Später kann nur noch marginal in das Kostengerüst eingegriffen werden. Die ersten belastbaren Kostenschätzungen auf der Grundlage von Richtwerten und unter Berücksichtigung besonderer zusätzlicher Kosten geben Auskunft, ob die Budgetvorstellungen erfüllt werden können. Wenn nicht, darf das Projekt nicht „schön gerechnet" werden, vielmehr muss der Umfang der Baumaßnahme reduziert oder das Budget angehoben werden.

Nach der Grundlagenermittlung wird das beste Entwurfskonzept in der Regel über alternative Planungsverfahren, wie die Auslobung eines Architektenwettbewerbs gesucht. In einer offenen Diskussion zwischen Bauherren, Nutzern, Architekten, Finanziers und Behörden werden alle Aspekte der jeweiligen Maßnahme ausführlich abgewogen. Auch hier gilt, je besser und je intensiver das Wettbewerbsverfahren vorbereitet wird, desto erfolgreicher wird auch das Ergebnis sein. Das Raumprogramm ist nach Nutzungsbereichen und deren Beziehungen zueinander zu ordnen und die Vorgaben hinsichtlich technischer Ausstattung und konstruktiver Vorgaben sind zu nennen.

Dabei sind auch die sogenannten Laborlandschaften zu diskutieren. Was können diese großräumlichen Strukturen leisten? Aber auch für welche Forschungsaufgaben, Forschungsfelder sind kleinere Einheiten sinnvoller? Es muss erörtert werden, ob ein nebeneinander beider Entwurfsansätze sinnvoll ist und Laborlandschaften später auch in kleinere Einheiten unterteilt werden können. Diese Flexibilität ist immer von Vorteil, weil sich Randbedingungen unvorhersehbar ändern können. Die Coronapandemie wird auch hier neue Aspekte liefern.

Für diese Untersuchungen und Diskussionen ist die Auseinandersetzung mit Gebäudetypologien für Forschungsbauten hilfreich. → 046–052

Floor-plan typology

Grundrisstypologien

■ **Analysis zone**
Auswertezone

□ **Laboratory zone**
Laborzone

■ **Service zone**
Servicezone

▨ **Office zone**
Bürozone

▨ **Circulation**
Verkehrsfläche

**See examples of
floor-plan typologies
on pages 66–69**
Siehe Beispiele zu
den Grundrisstypologien
auf den Seiten 66–69

046
Sketch 1
Skizze 1

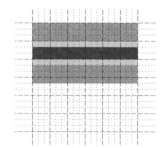

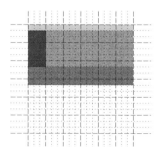

047
Sketch 2
Skizze 2

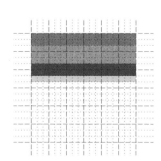

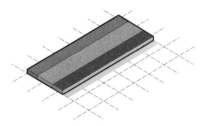

048
Sketch 3
Skizze 3

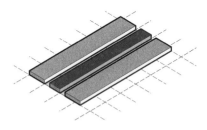

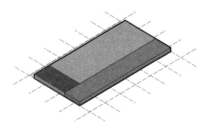

049
Sketch 4
Skizze 4

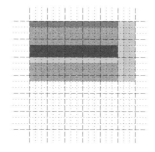

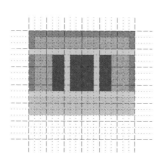

050
Sketch 5
Skizze 5

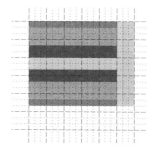

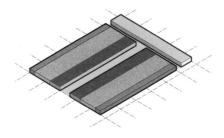

051
Sketch 6
Skizze 6

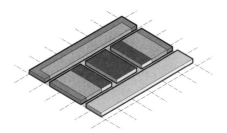

052
Sketch 7
Skizze 7

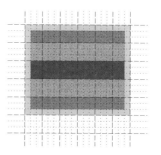

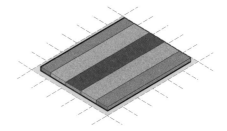

Floor-plan typology

Research-building typologies
→ support dialogue on the spatial programme and its specification
→ form the basis of initial reliable cost estimates
→ define the requirements of research work
→ are indicators for communication
→ are a database for structured research-building development

The field of science for research buildings in the scientific fields of biology, chemistry and physics consist of laboratory zones, analysis areas, service and auxiliary zones, as well as offices and seminar rooms.

Biology, chemistry or physics experiments are carried out in the **laboratory zone,** be they preparatory measures by hand or computer, microscopic operations or laser experiments. The laboratory zone contains extractors, secure workplaces and other experiment facilities. Laboratory zones are highly installed and require great variability for scientific work. **Analysis areas** provide space to observe and assess operations at close proximity to the experiments. They are not permanent workplaces, but are often used for extended periods. Noise insulation and a certain degree of privacy should therefore be taken into account. **Service and auxiliary-room zones** for refrigerators, devices, noisy experiment facilities, gloveboxes etc. supplement the laboratory zones as "dark areas". For practical reasons, **office and meeting rooms** are situated near the laboratories. A definition of "near" should be discussed with the user.

The outlined building typologies for science areas present examples that can be discussed with respect to interdisciplinarity, communication, scientific work, privacy, safety, as well as the limits of adaptability according to objective and subjective criteria. → `053-059`

Until the 1990s, two- and three-winged floor plans were standard in the field of universities, with required corridors between the individual laboratories and service zones, depending on the building regulations. Analysis workplaces were arranged within the laboratory zone along the windows or in an extension of the laboratory desks.

Since the turn of the millennium, floor-plan concepts have increasingly used laboratory landscapes and analysis zones. Laboratory landscapes encourage interdisciplinarity and communication, by bringing together research groups from different fields at one location. Laboratory landscapes form a spatial continuum without the required partitioning corridors between the laboratory areas, analysis zones and service rooms. A glass partition wall between the laboratory and evaluation areas lowers noise levels resulting from

Zur Grundrisstypologie

Typologien im Forschungsbau
→ unterstützen die Raumprogrammdiskussion und Raumprogrammfixierung,
→ sind Grundlage für erste belastbare Kostenschätzungen,
→ definieren die Erfordernisse der Forschungsarbeiten,
→ sind Indikator für die Kommunikation,
→ sind Datenbank für strukturierten Forschungsbau.

Der Wissenschaftsbereich von Forschungsgebäuden für die naturwissenschaftlichen Disziplinen Biologie, Chemie und Physik setzt sich zusammen aus Laborzone, Auswertebereich, Service- und Nebenraumzone sowie Büroflächen und Seminarräumen.

In der Laborzone findet der biologische, chemische oder physikalische Versuch statt, ob präparativ per Hand oder Computer, ob mikroskopisch oder im Laserexperiment. In der Laborzone befinden sich Abzüge, Sicherheitswerkbänke und weitere Versuchseinrichtungen. Laborzonen sind hoch installiert und erfordern große Variabilität für das wissenschaftliche Arbeiten. Auswertebereiche bieten Platz, versuchsnah zu beobachten und auszuwerten. Sie sind keine Dauerarbeitsplätze, werden aber oft über einen längeren Zeitraum genutzt. Lärmschutz und ein gewisses Maß an Privatheit sind deshalb zu berücksichtigen. Service- und Nebenraumzonen für Kühlschränke, Geräte, laute Versuchseinrichtungen, Gloveboxen etc. ergänzen die Laborzonen als „Dunkelbereiche". In der Nähe der Labore befinden sich zweckmäßigerweise auch Büro- und Besprechungsräume. Die Definition „nah" ist mit dem Nutzer zu diskutieren.

Die skizzierten Gebäudetypologien für Wissenschaftsbereiche zeigen Beispiele, an denen die Gesichtspunkte Interdisziplinarität, Kommunikation, wissenschaftliches Arbeiten, Privatheit, Sicherheit, aber auch die Grenzen der Veränderbarkeit nach objektiven und subjektiven Kriterien diskutiert werden können. → `053-059`

Bis in die 1990er-Jahre waren im Universitätsbereich Zwei- und Dreibundgrundrisse mit notwendigen Fluren nach Bauordnung zwischen den Einzellaboren und der Servicezone der Regelfall. Dabei wird der Auswerteplatz innerhalb der Laborzone entlang den Fenstern oder in Verlängerung der Labortische ausgewiesen.

Seit der Jahrtausendwende werden vermehrt Grundrisskonzepte mit Laborlandschaften und Auswertezonen entwickelt. Laborlandschaften fördern die Interdisziplinarität und die Kommunikation, indem fachübergreifend Forschungsgruppen an einem Ort zusammengeführt werden. Laborlandschaften bilden ein Raumkontinuum ohne trennende notwendige Flure zwischen Laborbereich, Auswertebereich und Servicezone. Eine Glastrennwand zwischen Labor und Auswertebereich senkt den Lärmpegel, der aus der Lüftungsanlage und der Laborarbeit resultiert. Schiebetüren zwischen Labor und Auswertebereich

the ventilation system and laboratory work. Sliding doors between the laboratory and analysis areas are possible if a direct connection between the analysis area and the required corridor is necessary. Appropriate furniture supports privacy and concentration in the analysis area. The service zone is directly connected to the laboratory zone.

The COVID pandemic has shown how both ventilation and air filtering are aspects that must already be integrated into the preliminary design stage.

The maximum size of a laboratory landscape is primarily defined by fire-safety regulations. The Bavarian regulations (BayBO) stipulate limits in its Art. 28 with respect to firewalls, which must be constructed at a maximum distance of 40 metres. Art. 34 also states that the maximum size of use units is fixed at 200 m², within which no prescribed corridors are necessary. Supervisory authorities also permit use units for large-scale laboratories with sizes of 400 m² if additional measures are undertaken. For instance the concept for the large-scale laboratory at the Salk Institute is assessed according to Art. 28, whereby the maximum extension must also be coordinated with safety authorities concerning the overview of the laboratory, both indoors and outdoors. For fire safety, the maximum size of a laboratory landscape depends on the extent to which the analysis area, the laboratory zone or the auxiliary room zone have direct connections to the required corridor. The use unit then refers to the respective area.

Generally, in laboratory landscapes, the room depths of the analysis areas are between 2.40 m and 4.80 m, while laboratory zones are between 6.00 m and 10.80 m deep and service zones have a depth of 2.40 m to 4.80 m.

One key design criterion for determining the depth of laboratories is natural light. Light, noise, quietness and privacy determine user satisfaction with respect to workplaces and therefore the acceptance of laboratory landscapes. Guidance of natural light depends on the façade design, the room height and technical installations. The floor heights in laboratory buildings are also a key factor for the technical variability of a laboratory. The required floor heights depend on workplace regulations and the building technology. Minimum heights of 4.0 m can only be undercut in exceptional cases. According to today's standards, recommended floor heights for chemistry, biology and physics laboratories range between 4.2 m and 4.5 m. Special laboratories such as cleanrooms and measuring rooms require considerably greater floor heights.

The laboratory axes in a research building have measurements of 3.45 m (3 × 1.15 m) or 3.60 m (3 × 1.20 m). In universities with many students in the research area, a laboratory grid of 3.6 m is recommended.

sind möglich, wenn eine direkte Verbindung vom Auswertebereich zum notwendigen Flur besteht. Eine entsprechende Möblierung unterstützt die Privatheit und Konzentration im Auswertebereich. Die Servicezone schließt direkt an die Laborzone an.

Die Corona-Pandemie hat gezeigt, dass sowohl die Luftführung als auch die Luftfilterung Aspekte sind, die bereits in die Vorentwurfsphase einfließen müssen. Die maximale Größe einer Laborlandschaft wird in erster Linie durch die Auflagen des Brandschutzes bestimmt. Die Bayerische Bauordnung setzt hierfür einerseits Grenzen im Art. 28 zu den Brandwänden, die nach maximal 40 Metern zu errichten sind, und andererseits über den Art. 34, der die maximale Größe von Nutzungseinheiten mit 200 m² festschreibt, innerhalb derer keine Flure erforderlich sind. Mit zusätzlichen Maßnahmen stimmen Aufsichtsbehörden auch Nutzungseinheiten für Labore mit einer maximalen Größe von 400 m² zu. Beispielsweise ist das Konzept des Großraumlabors des Salk Institute nach Art. 28 zu beurteilen, wobei die maximale Ausdehnung auch hinsichtlich der Übersichtlichkeit des Labors innen und von außen mit den Sicherheitsbehörden abzustimmen ist. Die maximale Größe einer Laborlandschaft ist bei der Brandschutzbeurteilung abhängig von den Möglichkeiten, inwieweit der Auswertebereich, die Laborzone oder die Nebenraumzone direkte Verbindungen zum notwendigen Flur besitzt. Die Nutzungseinheit bezieht sich dann auf den jeweiligen Bereich.

In Laborlandschaften betragen in der Regel die räumlichen Tiefen der Auswertebereiche 2,40 m bis 4,80 m, in der Laborzone zwischen 6,00 m bis 10,80 m sowie in der Servicezone zwischen 2,40 m bis 4,80 m.

Ein wesentliches Entwurfskriterium für die Festlegung von Labortiefen ist Tageslicht. Licht, Lärm beziehungsweise Ruhe und Privatheit entscheiden über die Zufriedenheit mit dem Arbeitsplatz und damit über die Akzeptanz von Laborlandschaften. Die Tageslichtführung ist abhängig von der Fassadengestaltung, der Raumhöhe und der technischen Installation. Die Geschoßhöhen in Laborgebäuden sind auch entscheidendes Kriterium für die technische Veränderbarkeit eines Labors. Die erforderliche Geschosshöhe richtet sich nach der Arbeitsstättenrichtlinie und der Gebäudetechnik. Ein Mindestmaß von 4,0 m kann nur in Einzelfällen unterschritten werden. Nach heutigem Stand der Technik werden für chemische, biologische und physikalische Labore Geschosshöhen von 4,2 m bis 4,5 m empfohlen. Sonderlabore wie Reinräume oder Messräume benötigen auch wesentlich größere Geschosshöhen.

Die Laborachsen im Forschungsbau betragen 3,45 m (3 × 1,15 m) oder 3,60 m (3 × 1,20 m). Im Hochschulbereich mit vielen Studierenden im Forschungsbereich wird das Laborraster 3,60 m empfohlen.

Examples of floor-plan typologies

Sketch 1

presents the concept of the first building section for the Biology Faculty of the Ludwig-Maximilian-Universität in Munich-Martinsried. →053 Highly installed and low-installation building areas are clearly distinguished. The laboratory wings are linked in a comb structure to the connecting wing with offices, lecture theatres and a library. The laboratory work is organised in a conventional tripartite system, whereby the analysis areas are part of the laboratory zone. The central shafts from technical systems are situated in the laboratory and service zones.

Sketch 2

shows the standard floor of the Center for Stroke and Dementia Research (CSD) at the Ludwig-Maximilians-Universität München in Großhadern. →054 The laboratory landscapes, individual labs, offices and seminar rooms with communication areas are grouped around a square inner courtyard. The laboratory landscapes are accessed via the service zones. The evaluation, laboratory and service zones' direct connection to the required corridors makes it possible to conform to the 200 m² rule for use units. Central technical shafts in the service zone ensure five respective laboratory axes. The laboratory landscape can also be subdivided into smaller units. Supplementing the laboratory units with individual laboratories opens up opportunities for special laboratories. Alternating between single and three-winged building sections leads to varied, communicative mobility areas. Special attention was paid to the furniture in the analysis zone.

Sketch 3

demonstrates how laboratory landscapes of the Institute for Medical Systems Biology at the Humboldt Universität Berlin are accessed via the laboratory zones. →055 The direct visibility from the corridors into the laboratories opens up the labs to the outside environment. Laboratory and service areas are pooled in a single zone. The technical systems are supplied by central shafts. The floor plan enables a high degree of flexibility in organising the laboratory work and maximum transparency. The analysis zone is situated in a quiet area along the façade behind the laboratories.

Beispiele zu den Grundrisstypologien

In Skizze 1

wird das Konzept des ersten Bauabschnitts der Fakultät für Biologie der Ludwig-Maximilians-Universität in München-Martinsried vorgestellt. →053 Hochinstallierte und niedrig installierte Gebäudebereiche werden klar unterschieden. Die Labortrakte schließen kammförmig an den Verbindungsbaukörper mit Büroräumen, Hörsälen und Bibliothek an. Die Laborarbeit ist in einem konventionellen Dreibund organisiert, wobei die Auswerteflächen Teil der Laborzone sind. Die zentralen Technikschächte befinden sich in den Labor- und Servicezonen.

Skizze 2

zeigt das Regelgeschoß des Centrum für Schlaganfall- und Demenzforschung (CSD) der Ludwig-Maximilians-Universität München in Großhadern. →054 Die Laborlandschaften, die Einzellabore, die Büro- sowie die Seminarräume mit Kommunikationsbereichen gruppieren sich um einen quadratischen Innenhof. Die Laborlandschaften werden über die Servicezone erschlossen. Durch die direkte Anbindung der Auswerte-, der Labor- sowie der Servicezone an die notwendigen Flure wird die 200 m² Regel für Nutzungseinheiten eingehalten. Zentrale Technikschächte in der Servicezone versorgen jeweils fünf Laborachsen. Die Laborlandschaft kann auch in kleinere Einheiten geteilt werden. Die Ergänzung der Laborlandschaften durch Einzellabore eröffnet Möglichkeiten für Sonderlabore. Der Wechsel zwischen ein- und dreibündigen Bauteilen führt zu erlebnisreichen, kommunikativen Verkehrsflächen. Besondere Aufmerksamkeit wurde der Möblierung der Auswertzonen geschenkt.

Skizze 3

zeigt wie die Laborlandschaften des Institute for Medical Systems Biology der Humboldt Universität Berlin über die Laborzone erschlossen werden. →055 Mit dem direkten Einblick von den Fluren in die Labore öffnet sich die Forschung auch nach außen. Labor- und Serviceflächen werden in einer Zone zusammengefasst. Die technische Versorgung erfolgt über Zentralschächte. Der Grundriss ermöglicht eine hohe Flexibilität in der Organisation der Laborarbeit und höchste Transparenz. Die Auswertezone befindet sich im ruhigen Bereich an der Fassade hinter den Laboren.

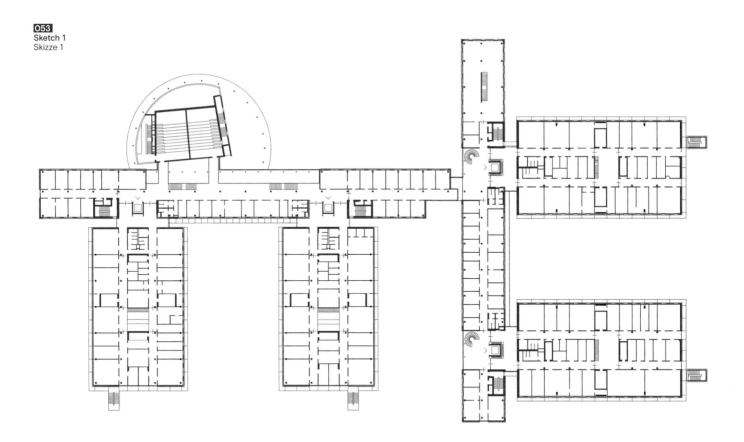

053
Biocenter of
the LMU, Munich–
Martinsried,
Fritsch + Tschaidse
Architekten,
completed in 2008
Biocenter der
LMU, München–
Martinsried,
Fritsch + Tschaidse
Architekten,
fertiggestellt 2008

054
Center for Stroke
and Dementia
Research (CSD) at
the LMU, Munich–
Großhadern,
Nickl & Partner
Architekten,
completed in 2014
Centrum für Schlag–
anfall- und Demenz–
forschung (CSD)
der LMU, München–
Großhadern,
Nickl & Partner
Architekten,
fertiggestellt 2014

055
Institute for
Medical Systems
Biology, Berlin,
Staab Architekten,
completed in 2019
Institute for
Medical Systems
Biology, Berlin,
Staab Architekten,
fertiggestellt 2019

054
Sketch 2
Skizze 2

055
Sketch 3
Skizze 3

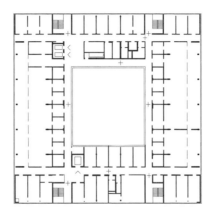

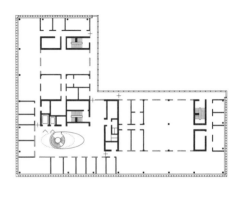

Sketch 4

presents the laboratory concept for the Research Centre for Molecular Biosystems at the Ludwig-Maximilian-Universität München in Großhadern. → 056 A central corridor connects three laboratory landscapes to the north, which can also be combined, as well as individual laboratories to the south. Direct connections between the analysis zones and the laboratory zones ensure great flexibility. Central technical shafts supply five to six laboratory axes respectively. Generous, communicative mobility areas connect the offices and seminar rooms.

Sketch 5

presents the floor plan of the Institute of Inorganic Chemistry at the Maximilian Universität Würzburg, with its opposite laboratory landscapes and a building depth of 33 m. → 057 The internal corridor connects the laboratories with the office spaces and leads to communication areas. The central technical shafts are situated at the front ends of the laboratory and service zones. Evaluation, laboratory and service zones are directly connected to the mobility areas.

Sketch 6

The Biomedical Centre at the Ludwig-Maximilian-Universität München in Martinsried consists of two research buildings and a lecture-theatre wing, which are grouped around a courtyard and integrate space for a further research building in the future. Sketch 6 shows one of the research buildings for a similarly deep floor-plan, as developed in Example 5. → 058 Based on a three-winged structure, two laboratory landscapes with an atrium are inserted into the core area between the office and seminar zone and a generous area for individual laboratories. Additionally required service areas are provided in the laboratory landscapes. Spacious mobility areas lead to communication spaces and connect the building's different wings.

Sketch 7

shows the floor-plan principle of the standard floor of a laboratory building on the Novartis Campus to the north of Basel, which was developed according to a master plan by Vittorio Lampugnani. → 059 Two laboratory landscapes with a common service zone are accessed via bright analysis areas in front of them, which have been designed to suit their special location. Also in front of them, the individual shafts allow future conversion with a high degree of independence. Office spaces and communication zones are located at the front ends of the building outside the highly installed laboratory zone.

In Skizze 4

wird das Laborkonzept des Forschungszentrums für Molekulare Biosysteme der Ludwig-Maximilians-Universität München in Großhadern erläutert. → 056 Ein Mittelflur erschließt nach Norden drei Laborlandschaften, die auch zusammengefasst werden können und nach Süden Einzellabore. Die direkte Anbindung der Auswertezonen und Laborzonen an die Verkehrsflächen ermöglicht eine große Flexibilität. Zentrale Technikschächte versorgen jeweils fünf bis sechs Laborachsen. Über großzügige, kommunikative Verkehrsflächen werden die Büro- und Seminarräume angebunden.

Skizze 5

zeigt den Grundriss mit gegenüberliegenden Laborlandschaften des Instituts für Anorganische Chemie der Julius-Maximilian-Universität mit einer Gebäudetiefe von 33 m. → 057 Der innenliegende Flur verbindet die Labore mit den Büroräumen und mündet in Kommunikationsorte. Zentrale Technikschächte befinden sich an den Stirnseiten der Labor- und Servicezonen. Auswertezonen, Laborzonen und Servicezonen sind direkt an die Verkehrsflächen angebunden.

Skizze 6

Das Biomedizinische Zentrum der Ludwig-Maximilians-Universität München in Martinsried besteht aus zwei Forschungsbauten und einem Hörsaaltrakt, die sich um einen Hof gruppieren und Raum für einen weiteren Forschungsbau vorsehen. Skizze 6 zeigt einen der Forschungsbauten, für den ein ähnlich tiefer Grundriss wie im Beispiel 5 entwickelt wurde. → 058 Basierend auf einem Dreibund werden zwischen eine Büro-, Seminarzone sowie eine großzügige Einzellaborzone im Kernbereich zwei Laborlandschaften mit einem Lichthof eingefügt. Zwischen den Laborlandschaften werden zusätzliche notwendige Serviceflächen bereitgestellt. Großzügige Verkehrsflächen münden in Kommunikationsbereiche und verbinden die Gebäudetrakte.

Skizze 7

zeigt das Grundrissprinzip des Regelgeschosses eines Laborgebäudes auf dem Novartis Campus nördlich von Basel, der nach dem Masterplan von Vittorio Lampugnani entwickelt wird. → 059 Zwei Laborlandschaften mit gemeinsamer Servicezone werden über helle, vorgelagerte Auswerteplätze, die der besonderen Lage entsprechend gestaltet wurden, erschlossen. Die vorgelagerten Einzelschächte erlauben bei Umbauten ein hohes Maß an Unabhängigkeit. Büroräume und Kommunikationsorte befinden sich an den Stirnseiten außerhalb der hochinstallierten Laborzone.

056
Research Centre for
Molecular Biosys-
tems at the LMU,
Munich-Großhadern,
Fritsch + Tschaidse
Architekten,
constructed in 2016
Forschungszentrum
für Molekulare
Biosysteme der
LMU, München-
Großhadern,
Fritsch + Tschaidse
Architekten,
fertiggestellt 2016

057
Inorganic Chemistry
C2, Universität
Würzburg, Schuster
Pechtold Schmidt
Architekten,
constructed in 2018
Anorganische
Chemie C2,
Universität Würzburg,
Schuster Pechtold
Schmidt Architekten,
fertiggestellt 2018

058
LMU Biomedical
Centre, Munich-
Martinsried,
K9 Architekten
Borgards Lösch
Piribauer,
constructed in 2015
Biomedizinisches
Centrum der
LMU, München-
Martinsried,
K9 Architekten
Borgards Lösch
Piribauer,
fertiggestellt 2015

059
Laboratory building,
Novartis Campus
Basel, Rafael Moneo
with HENN,
completed in 2008
Laborgebäude,
Novartis Campus
Basel, Rafael Moneo
mit HENN,
fertiggestellt 2008

056
Sketch 4
Skizze 4

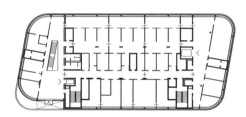

058
Sketch 6
Skizze 6

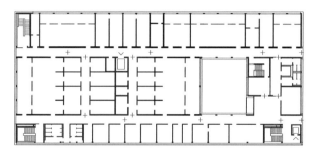

057
Sketch 5
Skizze 5

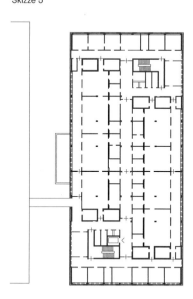

059
Sketch 7
Skizze 7

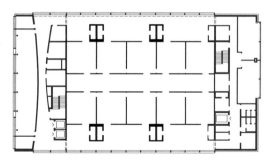

Flexibility and building technology, standard and limits

Laboratory landscapes encourage interdisciplinary work, but must be organised in a way to enable different working methods, allowing concentration and privacy even in large room units. On the one hand, natural light must shine deep into the laboratory zone, while on the other, rooms must be usable in darkness for laser experiments. In addition to deep spatial structures, individual laboratories should also be planned or retrofittable. The façade and load-bearing structure must react accordingly.

A research building requires generous spaces for technology in the basement and above the highest laboratory level. Exceptions can confirm the rule, but always entail significant technical and financial investment. The technical areas of today's highly installed research buildings represent between 40 % and 60 % of the usable space in accordance with DIN 277. Generous combined shafts supply all laboratory levels. When determining the dimensions of technical areas, the laboratory building's potential for change and flexibility is also a factor. The floor height of contemporary science research buildings should be between 4.20 m and 4.50 m. The combined shafts run in a linear fashion along the laboratory and service zones, to prevent intersections with the ventilation shafts. The depth of the shafts depends on the laboratory grid. Retrofitting and adaptations to the installations should be planned in advance.

The limits of flexibility are generally set by economic factors. It is not always possible to design technical areas in dimensions that are, for instance, large enough to accommodate a highly-installed environment for keeping SPF animals, or to choose floor heights that enable large cleanroom spaces with very high air cleanliness. But perhaps it is more accurate to say this is not yet standard practice. The great flexibility of the Salk Institute's building structure, with a technical floor above each laboratory level, should at least be discussed during every new construction project.

Communication, address, sustainability

Communication, the exchange of ideas, either within a group or in a one-on-one meeting, is a pillar of insight in science and has top priority during all stages of design planning: in urban planning when designing squares and forming representative addresses, in floor-plan concepts that equally provide laboratory landscapes and corridors with light and views outside, thereby inviting people to have a spontaneous conversation, as well as in wayfinding systems that encourage chance encounters.

Flexibilität und Gebäudetechnik, Standard und Grenzen

Laborlandschaften fördern das interdisziplinäre Arbeiten, müssen aber so konzipiert werden, dass unterschiedliche Arbeitsweisen möglich sind und Konzentration wie Privatheit auch in großen Raumeinheiten gegeben ist. Einerseits soll natürliches Tageslicht tief in die Laborzone reichen, andererseits müssen Räume auch für Laserversuche in Dunkelheit nutzbar sein. Neben tiefen Raumstrukturen für Laborlandschaften, sollten auch Einzellabore eingeplant werden oder nachträglich möglich sein. Fassade und Tragstruktur müssen darauf reagieren.

Ein Forschungsbau benötigt großzügige Technikflächen im Untergeschoss und oberhalb der obersten Laborebene. Ausnahmen bestätigen zwar die Regel, sind aber immer mit großem technischem und finanziellem Aufwand verbunden. Die Technikflächen von hochinstallierten Forschungsbauten betragen heute zwischen 40 % und 60 % der Nutzfläche nach DIN 277. Großzügige Sammelschächte erschließen alle Laborebenen. In der Dimensionierung der Technikflächen steckt auch das Veränderungs-/Flexibilitätspotential eines Laborgebäudes. Die Geschosshöhe von naturwissenschaftlichen Forschungsbauten sollte heute 4,20 bis 4,50 m betragen. Die Sammelschächte liegen linear zur Labor und zur Servicezone, um Kreuzungen der Lüftungskanäle zu vermeiden. Die Schachttiefe entspricht dem Laborraster. Es müssen Nach- und Änderungsinstallationen mit eingeplant werden.

Die Grenzen der Flexibilität werden in der Regel durch die Wirtschaftlichkeit gesetzt. Technikflächen so groß zu dimensionieren, dass zum Beispiel nachträglich hochinstallierte SPF-Tierhaltungen oder Geschosshöhen für große Reinraumflächen mit sehr hohen Anforderungen an die Luftreinheit eingerichtet werden können, ist nicht immer möglich. Vielleicht muss die Antwort aber lauten, ist noch nicht üblich. Die hohe Flexibilität der Gebäudestruktur des Salk Instituts mit einem Technikgeschoss über jeder Laborebene sollte bei jedem Neubauprojekt zumindest andiskutiert werden.

Kommunikation, Adresse, Nachhaltigkeit

Die Kommunikation, der Gedankenaustausch in der Gruppe wie im Vier-Augen-Gespräch sind Pfeiler für Erkenntnisse in der Wissenschaft. Diese Vorgabe hat bei der Planung in allen Entwurfsphasen höchste Priorität. Dies reicht vom Städtebau mit Platzgestaltung und Adressbildung, über Grundrisskonzepte, die Laborlandschaften genauso ermöglichen, wie den Flur mit Licht und Ausblick, der zum spontanen Gespräch einlädt oder Wegeführungen, die zum zufälligen Treffen einladen.

Forschungsbauten sind keine kurzfristigen Zweckbauten, sondern besitzen eine eigene Identität, mit der sich die Nutzer identifizieren können.

Instead of being short-term functional structures, research buildings have their own identity, to which users can relate. They are creative locations that also affect the outside environment, while combining qualities of a workplace and home. Science facilities operate twenty-four seven, so planners must take into account that they will be used outside usual working hours. Today, modern, flexible buildings with their own identity are also an important factor of recruitment policy.

Sustainability in laboratory building means providing adaptable floor-plans, in order to be able to react to developments in the research landscape that were unknown or unforeseeable during the planning stage. This aspect should be integrated in designs for the load-bearing structure, floor heights, technical areas and façade. Research buildings should be extendible. But sustainability also means designing a location for science where people enjoy working and meet up, allowing the facility to become part of the science landscape. Research buildings must react to the changing climate, for instance by choosing solid, heat-storing materials for all building elements that do not need to be adaptable. Sustainability in research buildings means always investigating whether existing buildings can be adapted to today's requirements. This above all also applies to laboratory buildings from the first major university construction wave in the 60s and 70s. For instance, it was possible to integrate laboratory landscapes into the buildings of the Chemistry Faculty at the Technische Universität München, incorporating them into the existing load-bearing structure, while also improving communication and orientation inside the building.

Planning and building a forward-looking, sustainable research facility requires close, trusting cooperation between the client, users and architect, as exemplified in the ingenious collaboration between Jonas Salk and Louis Kahn. 50 years after its completion, the Salk Institute is receiving a general refurbishment. There was no discussion on the matter. There can be no greater endorsement of the quality of a building.

1
Salk, Jonas.
"An Homage to
Louis I. Kahn",
Memorial
Convocation,
University of
Pennsylvania
1974 April 2.

Sie wirken als kreativer Ort auch nach außen, der Arbeitsstätte und Heimat zugleich ist. Twenty-four-seven beschreibt in der Wissenschaft die Nutzungsdauer, das heißt das Gebäude muss auch dem Umstand Rechnung tragen, dass es auch außerhalb der üblichen Arbeitszeiten genutzt wird. Moderne flexible Forschungsbauten mit eigener Identität sind heute auch wichtiges Argument einer erfolgreichen Berufungspolitik.

Nachhaltigkeit im Laborbau bedeutet, dass Gebäudegrundrisse veränderbar sind, um auf Entwicklungen in der Forschungslandschaft reagieren zu können, die während der Planungsphase nicht bekannt und vorhersehbar waren. Diese Tatsache ist in der Tragstruktur, bei den Geschosshöhen, den Technikflächen und der Fassade zu berücksichtigen. Forschungsbauten sollten erweiterbar sein. Nachhaltig heißt aber auch, einen Ort für die Wissenschaft zu gestalten, an dem man gerne arbeitet, sich trifft und der Teil der Wissenschaftslandschaft ist. Forschungsbauten müssen auf das sich ändernde Klima reagieren, indem zum Beispiel alle Bauteile, die nicht veränderbar sein müssen, aus massiven wärmespeichernden Materialien bestehen.

Nachhaltigkeit im Forschungsbau heißt immer zu untersuchen, ob Bestandsgebäude an heutige Erfordernisse angepasst werden können. Dies betrifft vor allem auch die Laborbauten aus der ersten großen Hochschulbauwelle in den 60er und 70er Jahren. So war es zum Beispiel möglich in den Gebäuden der Fakultät für Chemie der Technischen Universität München Laborlandschaften innerhalb der vorhandenen statischen Struktur zu integrieren und gleichzeitig die Kommunikation und Orientierung im Gebäude zu optimieren.

Voraussetzung für die Planung und den Bau eines in die Zukunft gerichteten, nachhaltigen Forschungsbaus ist eine enge, vertrauensvolle Zusammenarbeit zwischen Auftraggeber, Nutzer und Architekt. Das geniale Wirken zwischen Jonas Salk und Louis Kahn ist ein Beispiel, wie man dies erreichen kann. 50 Jahre nach Fertigstellung wird das Salk Institut generalsaniert. Hierüber gab es keine Diskussion. Ein größeres Kompliment an die Qualität eines Gebäudes kann es nicht geben.

1
Salk, Jonas.
"An Homage to
Louis I. Kahn",
Memorial
Convocation,
University of
Pennsylvania
2. April 1974

2.2 Research towers

The tower is literally an outstanding research-building type. The silhouette of a tower structure is a wonderful and very visible symbol of human striving to achieve higher goals. The gestures of the medieval towers in Tuscany, as well as today's race to build the world's tallest building, are always an expression of knowledge, the power that comes with it and technological advantage. Like the famous example of the Tower of Babel, today's towers can also be interpreted as a reflection of such detachment from ignorance and a striving for knowledge – hopefully with less fatal consequences than the Biblical example. Mankind rises above ignorance and strives to achieve a state of knowing – one could call it a godlike condition. The research tower, like the spires of a temple or church, reach up to the heavens.

A research tower can be built for a wide range of reasons. The tall building may be necessary to carry out a specific type of research: the tower as a means to a scientific end, for instance to study elevator facilities or wind flow properties. The artist Hendrik Christian Andersen and the architect Ernest Hébrard designed their concept for a centre mondial de communication around a gigantic "tower of progress", a radio tower broadcasting human advancement to all corners of the world. The design also reveals a second aspect of a tower as a widely visible symbol of prestige. →060

Nevertheless, laboratory and research towers are rare, since they offer limited floor space per storey and little potential for flexible use or expansion. Wherever they have been constructed, they enjoy special attention, since they have led to especially radical or intelligent designs, as the examples presented below demonstrate.

The tower as a research instrument
Fruitful collaboration between scientists and an architect led to the construction of one of the world's iconic research buildings: the astrophysicist Erwin Finlay Freundlich convinced his friend Erich Mendelsohn to design a solar observatory, which was constructed between 1919 and 1922 on the top of Potsdam's Telegrafenberg. The building was planned in close coordination with the demands of its technical devices, allowing it to be functionally tailored to its research task. The integrated telescope received its own foundation and is structurally autonomous from the building, which purely serves as a protective shell. Freundlich's goal was to find practical evidence of Einstein's Theory of Relativity by proving a shift in spectral lines in the gravitational field of the sun. The project was implemented in

72

2.2 Forschungstürme

Unter den Gebäuden für die Forschung, ist der Turm im wahrsten Sinne des Wortes herausragend. In der Silhouette eines Turmbaus manifestiert sich wunderbar und sehr anschaulich das menschliche Streben nach Höherem. Die Geste der toskanischen Geschlechtertürme, genauso wie das heutige Wettrennen um das höchste Gebäude der Welt, ist immer Ausdruck von Wissen und damit verbundener Macht und zivilisatorischem Vorsprung. Gleich jenem berühmten Vorbild in Babel können auch heutige Türme als Ausdruck dieses Loslösens aus der Unwissenheit und als Streben nach Wissen gelesen werden – mit hoffentlich weniger fatalen Folgen, als den biblisch überlieferten. Der Mensch erhebt sich aus der Unwissenheit und strebt nach einem wissenden – oder wenn man so will, gottähnlichen – Zustand. Der Forscherturm, wie die Türme eines Tempels oder einer Kirche, streben gen Himmel.

Es kann ganz unterschiedliche Gründe dafür geben, der Forschung einen Turm zu errichten. Es kann der Zweck der Forschung sein, der ein hohes Gebäude benötigt, um ausgeführt zu werden. Der Turm als Mittel zum wissenschaftlichen Zweck, wie es Türme zur Erforschung von Aufzugsanlagen oder Windströmungseigenschaften sind. So entwarfen der Künstler Hendrik Christian Andersen und der Architekt Ernest Hébrard ihre Vision eines Centre mondial de communication rund um einen mächtigen „Turm des Fortschritts", der als Sendemast die Errungenschaften der Menschheit in alle Welt übertragen sollte. In dem Entwurf tritt auch gleich die zweite Eigenschaft eines Turms deutlich zu Tage, er ist weithin sichtbares Prestigeobjekt. →060

Dennoch sind Labor- oder Forschungstürme selten, bietet doch die geringe Grundrissfläche pro Geschoss wenig Möglichkeiten zur flexiblen Nutzung oder zur Expansion. Dort, wo sie realisiert wurden, verdienen sie jedoch oft besondere Beachtung, denn sie führten zu besonders radikalen oder intelligenten Entwürfen, wie die folgenden ausgewählten Beispiele zeigen.

Der Turm als Forschungsinstrument
Eine glückliche Kooperation von Wissenschaftlern und Architekt führte zu einer Ikone der Forschungsbauten. Der Astrophysiker Erwin Finlay Freundlich überredete seinen Freund Erich Mendelsohn zum Entwurf eines Sonnenobservatoriums, der zwischen 1919 und 1922 auf dem Potsdamer Telegrafenberg realisiert wurde. Das Gebäude ist in enger Abstimmung auf die Anforderungen der technischen Geräte geplant worden und so in seiner Funktion ganz auf die Forschungsaufgabe abgestimmt. Das integrierte Teleskop erhielt ein eigenes Fundament und ist konstruktiv völlig unabhängig vom Gebäude, das lediglich als schützende Hülle dient. Freundlichs Ziel war

ANNO 1912
AN
INTERNATIONAL · WORLD · CENTRE.
PERSPECTIVE GENERALE VUE A VOL D'OISEAU.

HENDRIK. G. ANDERSEN.
ERNEST. M. HEBRARD. ARCHITECTE.

060

060
Andersen, Hébrard,
International
World Centre, 1912
The "tower of
progress" stands
at the centre
of the ideal city.
Andersen, Hébrard,
International
World Centre, 1912
Der „Turm des
Fortschritts"
im Zentrum der
Idealstadt.

73

close collaboration between Freundlich, Mendelsohn and Einstein, and to this day, the building's name of "Einsteinturm" bears witness to the role played by the expressionist architecture. The tower's status is also the result of its organically sweeping form, window details and base section. Mendelsohn wanted his design to sound out the potential of new reinforced concrete construction and translate it into a completely new architectural language. Working with his researching colleagues was an inspiration to him: *"For the first time, I am applying function and dynamics to the field of architecture as a pair of opposites. Such a scientific approach is the result of my frequent presence at discussions between Einstein and his employees."*

It was neither possible to construct the building completely out of reinforced concrete, nor was it able to prove Einstein's Theory of Relativity, yet the Einsteinturm nevertheless became internationally renowned and is still used for research today by the Leibniz-Institut für Astrophysik Potsdam. → 061-064

The prestige building

Unlike the Einsteinturm, Frank Lloyd Wright's Research Tower for SC Johnson can by no means be regarded as a building type that was adapted to suit its purpose. Instead, the laboratory building is a proud symbol of the innovative drive of a family-owned corporation, rising above the adjoining administrative building, which Wright had built in Racine ten years earlier for the prospering manufacturer of cleaning agents and insecticides. The tower is beautifully staged. Visible from afar, it elevates the researchers in a shimmering glass "ivory tower" over the low surrounding buildings. Not even the ground touches the tower. It rests on a slim base and is accessed via a bridge to the first floor.

The structure thereby represents a strong contrast to the horizontal administrative complex, with its brick façades and the cathedral-like Great Workroom, an enormous open office space with a glass roof and surrounding mezzanines. The laboratory-tower levels, however, are compact and concentrated. Nevertheless, both buildings have the common aspect of relating to a natural element. Mushroom-shaped columns and rounded forms characterise the architecture of the administrative building. Wright himself described the laboratory tower as a tree-like structure. From a central trunk that pools the elevator, staircase, toilet and all supply and disposal channels at its centre, projecting levels branch out, their thicknesses narrowing towards the edge. Round mezzanines alternate with rectangular floor spaces.

der praktische Beleg von Einsteins Relativitätstheorie durch den Nachweis der Verschiebung von Spektrallinien im Schwerefeld der Sonne. Das Projekt entstand in enger Zusammenarbeit zwischen Freundlich, Mendelsohn und Einstein und ist bis heute unter dem Namen „Einstein-Turm" als ein Zeugnis expressionistischer Architektur bekannt. Diesen Stellenwert verdankt es der organisch geschwungenen Form von Turm, Fensterdetails und Sockelgeschoss. Mendelsohn wollte mit seinem Entwurf die Möglichkeiten der neuen Stahlbetonbauweise ausschöpfen und sie in eine völlig neue Architektursprache übersetzen. Er selbst sah sich durch seine Arbeit mit den Forschern dazu inspiriert: *„Ich übertrage zum ersten Mal Funktion und Dynamik als Gegensatzpaar auf das Gebiet der Architektur. Ich schulde diese wissenschaftliche Überlegung meiner häufigen Anwesenheit bei Diskussionen zwischen Einstein und seinen Mitarbeitern".*

Zwar konnte das Gebäude weder komplett als Stahlbetonbau realisiert noch der Nachweis von Einsteins Relativitätstheorie erbracht werden, doch der Einstein-Turm erlangte internationale Berühmtheit und noch heute nutzt das Leibniz-Institut für Astrophysik Potsdam das Observatorium zu Forschungszwecken. → 061-064

Das Prestige-Objekt

Ganz anders als der Einsteinturm kann von Frank Lloyd Wrights Research Tower für SC Johnson nicht die Rede davon sein, der Gebäudetyp sei dem Zweck angepasst. Hier erhebt sich das Laborgebäude als stolzes Symbol der Innovationskraft eines Familienunternehmens über das angegliederte Verwaltungsgebäude. Dieses hatte Wright bereits zehn Jahre zuvor in Racine für den prosperierenden Hersteller von Reinigungsmitteln und Insektenvertilgern gebaut. Der Turm ist schönste Inszenierung. Weithin sichtbar ragt er empor, erhebt die Forscher gleichsam in einen gläsern schimmernden Elfenbeinturm über die flachen Umgebungsbauten. Nicht einmal den Boden berührt der Turm. Er sitzt auf einem schlanken Fuß und wird über die Brücke in der ersten Etage erschlossen.

Damit bildet er einen krassen Gegensatz zum horizontalen Verwaltungsbau, mit seinen backsteinernen Fassaden, und dem kathedralen-ähnlichen Great Workroom, einem enormen offenen Büroraum mit gläsernem Dach und Mezzaninen rundum. Die Ebenen des Laborturms hingegen sind kompakt und konzentriert. Beide Gebäude vereint jedoch ihre Anspielung auf Naturelement. Pilzförmige Säulen und Rundungen prägen die Architektur des Verwaltungsbaus. Von der Struktur des Laborturms sprach Wright selbst als einer baumartigen Konstruktion. Von einem zentralen Stamm, welcher Aufzug, Treppenhaus, WC und sämtliche Ver- und Entsorgungsstränge in der Mitte konzentriert, spreizen sich auskragende Ebenen, deren Durchmesser sich zum Rand hin verjüngt. Runde Mezzanine alternieren mit quadratischen Geschossflächen.

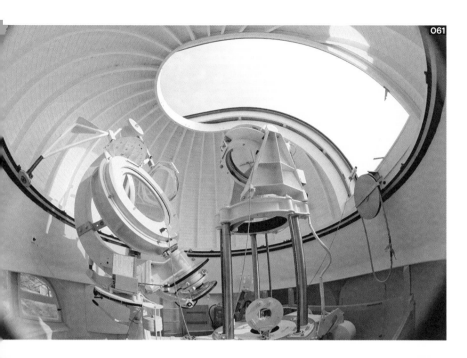

061

062

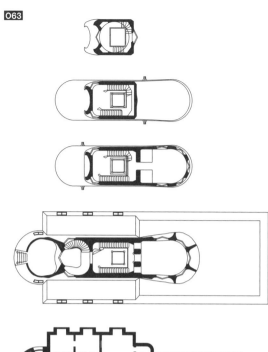

063

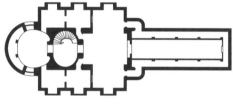

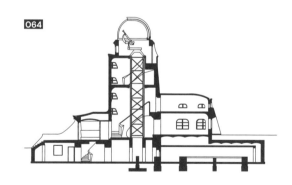

064

061–062
Einsteinturm,
Erich Mendelsohn,
Potsdam, 1919–22
Einsteinturm,
Erich Mendelsohn,
Potsdam, 1919–22

063–064
Floor plans and
sectional views,
Einsteinturm
Grundrisse
und Schnitte,
Einsteinturm

No sharp angles exist in the entire tower, since all corners are rounded and even the elevator and toilet are circular.

Due to the mezzanines, the glass façade bands respectively frame two levels. As soon as the tower is illuminated from within, the building itself has the appearance of a piece of apparatus. The image is strengthened by the distorting effect of the curved Pyrex glass tubing that forms the window bands. These Pyrex tubes may be regarded as an especially apt reference to laboratory equipment, but in fact, Wright had already used them a decade earlier for the administrative building, for glass roofing, windows and partition walls. The tailored laboratory tables were integrated along the brick-clad balustrade bands.

Architects may have celebrated the building, but its utilisation revealed problems. It is reported that researchers could initially only work wearing sunglasses, since the Pyrex tubing refracted the incident sunlight several times, making it necessary to install curtains. The individual floors are only connected via the elevator or the tiny staircase, which was not exactly conducive to interaction between the researchers. The constricted spatial conditions and poor accessibility were also a problem when new laboratory equipment had to be installed. Growing demands for heating, cooling and fire safety have ultimately prevented the Johnson Research Tower from being used as a laboratory building since the 1980s. → 065-069

Tower ensemble

How can one compensate for the clear disadvantage of limited usable space on each floor in a research tower? By placing several towers beside each other and connecting their respective floors. Louis Kahn used the solution for his design of the Richard Medical Research Laboratories at the University of Pennsylvania in Philadelphia – simply known as Penn. Together with the adjoining Goddard Laboratories, which were constructed later, the ensemble comprises six slim volumes, of which one serves as a functional and distribution area. Furthermore, externally docked-on towers for staircases and ventilation shafts protrude from the main structure. While these are entirely clad in brickwork, the laboratory towers are characterised by the visible concrete structure and glass corners.

In the late 1950s, the exposed concrete volume represented a milestone in the use of prestressed, prefabricated concrete elements. The individual elements were produced with extreme precision in a nearby factory and only had to be fixed on location. Since all structural elements and auxiliary functions, such as staircases and shafts, are situated on the façade, the actual laboratory areas

In dem gesamten Turm ist kein scharfer Winkel zu finden, alle Ecken sind abgerundet, sogar Aufzug und WC kreisförmig.

Dank der Mezzanine fassen die gläsernen Fassadenbänder jeweils zwei Ebenen zusammen. Sobald der Turm von innen erleuchtet wird, erscheint das Gebäude selbst wie ein wissenschaftliches Gerät. Verstärkt wird das Bild durch den verzerrenden Effekt der gebogenen Pyrex-Glasröhren, aus denen die Fensterbänder bestehen. Diese Pyrex-Röhren mögen für eine besonders gelungene Referenz an Labor-Utensilien gehalten werden, tatsächlich hatte Wright sie bereits eine Dekade zuvor im Verwaltungsgebäude als Glasdächer, Fenster und Raumteiler eingesetzt. Entlang der mit Backstein verkleideten Brüstung wurden die Labortische an den Brüstungsbänder maßgefertigt integriert.

Von Architekten gefeiert, hat die Nutzung des Gebäudes jedoch Probleme offenbart. So heißt es, dass die Forscher anfangs nur mit Sonnenbrillen arbeiten konnten, da die Pyrex-Röhren das einfallende Sonnenlicht mehrfach brachen, bis schließlich Vorhänge angebracht wurden. Die einzelnen Etagen sind nur über den Aufzug oder das winzige Treppenhaus miteinander verbunden, was nicht gerade zur Interaktion unter den Forschenden einlud. Auch stellten die beengten Platzverhältnisse und die schlechte Zugänglichkeit ein Problem dar, wenn es darum ging, neue Labortechnik zu installieren. Wachsenden Anforderungen an Heizen, Kühlen und Brandschutz führten schließlich dazu, dass der Johnson Research Tower seit den 80er Jahren nicht mehr als Laborgebäude genutzt wird. → 065-069

Turm-Ensemble

Wie kann der offensichtliche Nachteil einer kleinen Nutzfläche pro Geschoss bei einem Forschungsturm umgangen werden? Man stellt mehrere Türme nebeneinander und verbindet sie geschossweise. Zu dieser Lösung kam Louis Kahn für seinen Entwurf der Richard Medical Research Laboratories der University of Pennsylvania – kurz Penn – in Philadelphia. Das Ensemble umfasst zusammen mit den später entstandenen, angrenzenden Goddard Laboratories sechs schlanke Volumen, wovon eines als Funktions- und Verteilerfläche dient. Darüber hinaus ragen außen angedockte Türme für Treppenhäuser, Zu- und Abluftschächte. Während diese ganz in Backstein gefasst sind, charakterisieren die Labortürme deren sichtbare Betonkonstruktion und gläserne Ecken.

Die offenliegende Betonkonstruktion war Ende der 50er Jahre ein Meilenstein in der Verwendung vorgespannter Beton-Fertigteile. Die einzelnen Bestandteile wurden in einer nahegelegenen Fabrik mit äußerster Präzision vorgefertigt und mussten vor Ort nur noch fixiert werden. Da sämtliche konstruktive Elemente und andienende Funktionen, wie Treppenhäuser und Schächte, an die Fassade verlegt

O65

O65
SC Johnson
Research Tower,
Sectional view,
Frank L. Wright,
Racine, Wisconsin,
USA 1950
SC Johnson
Research Tower,
Querschnitt,
Frank L. Wright,
Racine, Wisconsin,
USA 1950

O66
1st floor plan
Grundriss
1. Obergeschoss

O67
Standard floor
plan of the
laboratory tower
Grundriss
Regelgeschoss
des Laborturms

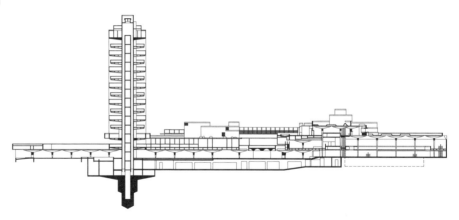

O66

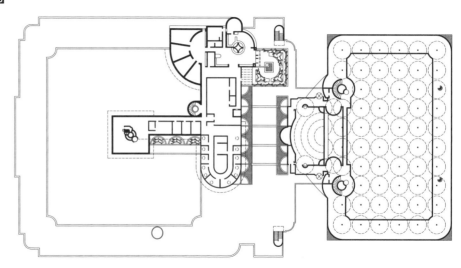

O67

069

068–069
"Helio Lab" and
exterior view,
SC Johnson
Reserach Tower
„Helio-Lab" und
Außenansicht des
SC Johnson
Research Tower

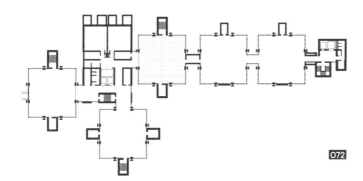

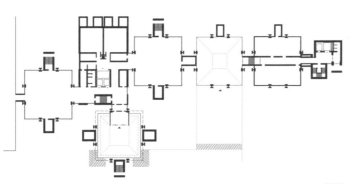

070–071
Richards Medical
Research
Laboratories,
interior with glass
corner following
renovation in 2018,
Louis Kahn,
Philadelphia,
USA 1957–61
Richards Medical
Research
Laboratories,
Innenraum nach
Renovierung 2018,
gläserne Ecke
Louis Kahn
Philadelphia,
USA 1957–61

072–073
Ground floor plan
and standard foor
plan, including load-
bearing structure
Grundriss
Erdgeschoss
und Grundriss
Regelgeschoss
mit Darstellung
des Tragwerks

require no supports at all, allowing their flexible use. However, when the first research groups moved into the building in the 1960s, a number of fittings and suspended ceilings were added. The open architectural language was not always compatible with the requirements of a wet lab.

The entrance situation is notable. The entire ground floor of one of the towers was kept open for the purpose, allowing one of the levels to serve as a covered forecourt in front of the actual entrance in the functional tower. Today, the ensemble is listed as a National Historic Landmark and continues to be used for medical research at Penn – albeit no longer for wet labs. → `070-073`

The connecting element

Two laboratory towers in Copenhagen and Basel are outstanding examples of more recent European projects, pursuing contrasting design approaches with similar concepts.

The Maersk Tower at the University of Copenhagen, with its 24,700 m² of laboratory space for medical research, stands in the northern part of the city between the Rigshospitalet and the centre. It is directly connected to the building of the Faculty of Medicine and Health Sciences, a colossal Brutalist structure from the 1970s. The tower is not only aimed at creating laboratory space for researchers and students, but also accommodates a broad programme including a conference centre, show labs, gathering areas and places for people to meet. These are concentrated in the low base section, which also serves as the connector to the Medical Faculty, its many long arms stretching into the diverse park landscape of terraces, footpaths and green spaces.

The thought of connecting various zones and the public park with places for students to learn, as well as withdrawn research areas, is a consistent theme throughout the entire building. The choice of a tower typology made it possible to preserve a public green space all around the building, through which a footpath meanders, thereby connecting two districts on either side of the building's base section. The areas of the foyer and the conference centre are designed to merge into each other and remain open. It is difficult to say where the building ends and the park begins. Allowing people to meet each other by chance and exchange ideas was also a key factor in planning the towers. Thus, an oversized vertical atrium with a spiral staircase covers the entire height of the tower. In front of it, "science plazas", open meeting places, are aimed at encouraging informal conversations. The laboratories themselves are partially organised along the façades as open-plan or cell laboratories around an inner core that pools together the office and auxiliary rooms. In a reference to the copper-clad

wurden, sind die eigentlichen Laborflächen völlig stützenfrei und flexibel nutzbar. Als in den 1960er-Jahren die ersten Forschergruppen einzogen, kam mit ihnen allerdings auch einiges an Einbauten und Abhangdecken. Die offene Architektursprache war mit den Anforderungen an ein Nasslabor nicht immer vereinbar.

Bemerkenswert ist die Eingangssituation. Das komplette Erdgeschoss einer der Türme wurde dafür offengelassen, so dass diese Ebene als überdachter Vorplatz zum eigentlichen Eingang im Funktionsturm dient. Das Ensemble ist inzwischen als National Historic Landmark eingestuft und wird weiterhin für die Medizinische Forschung an der Penn genutzt – wenn auch inzwischen nicht mehr mit Nasslaboren. → `070-073`

Das verbindende Element

Unter den europäischen Projekten jüngeren Datums stechen zwei Labortürme in Kopenhagen und Basel hervor, die ähnliche Konzepte in unterschiedlichen Gestaltungsansätzen verfolgen.

Der Maersk Tower der Universität Kopenhagen mit seinen 24.700 m² Laborfläche für medizinische Forschung erhebt sich im Norden der Stadt zwischen Rigshospitalet und Zentrum. Er ist direkt an das Gebäude der Fakultät für Medizin und Gesundheitswissenschaften angeschlossen, ein brutalistischer Koloss der 1970er-Jahre. Mit dem Turm sollten nicht nur Laborflächen für Forschende und Studierende entstehen, sondern zudem ein breitgefächertes Programm aus Konferenzzentrum, Schau-Laboren Versammlungs- und Begegnungsflächen. Sie konzentrieren sich in dem flachen Sockelgebäude, welches gleichzeitig den Verbindungsbau zur medizinischen Fakultät herstellt und mit weiten Auslegern in eine vielfältige Parklandschaft aus Terrassen, Wegen und Grünflächen hineinragt.

Dieser Gedanke des Verbindens verschiedener Bereiche, des öffentlichen Parks mit Orten studentischen Lernens und zurückgezogenen Forschens, zieht sich als durchgängiges Zitat durch das gesamte Gebäude. Durch die Wahl einer Turmtypologie konnte rund um den Bau eine öffentliche Grünfläche erhalten werden, durch die ein Weg mäandert, der über das Sockelgebäude hinweg zwei Stadtteile miteinander verbindet. Die Flächen von Foyer und Konferenzzentrum sind ineinanderfließend und offen gestaltet. Wo das Gebäude aufhört und der Park anfängt, ist schwer auszumachen. Auch in den Laboretagen des Turms sollte der Austausch, die zufällige Begegnung Leitthema sein. So zieht sich ein überdimensionales vertikales Atrium mit einer Wendeltreppe durch die gesamte Höhe des Turmes. Diesem sind etagenweise „sience plazas" vorgelagert, offene Treffpunkte, die zum informellen Austausch anregen sollen. Die Labore selbst erstrecken sich jeweils entlang der Fassaden als Großraum- oder Zellenlabore rund um einen innenliegenden Kern, der Büro- und Nebenräume konzentriert. Als Referenz an die kupfergedeckten Kirchturmspitzen Kopenhagens wurden die Sonnenschutzlamellen ebenfalls aus kupferbeschichteten,

074–075
Maersk Tower,
C.F. Møller Architects
Copenhagen
2010–17
Maersk Tower,
C.F. Møller Architects
Copenhagen
2010–17

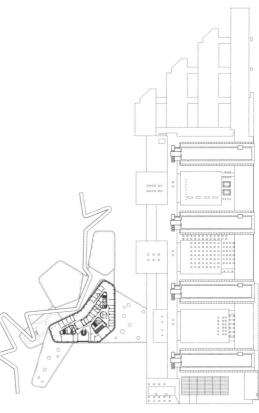

076–077
Science Plaza and
laboratories in the
Maersk Tower
"Science Plaza"
und Labor im
Maersk Tower

83

church spires in Copenhagen, the sun-blind lamellae are also made of copper-coated, perforated panels. They open and close automatically depending on the position of the sun, to regulate the heat radiation into the building. The lamella façade is only interrupted by a glass band along the vertical atrium, thereby also demonstrating the lab tower's communicative artery to the outside. → 074–077

A similar programme was implemented at the Biocentre on the Schällemätteli Campus in Basel. The Life Science Campus of the University of Basel is currently under construction there, including several buildings for medical and biological research in the direct vicinity of the Basel University Hospital (see Chapter 2.1). The compact volume of the new Biocentre, with its 16 floors, would hardly be considered a tower in a different context. However, it is conspicuously tall against the backdrop of Basel's city centre. Built on the site of a former prison, its 23,400 m² floor space has a similar variety of zones to its counterpart in Copenhagen, accommodating laboratory zones, seminar rooms, lecture theatres, a computer centre and an extensive foyer with a cafeteria. It also aims to encourage exchanges between researchers, in this case by respectively combining two layers over an open space at the centre of the laboratory floors. The result is an efficient, concentric floor plan: with desk-workplaces along the façades, laboratory tables further inside, and at the centre, four access and supply cores that surround a communal communication zone. The load-bearing structure forms a crown around the floor levels and is connected to four cores using Vierendeel girders to allow the expansive laboratories and the central zone to remain completely support-free. Fair-faced concrete and glass dominate on the laboratory floors. By contrast, the monochrome white, three-storey foyer with rounded balconies and mezzanines has an airy, playful atmosphere.

The examples in Copenhagen and Basel demonstrate how flexibility and communication can be planned in laboratory buildings despite the limited space of a tower. In view of the densification of research locations, combined with the trend of science facilities returning to city centres (see Chapter 1.1), this building type is likely to feature more frequently on research campuses, acting as towering lighthouses of science. → 078–083

perforierten Paneelen gefertigt. Sie öffnen und schließen sich je nach Sonnenstand automatisch, um den Hitzeeintrag in das Gebäude zu regulieren. Lediglich entlang des vertikalen Atriums wird die Lamellenfassade von einem gläsernen Band durchbrochen. Es demonstriert auch nach außen die kommunikative Ader des Laborturms. → 074–077

Ein ähnliches Programm wurde im Biozentrum am Campus Schällemätteli in Basel umgesetzt. Dort entsteht derzeit der Life Science Campus der Universität Basel mit mehreren Gebäude der medizinischen und biologischen Forschung in unmittelbarer Umgebung des Basler Universitätsspitals. (siehe Kapitel 2.1) Die gedrungene Gestalt des neuen Biozentrums mit seinen 16 oberirdischen Geschossen würde in einem anderen Kontext kaum noch als Turm durchgehen. Vor der Kulisse der Basler Innenstadt ragt er jedoch weithin sichtbar empor. Auf dem Grundstück einer ehemaligen Strafanstalt entstanden auf 23.400 m², ähnlich wie in Kopenhagen, neben den Laborflächen auch Seminarräume und Hörsäle, ein Rechenzentrum und ein ausgedehntes Foyer mit Cafeteria. Auch hier wurde versucht, den Austausch der Forschenden untereinander zu fördern, indem jeweils zwei Ebenen über einen Luftraum im Zentrum der Laboretagen zusammengefasst wurden. So entstand ein effizienter, konzentrischer Grundriss: entlang der Fassaden die Schreibtischarbeitsplätze, dann die Labortische, in der Mitte vier Erschließungs- und Versorgungskerne, die eine gemeinsame Kommunikationszone umschließen. Die tragende Struktur bildet einen Kranz rund um die Geschossebenen und ist über Vierendeel-Träger mit den vier Kernen verbunden, so dass die weitläufigen Labore und die Mittelzone komplett stützenfrei ausgebildet werden konnten. Sichtbeton und Glas dominieren in den Laboretagen. Im Kontrast dazu wirkt das monochrom weiße dreigeschossige Foyer mit seinen runden Balkons und Mezzaninen luftig und verspielt.

Die Beispiele aus Kopenhagen und Basel zeigen, wie auch auf der begrenzten Fläche eines Turms, Flexibilität und Kommunikation in Laborbauten geplant werden können. Im Zuge der Verdichtung von Forschungsstandorten und des Wiedereinzugs von wissenschaftlichen Einrichtungen in die Innenstädte (siehe Kapitel 1.1) wird dieser Gebäudetyp womöglich demnächst öfter als Leuchtturm der Wissenschaft einen Forschungscampus überragen. → 078–083

079

080

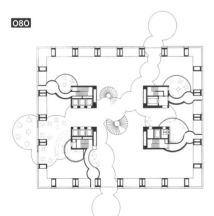

078

081–083
Foyer and
laboratory floors,
Biocentre on the
Schällemätteli
Campus, Ilg Santer
Architekten,
Basel, 2021
Foyer & Laboretagen
mit zentraler
Kommunikationszone
Biozentrum Campus
Schällemätteli, Ilg
Santer Architekten,
Basel, 2021

2.3 Laboratory workplace – Laboratory module – Integral planning

CHRISTOPH HEINEKAMP

A retrospective view often has the connotation of being behind the times. That is certainly true if all that remains of experience is "habit", and if the idea that "we've always done it that way" has lost the reason why. Today, some projects are developed with the header "Planning for the second user". To that aim, we can learn from past projects for which a second use has already been planned or developed.

New laboratory structures with existing cores

Core refurbishments reveal the quality of the building structure for the future and expose its weaknesses. The refurbishment of the high-rise building used by the DKFZ (Deutsches Krebsforschungszentrum) in Heidelberg is a good example. The classic three-winged building with a clear 7.20 m load-bearing structure required a general overhaul after 30 years of use. In accordance with the state of the art at the time, the load-bearing structure and the interior finishing were separated in exemplary fashion. The same applied to the emergency exit balconies for the laboratory building. During its use, the building's maintenance and thermal bridges proved to be a problem. From today's perspective, the efficiency of the laboratory areas can be improved by combining the interior finishing and the load-bearing structure. →084

Generally, the development of fire-safety regulations and the resulting requirements for a building could not and cannot be foreseen. However in this case, the lack of specific space, i.e. too small shafts and also the organisation of the shafts for building technology, can more reasonably be regarded as a conceptual error. Above all the original reduction of floor heights, which was decided upon during planning as a way of saving costs, proved to be a particular problem for the building's future use. The building technology, above all the ventilation, requires a certain installation height. The lack of clearly separated installations according to departments, especially in the case of electrical and IT technology, made it difficult to refurbish the building in individual sections.

A building should not only be planned for its second user, but also enable the future replacement of its entire technology. During the life cycle of a laboratory building, its technical systems must be replaced several times. Ring systems with several supply sources and partially

88

2.3 Laborarbeitsplatz – Labormodul – Integrale Planung

CHRISTOPH HEINEKAMP

Ein Rückblick hat oft den Ruf von rückständig. Wenn aus Erfahrung nur noch „eingefahren" übrigbleibt und bei der Aussage „Haben wir schon immer so gemacht" der Grund vergessen wurde, ist das sicher richtig. Heute gibt es Projekte mit der Planungsüberschrift „Für den zweiten Nutzer planen". Für diese Anforderung kann man aus Projekten lernen, für die bereits eine zweite Nutzung geplant und gebaut wurde.

Neue Laborstrukturen mit Bestandskern
Kernsanierungen zeigen die Qualität der Gebäudestruktur für die Zukunft und offenbaren Schwachpunkte. Anhand der Sanierung des Hochhauses des DKFZ (Deutsches Krebsforschungszentrum) in Heidelberg kann man das gut aufzeigen. Das klassische Dreibundgebäude mit einer klaren 7,20 m Tragwerkstruktur musste nach über 30 Jahren kernsaniert werden. Gemäß damaligem Kenntnisstand erfolgte lehrbuchmäßig die Trennung von Tragwerk und Ausbau sowie der Bau von Fluchtbalkons für das Laborgebäude. Der Wartungsaufwand und Kältebrücken haben sich während der Nutzungszeit als Problem erwiesen. Für die Nutzungseffizienz der Laborflächen ist es jedoch nach heutigen Erkenntnissen besser, den Ausbau und das Tragwerk zu verbinden. →084

Die Entwicklung von Brandschutzrichtlinien und die sich daraus ergebende Notwendigkeiten an ein Gebäude konnten und können nicht vorhergesehen werden. Fehlende Flächen, zum Beispiel zu kleine Schächte und auch die Anordnung der Schächte für die Gebäudetechnik, sind schon eher als konzeptioneller Fehler einzustufen. Besonders die damalige Reduktion der Geschosshöhe, als Einsparung in der Planung beschlossen, erwies sich für die zukunftsfähige Nutzung des Gebäudes als besonderes Problem. Die Gebäudetechnik, insbesondere die Lüftung, benötigt die Installationshöhe. Die nicht klare Trennung der Installation nach Bereichen, besonders bei der Elektro- und EDV-Technik, erschwerte die abschnittsweise Sanierung.

Ein Gebäude sollte nicht nur für den zweiten Nutzer, sondern für den Austausch der gesamten Technik geplant werden. Im Lebenszyklus eines Laborgebäudes muss die Gebäudetechnik mehrfach ersetzt werden. Ringsysteme mit mehrfachem Einspeisen und teilredundante Zentralgeräte, wie sie in den Nachhaltigkeitszertifizierungen von Laborgebäuden gefordert werden, ermöglichen die technische Sanierung im Teilbetrieb.

In der Dreibund-Struktur des DKFZ lagen 30 % der Fläche im Bereich des Innenbundes und waren somit Dunkelzonen, als Konsequenz aus fehlenden

Deutsches Krebs-
forschungszentrum
(dkfz) Heidelberg,
Heinle, Wischer und
Partner, built in 1972,
refurbished in 2021
Deutsches Krebs-
forschungszentrum
(dkfz) Heidelberg,
Heinle, Wischer und
Partner, erbaut 1972,
saniert 2012

redundant central appliances, as demanded by sustainability certification for laboratory buildings, enable the technical refurbishment during partial operations.

In the three-winged structure of the DKFZ building, 30 % of the usable space was situated in the inner wing, making it a dark zone. Due to a lack of capacity, these areas were nevertheless filled with workplaces, despite their need for natural light. The reality experienced in many laboratories – with open laboratory doors and refrigerators in the hallway due to a lack of space – was also apparent at the DKFZ.

In the new planning concept, one of the existing corridors was integrated into the laboratory landscape and another hall was reduced in size, in order to prevent renewed improper use. The documentation workplaces were also integrated into the laboratory landscape. From a fire-safety perspective, utilisation units were created to enable flexible occupation. → **085**

The 16 decentralised washing kitchens were pooled to create three new central laboratory washing areas, while the laboratory building is supplied via a box-shaped conveyor system. The laboratory building has already been in operation for 10 years and the planning concepts chosen for the general overhaul have proven to be sustainable. → **086**

From an individual laboratory to a laboratory module

In the 1990s, new laboratory development focused on systematising individual laboratories and optimising the laboratory grid from 1.20 m to 1.15 m and laboratory depths of 7 m, as well as technical connections using "individual rather than central shafts". Individual rooms were combined to produce larger laboratories and laboratory areas. Depending on the field of research, laboratories were built as three-winged (biology / biomedicine) or two-winged (chemistry, physics) structures. Today, interdisciplinary research teams are becoming increasingly prevalent, as can be seen in the institutes' names: biophysics, biochemistry, chemistry of solid materials. The focus of research changes faster today, so flexibility in a laboratory building is frequently demanded, but without defining its content. Does flexibility mean the ability to exchange furniture, retrofit media and fittings, or relocate walls easily? To me, flexibility means adaptability to future demands. Thus from my perspective, it is less important to know what a laboratory/building can do than what a laboratory building cannot do. Determining grids, building heights, building depths and shaft sizes define limits (often) without basing them on conscious decisions. For instance, the arrangement of shafts and the building height limit the potential volume of air and therefore the ability to use extractors or other

Arbeitsplätzen wurden in diese Flächen trotzdem Arbeitsflächen mit Tageslichtanforderung verschoben. Die Realität, die man in vielen Laborgebäude erlebt – die Labortüren stehen auf und die Kühlschränke stehen aus Platzmangel auf dem Flur – war im DKFZ auch gegeben.

In der neuen Planungskonzeption wurde einer der bestehenden Flure in die Laborlandschaft integriert, der andere Flur wurde verkleinert, um eine erneute Fehlnutzung zu verhindern. In die Laborlandschaft wurden auch die Dokumentationsarbeitsplätze integriert. Brandschutztechnisch wurden Nutzungseinheiten gebildet, die eine flexible Belegung ermöglichen. → **085**

Die 16 dezentralen Spülküchen wurden zu drei neuen zentralen Laborspülküchen zusammengefasst, die Versorgung des Laborgebäudes erfolgt über eine Kastenförderanlage. Das Laborgebäude ist inzwischen schon wieder 10 Jahre in Betrieb und die gewählten Planungskonzeptionen für die Kernsanierung haben sich als zukunftsfähig erwiesen. → **086**

Vom Einzellabor zum Labormodul

In den 1990er-Jahren waren die Systematisierung des Einzellabors mit Optimierung des Laborrasters von 1,20 m auf 1,15 m und Labortiefen von 7 m sowie technische Erschließungen, „Einzelschacht versus Zentralschacht", die Themen im Laborneubau. Die Addition von Einzelräumen bzw. Kopplung von Einzelräumen ergaben größere Labore bzw. Laborbereiche. Je nach Forschungsrichtung wurden Labore als Dreibund (Biologie / Biomedizin) oder Zweibund (Chemie, Physik) gebaut. Heute entstehen in der Forschung interdisziplinäre Forschungsteams, was auch an Institutsbezeichnungen – Biophysik, Biochemie, Chemie fester Stoffe – offensichtlich wird. Die Forschungsschwerpunkte wechseln heute schneller, daher ist Flexibilität im Laborbau eine oft benutzte Vokabel, allerdings ohne, dass der Inhalt definiert wird. Bedeutet Flexibilität die Möglichkeit zum Austausch von Möbeln, die Nachrüstung von Medien und Armaturen oder das leichte Versetzen von Wänden? Flexibilität bedeutet für mich Anpassbarkeit für zukünftige Anforderungen. Dafür ist es aus meiner Sicht weniger wichtig, zu betonen, was ein Labor/Gebäude kann, sondern was das Laborgebäude nicht leisten kann. Festlegungen zu Raster, Gebäudehöhe, Gebäudetiefe und Schachtgrößen definieren Grenzen, ohne dass dabei (häufig) eine bewusste Entscheidung zu Grunde lag. Die Anordnung der Schächte und die Gebäudehöhe begrenzen zum Beispiel die mögliche Luftmenge und damit die Möglichkeit, Abzüge oder andere Verbraucher zu betreiben. Auch automatisierte „Laborstraßen" in der klinischen Chemie zeigen, dass im Grundriss die Ausdehnung in drei Richtungen notwendig ist und bedacht werden muss.

Die Integration von Verkehrswegen in Sicherheits- oder Hygienebereiche, die dann nicht mehr als allgemeine Rettungswege im Gebäude genutzt

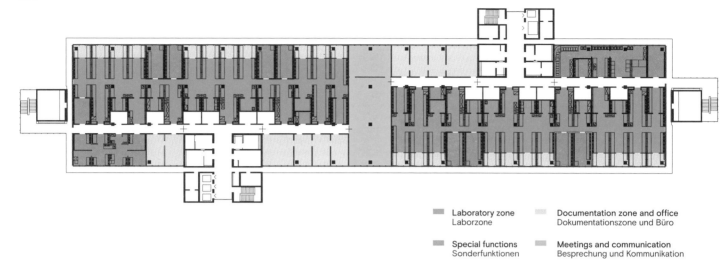

	Laboratory zone		Documentation zone and office
	Laborzone		Dokumentationszone und Büro
	Special functions		Meetings and communication
	Sonderfunktionen		Besprechung und Kommunikation

085
Zoning concept for
the refurbishment of
the high-rise DKFZ
building, 2004–2010,
Heinle, Wischer
und Partner
Freie Architekten
Zonierungskonzept
für die Sanierung des
DKFZ-Laborhoch-
hauses, Heidelberg,
Heinle, Wischer
und Partner
Freie Architekten,
2004–2010

086
Refurbishment
of the DKFZ
high-rise building,
Heinle, Wischer
und Partner
Freie Architekten
Laborhochhaus-
sanierung DKFZ,
Heidelberg, Heinle,
Wischer und Partner
Freie Architekten

consuming appliances. Automated "laboratory streets" in clinical chemistry also show that floor-plan expansion in three directions is necessary and must be taken into account. The integration of mobility routes in security or hygiene areas, which can then no longer be used as general emergency exits in the building, are further demands for new laboratory buildings, requiring an appropriate building depth. The development of laboratory modules is a response to these challenges. A continuous space of 300 to 400 m², representing single utilisation in terms of fire safety, forms one module. It must provide two emergency exits, one of which must be shorter than 35 m. Such a laboratory module is supplied by two central shafts, enabling a ring-shaped connection for ventilation systems and media access. Connection to two shafts reduces the required floor height, since the channels in the module can be connected at the same height from two sides, thereby also minimising intersecting channels. Supply hotspots and air volumes can be moved around the ring as required. Ring-shaped supplies reduce the required loss of pressure in the ventilation system, thereby saving energy costs, since a reduced pressure of 100 Pa reduces overall energy costs by approximately 10 %. The noise levels in the laboratory are also lower, since less pressure must be reduced at the volumetric flow regulators.

Provisions for the future are not usually sensible, since often, the assumptions made during planning do not come about. In ventilation systems however, it is always sensible, especially for the channel network, to avoid simultaneity, despite the fact that it is often seen as a source of potential savings. In fact, a larger channel diameter increases the flexibility for the future and the overall system can be operated at lower airflow speeds, which also saves energy and therefore operating costs.

Flexible partitioning

Laboratory modules are not open-plan laboratories. Instead, they are laboratory landscapes that are designed according to requirements. It must be possible to divide them into different security levels, provide shielding from noisy devices and work in a clean environment during running operations. Wherever possible, a good laboratory module should be surrounded on three sides by access corridors. A hall between the shafts and the laboratory modules allows the laboratory entrance to be positioned as required. Due to the shafts' direct proximity to the laboratory and the large space for inducing channels and installations, it is possible to distribute and connect the building technology in an ideal way, thereby reducing the required installation heights in the laboratory and enabling an organised, open installation. In

werden können, sind weitere Anforderungen an neue Laborgebäude, für die eine entsprechende Gebäudetiefe benötigt wird. Die Schaffung von Labormodulen ist die Antwort auf diese Herausforderungen. Eine zusammenhängende Fläche mit 300 bis 400 m², die eine brandschutztechnische Nutzungseinheit darstellt, bildet ein Modul. Aus diesem Labormodul müssen zwei Fluchtwege, wovon einer kürzer als 35 m sein muss, zur Verfügung stehen. Solch ein Labormodul wird mit zwei Zentralschächten versorgt, die eine ringförmige Erschließung für die Lüftungstechnik und Medienversorgung ermöglichen. Die Erschließung aus zwei Schächte reduziert die notwenige Geschosshöhe, da die Kanäle im Modul mit gleicher Höhe von zwei Seiten eingespeist werden und auch Kreuzungen von Kanälen minimiert werden. Versorgungsschwerpunkte und Luftmengen können an dem Ring bedarfsgerecht verschoben werden. Die Ringversorgung reduziert den notwendigen Druckverlust, der mit der Lüftungsanlage generiert werden muss, wodurch Energiekosten gespart werden, da eine Reduktion des Drucks von 100 Pa ca. 10 % niedrigere Gesamtenergiekosten bedeutet. Zusätzlich wird der Lärm im Labor verringert, da weniger Druck an den Volumenstromreglern reduziert werden muss.

Vorhaltungen für die Zukunft sind meistens wenig sinnvoll, da dafür gemachte Planungsannahmen häufig nicht eintreffen. In der Lüftungstechnik ist es allerdings immer sinnvoll, insbesondere für das Kanalnetz, keine Gleichzeitigkeit anzusetzen, obwohl diese Reduzierung der Kanalgröße als vermeintliches Einsparpotential während der Planungsphase oft herangezogen wird. Dabei bietet ein größerer Kanalquerschnitt die Flexibilität für die Zukunft, und die Gesamtanlage kann zusätzlich mit einer geringeren Strömungsgeschwindigkeit betrieben werden, wodurch Energie und somit Betriebskosten gespart werden.

Flexibel aufteilbar

Labormodule sind keine Großraumlabore, sondern Laborlandschaften, die bedarfsgerecht gestaltet werden. Eine Aufteilung in unterschiedliche Sicherheitsstufen oder Abgrenzung von lärmenden Geräten bzw. sauberem Arbeiten ist im laufenden Betrieb erforderlich. Ein gutes Labormodul sollte möglichst dreiseitig von Erschließungsfluren umgeben sein, ein Flur zwischen den Schächten und dem Labormodul ermöglicht die Positionierung des Laboreingangs an bedarfsgerechter Stelle. Durch die unmittelbare Nähe der Schächte zum Labor mit einer großen Fläche für das Ausfädeln von Kanälen und Installationen wird eine optimale Verteilung der gebäudetechnischen Erschließung erreicht, was die benötigte Installationshöhe im Labor reduziert und eine geordnete offene Installation ermöglicht. Im Labormodul selbst werden Wände und Türen nur dort gesetzt, wo es die Nutzung erfordert. Die Anpassung dieser Abgrenzung z. B. für saubere Arbeiten wie Zellkulturen ist oft auch im laufenden Betrieb notwendig. Allerdings bedeuten

the laboratory module itself, walls and doors are only positioned according to the demands of use. The adaptation of such partitions, for instance for clean work on cell cultures, is often also necessary during running operations. However, even light partition walls represent a building measure, while penetrating installation channels to retrofit partitioning systems are very work-intensive. Our planning response to this question is the development of laboratory boxes that are set up as furniture in the laboratory space, with connections to air inflows and outflows. These boxes can be fitted with closed wall elements or glazing, as required. These approaches create laboratory landscapes that provide the different functionally equipped workplaces for the laboratory tasks. Various concepts exist for flexible laboratory interior fittings, all of which can be applied sustainably, as long as the following underlying principles are considered:
→ Connections to media, electronics and IT come from above. Only wastewater flows downwards. Lifting systems should not be installed as standard. The wastewater points should either be located at the supports or in peripheral areas, to provide open spaces in the centre of the laboratory for retrofitting, large appliances and the like. Wash basins with floor connections arranged in the space often represent fixed points that, in the case of required rearrangement, make it difficult or impossible to set up standing units such as a pipetting robot.
→ Fittings are not fixed to the floor. Substructures are wheeled and tables can be easily dismantled, to ensure that space for appliances can be created easily.
→ The laboratory furniture is developed in a modular way and has flexible retrofitting potential, both with respect to the installation paths and to the integration of mountings and power sockets.

Communication and documentation

Writing and documentation work is becoming increasingly important in everyday laboratory life. Technical personnel work over 60 % of their time at the computer. However, that does not mean they spend three hours at the computer and then one hour in the laboratory. Instead, their work consists of a constant back and forth between their workplaces. A short distance between the writing workplace and the laboratory workplace is therefore especially important. A second aspect lies in the fact that by splitting workplaces for writing and laboratory work, solo work in the laboratory can become standard practice, but this is not permitted for security reasons. A solution is provided by placing documentation areas in front of the laboratory landscape, which can be separated from each other by a glass wall. →**087** The writing

selbst leichte Trennwände eine Baumaßnahmen, und Durchdringungen von Installationsleitungen sind im Nachgang mit Trennwandsystemen nur mit sehr hohem Aufwand möglich. Unsere planerische Antwort auf diese Fragestellung ist der Aufbau von Laborboxen, die als Möbel mit Anschluss für Zu- und Abluft in der Laborfläche aufgestellt werden. Die Boxen können je nach Bedarf mit geschlossenen Wandelementen oder Verglasungen ausgeführt werden. Mit diesen Ansätzen entstehen Laborlandschaften, in denen unterschiedliche funktionell ausgestattete Arbeitsplätze für die Laborarbeit angeboten werden. Für den flexiblen Labormöbelausbau gibt es verschiedene Konzepte, die alle zukunftsfähig eingesetzt werden können, wenn nachfolgende Grundanforderungen bedacht sind:
→ Die Anbindung durch Medien sowie Elektro und EDV erfolgt von oben. Nur Abwasser fließt nach unten, Hebeanlagen sollten nicht die Standardinstallation sein. Die Abwasserpunkte sollten sich jedoch entweder an den Stützen oder am Randbereich befinden, um für Umrüstungen, große Geräte und ähnliches freie Fläche in der Labormitte zu haben. Mittig im Raum angeordnete Stirnspülen mit Anbindung von unten bilden bei Umbauten oft Fixpunkte, die eine erforderliche Umgestaltung für bodenständige Geräte wie z.B. für die Aufstellung eines Pipettierroboters schwierig oder unmöglich machen.
→ Die Einrichtung wird nicht am Boden befestigt. Unterbauten sind fahrbar und Tische leicht demontierbar, um leicht Aufstellflächen für Geräte schaffen zu können.
→ Die Labormöbel sind modular aufgebaut und haben eine flexible Nachrüstmöglichkeit sowohl für Installationswege als auch Integration von Armaturen und Steckdosen.

Kommunikation und Dokumentation

Im Laboralltag wird die Schreib- und Dokumentationsarbeit immer wichtiger. Technisches Personal arbeitet mehr als 60 % am Computer. Das bedeutet aber nicht, dass drei Stunden am Computer verbracht werden und eine Stunde im Labor, sondern ein stetes Pendeln zwischen den Arbeitsplätzen. Der kurze Weg vom Schreibplatz zum Laborplatz ist deshalb besonders wichtig. Ein zweiter Aspekt besteht darin, dass durch die Splittung von Arbeitsplätzen für Schreib- und Laborarbeit Alleinarbeit im Labor zur Regel werden kann, die allerdings aus Sicherheitsgründen nicht erlaubt ist. Die Lösung sind die der Laborlandschaft vorgelagerten Dokumentationsbereiche, die über eine Glaswand vom Labor abgetrennt werden. →**087** Die Schreibbereiche bekommen einen direkten Zugang von einem Flur, damit sind auch Schiebetüren zwischen Labor und Schreibbereich möglich. Die direkte Zugänglichkeit der Dokumentationszone ist auch für die interne Kommunikation besonders wichtig, da Mitarbeiter aus anderen Bereichen nicht das Labor durchqueren müssen, um eine Frage zu stellen. Der Schreibbereich wird mit Zuluft versorgt, wobei

O87

O87
Documentation
zone at the
Deutsches Zentrum
für Neurodegene-
rative Erkrankungen
in Bonn,
Wulf architekten
gmbh, 2017
Dokumentationszone
im Deutschen
Zentrum für
Neurodegenerative
Erkrankungen
in Bonn,
Wulf architekten
gmbh, 2017

areas have direct access to a corridor, thereby enabling sliding doors between the laboratory and the writing area. This direct access to the documentation zone is also especially important for internal communication, since employees from other departments do not need to walk through the laboratory to ask a question. The writing area is ventilated using a throttle that allows the writing area to receive at least part of its induced air from the laboratory ventilation. The cooled induced air in the documentation area does not need to be created separately, since this air volume is required to balance out the extracted air in the laboratory. The pressure created in this way in the documentation zone prevents toxic substances from entering.

Interaction between the laboratory and office is especially important in a laboratory building. Above all, the threshold between the documentation zone and the office areas provides an ideal meeting place to exchange ideas. In the 1990s, we had the office workplace in the laboratory. Later, a computer workplace was set up in the documentation zone directly beside the laboratory. In future, will we have a laboratory within an office? That is unlikely from our perspective: laboratory areas may be framed by office areas, documentation zones and small developmental laboratories integrated on an office floor. Automation will further reduce work times in the laboratory, so the proximity to classic writing areas will become even more important. Laboratories already exist today – especially in the field of physics – where extensive measurements are taken and then analysed in the office. In such laboratories, the immediate proximity to the writing place / laboratory workplace is not necessary and is even undesirable in the case of laser workplaces, for instance, due to security considerations.

Laboratory landscapes with clear zoning – documentation, workplaces and support – as well as a rectangular organisation of fittings and appliances, can be up to 25 m deep when they are naturally lit from one side. Flexible work areas are created to utilise the space, with short walking distances and clearly separated security. The great depth of the building reduces the façade area and enables very economic building technology connections.

The dimensions of the laboratory modules, with 20 × 15 m or up to 28 × 25 m, also provide the free space with which to automate and optimise internal work processes.

The laboratory building of the future has communication areas, calm and creative workplaces and compact laboratory zones to ensure the safe handling of hazardous substances, special equipment and biological material. A good laboratory building facing these challenges can only be constructed successfully by a competent, integral planning team in cooperation with the client and the user.

möglichst mit einer Drossel ein Teil der Laborzuluft den Schreibbereich belüftet. Die gekühlte Zuluft im Dokumentationsbereich muss nicht separat erzeugt werden, da diese Luftmenge zum Ausgleich der Abluftmenge im Labor benötigt wird. Durch den auf diese Weise erzeugten Überdruck in der Dokumentationszone ist ausgeschlossen, dass Schadstoffe in diesen Bereich gelangen.

Die Interaktion zwischen Labor und Büro ist im Laborgebäude besonders wichtig. Insbesondere an der Nahtstelle zwischen Dokumentationszone und Bürobereich ist der ideale Treffpunkt zum Austausch. In den 1990er-Jahren hatten wir den Büroarbeitsplatz im Labor, dann wurde der Computerarbeitsplatz in der Dokumentationszone direkt ans Labor platziert. Haben wir in der Zukunft das Labor im Büro? Aus unserer Sicht ist das eher unwahrscheinlich. Laborbereiche können jedoch von Bürobereichen bzw. Dokumentationszonen eingerahmt sein und kleine Entwicklungslabore in eine Büroetage integriert werden. Die Automatisierung wird die Arbeitszeiten im Labor weiter reduzieren, so dass die Nähe zu klassischen Schreibbereichen wichtiger wird. Bereits heute gibt es Labore – insbesondere in der Physik – wo aufwendige Messungen durchgeführt werden und anschließend die Auswertungen im Büro erfolgen. In diesen Laboren ist die unmittelbare Nähe zum Schreibplatz / Laborarbeitsplatz nicht notwendig und z.B. bei Laserarbeitsplätzen auch sicherheitstechnisch nicht gewünscht.

Laborlandschaften mit klaren Zonierungen – Dokumentation, Arbeitsbereiche und Support – sowie einer rechtwinkligen Anordnung der Einrichtung und Geräte können einseitig belichtet bis zu 25 m tief sein. Für die Nutzung entstehen flexible Arbeitsbereiche mit kurzen Wegen und klar abgegrenzten Sicherheitsbereichen. Die große Gebäudetiefe reduziert die Fassadenfläche und ermöglicht eine sehr wirtschaftliche Erschließung für die Gebäudetechnik.

Die Ausdehnungen der Labormodule mit 20 × 15 m bzw. bis 28 × 25 m schaffen auch den Freiraum für Automatisierung und Optimierung der internen Arbeitsabläufe.

Das Laborgebäude der Zukunft hat Kommunikationsflächen, ruhige und kreative Arbeitsplätze sowie kompakte Laborzonen für den sicheren Umgang mit Gefahrstoffen, Sondergeräten und biologischem Material. Ein gutes Laborgebäude mit diesen Herausforderungen kann nur von einem kompetenten integralen Planungsteam in Kooperation mit dem Bauherrn und Nutzer erfolgreich realisiert werden.

LUKAS SEMMLER

Planned flexibility in laboratory construction

Geplante Flexibilität im Laborbau

We are currently experiencing a period of rapid transformation. Individualisation is growing fast. Our new laboratory buildings must be able to cope with such accelerating changes. The importance of such flexibility is increasing, while maintaining order within that "flexibility" is becoming a considerable planning task.

Individual user requirements must be technically implementable both after a laboratory's first fitting and following many later "secondary fit-outs". The planning implementation takes place close to the user through laboratory planning and close to the infrastructure by the planners of the technical building equipment. All planners are therefore integrated into the process and topic of the defined flexibility.

What conditions can be created by a building to cope with continuously changing user requirements and usage?

Wir befinden uns in einer Phase des schnellen Wandels. Die Individualisierung nimmt rasant zu. Unsere neuen Laborgebäude müssen diese immer schneller werdenden Veränderungen aufnehmen können. Flexibilität wird immer wichtiger und das Bewahren einer Ordnung in der Flexibilität wird zu einer beachtlichen Planungsaufgabe.

Die individuellen Anforderungen der Nutzer und Nutzerinnen müssen in einem Laborgebäude in einer Erstausstattung und in vielen späteren „Zweitausstattungen" technisch umgesetzt werden können. Die planerische Umsetzung erfolgt dabei nahe am Nutzer durch die Laborplanung und nahe an der Infrastruktur durch die Planer der technischen Gebäudeausrüstung. Alle Planer sind somit in den Prozess und die Thematik der definierten Flexibilität eingebunden.

Welche Voraussetzungen können gebäudeseitig geschaffen werden, um den kontinuierlichen Nutzeranforderungs- und Nutzungsveränderungen gerecht zu werden?

The key factors in a successful project with respect to adaptability are guidelines and limits. At the start of a project, it must be clarified which functions and requirements are needed in which areas. To use a simple example, that means the extent to which an office area can be transformed into a laboratory area and vice versa. The period for additions and conversions must also be determined using scenarios. The final important aspects are initial investment costs, investment in changes, maintenance and dismantling. Investment in the defined flexibility is only attractive when considering the costs over the building's entire life cycle.

The buildings should perfectly support their users and use requirements. The specific adaptations and additions this requires are primarily carried out in the field of user installations. They are ideally supplied by the basic installations including building technology systems and structural elements. Required amounts, types and qualities of ventilation, cooling, media, electricity, walls, acoustic measures etc. are provided by the basic installations in the ceiling. It is important to form a simple, clear partition between basic and user installations. →088-089

Another factor is the organisation of the floor plan structure. For instance, diagonally arranged riser zones enable economic fire compartment formation, as well as clear and simple access to laboratory units. These are regarded as repeated grid structures and not as a room structure. Grid structures should be as large as possible to increase the variety of possible designs and utilisation in the user installation. The initial situation is an area that is only structured using partition walls when sensible or required for reasons of hygiene (different standards or zones), ergonomics (different noise levels) or energy saving (different exchange of air or lowering mode). →090-093

Conversion planning is based on new building planning

Planned flexibility is based on the following principles:

The bandwidth in which changes should be possible must be defined. The aim should be explicitly to enable neither "nothing" nor "everything". This bandwidth provides leeway for the initial installation and continuous conversion.

Planning results must be understandable. Employees from the fields of maintenance, upkeep and subsequent projects must understand the planning. Thus it is helpful to have rules that quickly provide the required insight both during planning and when making changes. Such rules must be simple and self-explanatory. Appropriate training to communicate these principles can and should provide effective support.

Ausschlaggebend für ein erfolgreiches Projekt in Bezug auf die Anpassungsfähigkeit sind Leitplanken und Grenzen. Beim Projektstart muss geklärt sein, welche Funktionen und Anforderungen in welchen Bereichen erforderlich sind. Dies bedeutet als einfaches Beispiel festzulegen, inwieweit ein Bürobereich zum Laborbereich werden kann und umgekehrt. Zudem ist die Zeitdauer für Ergänzungen und Umbauten anhand von Szenarien festzulegen. Der abschließende wichtige Punkt sind die Kosten für die Erstinvestition, die Veränderungsinvestition, die Wartung und den Rückbau. Erst im Zusammenhang mit der Betrachtung der Kosten im Gesamtlebenszyklus eines Gebäudes wird die Investition in die definierte Flexibilität interessant.

Die Gebäude sollen die Nutzer und die Nutzeranforderung optimal unterstützen. Die dazu erforderlichen spezifischen Anpassungen und Ergänzungen finden prioritär im Nutzerausbau statt. Dieser wird vom Grundausbau perfekt mit der technischen Gebäudeausrüstung und den baulichen Elementen versorgt. Lüftung, Kühlung, Medien, Strom, Wände, Akustikmaßnahmen … alles wird via Grundausbau in der Decke in der erforderlichen Art, Anzahl und Qualität zur Verfügung gestellt. Es ist wichtig, eine einfache und klare Trennung zwischen Grund- und Nutzerausbau auszubilden. →088-089

Ein weiterer Faktor ist die Gliederung der Grundrissstruktur. Beispielsweise diagonal angeordnete Steigzonen ermöglichen eine wirtschaftliche Brandabschnittsbildung sowie eine klare und einfache Erschliessung der Laboreinheiten. Diese werden als sich wiederholende Raster- und nicht als Raumstruktur betrachtet. Möglichst große zusammenhängende Rasterstrukturen erhöhen die Gestaltungs- und Nutzungsvarianten im Nutzerausbau. Die Ausgangslage ist eine Raumfläche, die nur dann mit raumabschließenden Trennwänden gegliedert wird, wenn dies infolge von (unterschiedliche Anforderungen oder Zonen), Ergonomie (unterschiedliche Schallpegel) oder Energiesparen (unterschiedlicher Luftwechsel oder Absenkbetrieb) sinnvoll oder erforderlich ist. →090-093

Umbauplanung basiert auf Neubauplanung

Die geplante Flexibilität beruht auf den folgenden Grundlagen:

Die Bandbreite, in der Veränderungen möglich sein sollen, muss definiert werden. Es gilt bewusst nicht nichts und nicht alles zu ermöglichen. Diese Bandbreite gibt den Spielraum für die Erstrealisation und die fortlaufenden Umbauten vor.

Die Planungsresultate müssen nachvollziehbar sein. Die Mitarbeitenden aus den Bereichen Wartung, Unterhalt und der Folgeprojekte müssen die Planung verstehen. Hier unterstützen Spielregeln, welche sowohl bei der Planung als auch bei den Veränderungen rasch den erforderlichen Einblick geben. Die Spielregeln müssen einfach und selbsterklärend sein.

O88

O88
Ceiling installation /
Basic installation
Deckeninstallation /
Grundausbau

O89
Base installation /
User Customisation
Grundausbau /
Nutzerausbau

Base installation
Grundausbau

Building operator
TGA / Betreiber

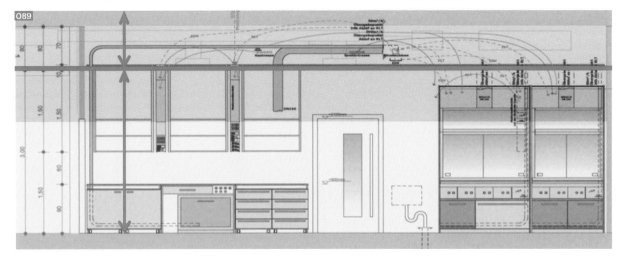

O89

User customisation
Nutzerausbau

User / Laboratory service
Nutzer / Laborservice

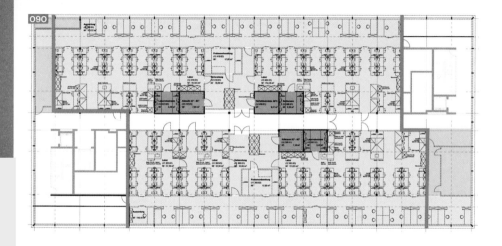

090
Laboratory
grid structure
Rasterstruktur
maximale
Laborfläche

091
Partition wall
positions
on the grid
Trennwand-
positionen im
Raster

092
Access from
the riser zone,
air exchange
Erschließung ab
Steigzone,
Luftwechsel

Grid n x1
Raster n x1

3   2   1

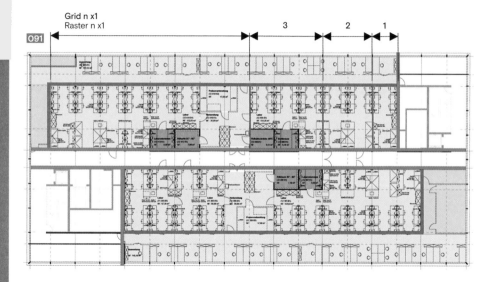

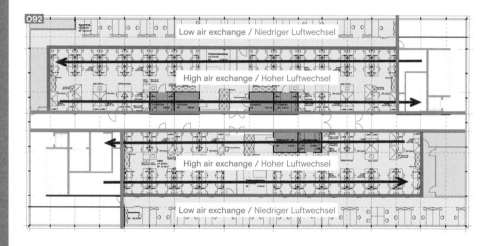

Low air exchange / Niedriger Luftwechsel

High air exchange / Hoher Luftwechsel

High air exchange / Hoher Luftwechsel

Low air exchange / Niedriger Luftwechsel

093
Analysis laboratory
Analytiklabor

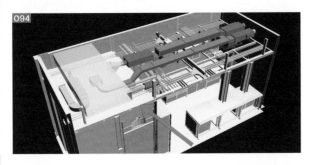

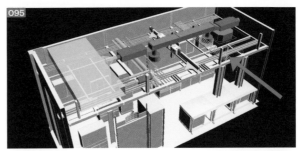

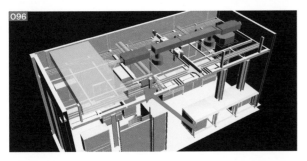

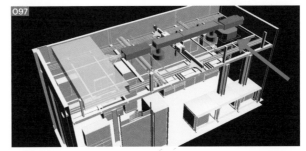

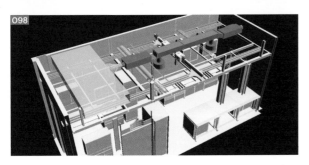

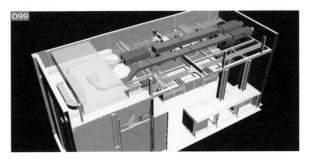

094–099
In the series of images, one defined building element (red arrow) is omitted respectively. The element is then not shown in the following image and the next element is marked with a red arrow for removal
In der Bildfolge wird jeweils ein definiertes Bauteil (roter Pfeil) weggelassen. Im folgenden Bild ist dann dieses Bauteil ausgeblendet und das nächste wegzunehmende Bauteil mit einem roten Pfeil markiert.

094
Omit auxiliary room (walls, air in & out)
Nebenraum weglassen (Wände, Zu- & Abluft)

095
Omit media (gases, cooling water)
Medien weglassen (Gase, Kühlwasser)

096
Omit source air out
Quellenabluftanschlüsse weglassen

097
Omit ventilation cooling unit
Umluftkühlgerät weglassen

098
All non-essentials omitted
Alles Nichterforderliche ist weggelassen

099
Use planning = Display and remove
Nutzungsplanung = Einblenden und Ausblenden

Order must be achieved. This order entails three factors: a thinking and planning process "from the roots to the branches", modular planning with recurring elements as the basis also for industrial prefabrication, and "planning by omission"

Planning by omission – A thought process

"Planning by omission" is based on the simple principle that all elements required on one floor/area are planned in a grid element or module and referenced into the building. By not showing the non-essential elements in an individual area/grid, the remaining elements are those that are built. Omission is very simple. The omitted elements can be reactivated at any time without design work. → 094 – 099

This thought process also enables implementation in stages. The stages are important because the building and its infrastructure should provide ongoing, ideal support for the work process. The resulting fast changes should be possible to implement at short notice. To that aim, maximum omission is applied in building stage one. Stage two is implemented perhaps straight away, tomorrow or never. Appropriate training provides support, since everyone's understanding and a specific way of thinking are decisive for the overall result.

Clear requirements must be defined to achieve the overall result at the initial installation stage and for subsequent conversions. These requirements are use-related, i.e. non-personal and defined with as much far-sighted leeway as possible. The responsible laboratory engineers and operators must know how the structure and infrastructure of the laboratory building can perform and be able to maintain that structure. During initial planning and subsequent changes, it is important to apply maximum perseverance with respect to adhering to the rules defined for the project. That approach enables swift statements on "what is feasible" and "what is impossible"; what can be achieved quickly and cheaply with limited investment, and what requires greater effort, appropriately more time and higher financial investment. The building, specifically flexible user installations, can and should adapt to its utilisation. However, should requirements go beyond the planned flexibility, the building may not be suitable for such use.

Such user installation is flexible due to the definition of requirements including leeway to ensure planned flexibility. The building and the user installation are prepared for "what could happen". We simply do not know today what will be needed in five or ten years. However, we do know that with hindsight, research, development and analysis have changed massively in some aspects. If automated systems and IT continue to develop in the same way, the future

Eine entsprechende Schulung der Prinzipien soll und darf hierbei wirkungsvoll unterstützen um eine Ordnung zu erreichen.

Eine Ordnung muss erreicht werden. Diese Ordnung beinhaltet drei Faktoren: Einen Denk- und Planungsprozess „von der Wurzel in die Äste hinein", eine modulare Planung mit wiederkehrenden Elementen als Basis auch für eine industrielle Vorfertigung und eine „Planung durch Weglassen".

Planung durch Weglassen – Ein Denkprozess

Die „Planung durch Weglassen" basiert auf dem einfachen Prinzip, dass alle in einem Geschoss/Bereich erforderlichen Elemente in einem Rasterelement oder Modul eingeplant und ins Gebäude referenziert werden. Durch Ausblenden der nicht erforderlichen Elemente im einzelnen Bereich/Raster verbleiben diejenigen Elemente, die gebaut werden. Weglassen ist ganz einfach. Die ausgeblendeten Elemente können jederzeit ohne Konstruktionsarbeit wieder aktiviert werden. → 094 – 099

Dieser Denkprozess ermöglicht zudem eine Realisation in Etappen. Diese Etappen sind wichtig, weil das Gebäude mit seiner Infrastruktur den Arbeitsprozess fortlaufend optimal unterstützen soll. Die daraus folgenden schnellen Veränderungen sollen in kurzer Zeit möglich sein. Hierzu wird maximal vom Weglassen in der Bauetappe eins profitiert. Die Etappe zwei wird vielleicht jetzt, morgen oder nie umgesetzt. Eine entsprechende Schulung ist unterstützend, denn das Verständnis und die Denkweise eines Jeden ist entscheidend für das Gesamtresultat.

Um dieses Gesamtresultat in der Ersterstellung und den darauffolgenden Umbauten erreichen zu können bedarf es klarer Anforderungen. Diese Anforderungen sind nutzungsbezogen, also unpersönlich und mit weitsichtigem Spielraum festgeschrieben. Die zuständigen Ingenieure und Betreiber für das Laborgebäude müssen wissen, was die Struktur und die Infrastruktur des Gebäudes leisten kann und diese Struktur wahren. Es ist wichtig, dass bei der Erstplanung und den Veränderungen ein höchstes Mass an Durchhaltewillen bezüglich der Einhaltung der für das Projekt festgelegten Spielregeln vorhanden ist. Dieses Verständnis erlaubt rasche Aussagen zum „Was geht" und „Was geht nicht". Was mit geringem Aufwand rasch und günstig und Was mit erhöhtem Aufwand in entsprechend längerer Zeit mit höherem finanziellem Aufwand umgesetzt werden kann. Das Gebäude, im Speziellen der flexible Nutzerausbau, darf und muss sich der Nutzung anpassen. Jedoch bei Anforderungen über den Rahmen der geplanten Flexibilität hinaus ist das Gebäude gegebenenfalls nicht geeignet.

Dieser Nutzerausbau ist flexibel durch die Anforderungsdefinition mit Spielraum, die geplante Flexibilität. Das Gebäude und der Nutzeraus-

will be very exciting and challenging, both for the buildings and ourselves. The structures, rules and everything we can foresee that has not been implemented in stage one all provide support throughout the building's life cycle. →100

Sustainability and planned flexibility

The life cycle is the all-encompassing element. A holistic perspective on requirements, planning, acquisitions, implementation, actuation, operation, maintenance and dismantling is decisive for a sustainable laboratory building. The entire infrastructure, from basic to user-specific installations, is developed further in conversion work, rather than being replaced. This is a key factor for sustainability.

The ability to make quick changes in a laboratory building is a key success factor in today's climate of rapid transformation. Conscious, coordinated and planned flexibility enhances the ability to change quickly. Following a brief conversion period, lasting weeks rather than months, employees can ideally carry out their tasks in a secure, ergonomic laboratory that is functionally tailored towards their requirements.

Planned flexibility in a laboratory building creates the conditions in which conceiving, planning, initially installing, operating, implementing all conversions and successful dismantling can be a source of great enjoyment, while continuously adapting to user requirements and changing utilisation.

bau sind vorbereitet auf das „Was kommen könnte". Wir wissen heute nicht, was in fünf oder zehn oder zwanzig Jahren erforderlich sein wird. Wir wissen jedoch, dass rückblickend sich die Forschung, Entwicklung und Analytik in Teilen massiv verändert haben. Wenn sich automatisierte Systeme und Informationstechnik weiter so entwickeln, wird die Zukunft sehr spannend und herausfordernd, für die Gebäude und für uns. Die Strukturen, die Spielregeln und alles, was wir vorgesehen und in Etappe eins nicht realisiert haben, unterstützen im gesamten Lebenszyklus. →100

Nachhaltigkeit und geplante Flexibilität

Mit dem Lebenszyklus schließt sich der Kreis. Die Gesamtbetrachtung, von der Anforderung, Planung, Einkauf, Realisation, Inbetriebnahme, Betrieb, Wartung bis hin zur Rückmontage, ist entscheidend für ein nachhaltiges Laborgebäude. Die gesamte Infrastruktur von Grund- und Nutzerausbau wird bei Ergänzungsarbeiten weitergebaut und nicht ersetzt. Das ist ein wichtiger Faktor für die Nachhaltigkeit.

Veränderungen in einem Laborgebäude rasch umsetzen zu können ist ein wesentlicher Erfolgsfaktor in der heutigen Phase des schnellen Wandels. Die bewusste und abgestimmte geplante Flexibilität unterstützt die Möglichkeit für schnelle Veränderungen. Die Mitarbeitenden können dementsprechend nach kurzen Umbauphasen, Wochen nicht Monate, in einem sicheren, ergonomischen und in der Funktion auf die Bedürfnisse abgestimmten Laborbereich ihrer Tätigkeit optimal nachgehen.

Die geplante Flexibilität im Laborbau schafft die Voraussetzungen, um mit viel Spaß und Freude bei der Auslegung, der Planung, der Erstrealisation, dem Betrieb, der Realisation aller Umbauten und dem Rückbau erfolgreich den kontinuierlichen Nutzeranforderungs- und Nutzungsveränderungen gerecht zu werden.

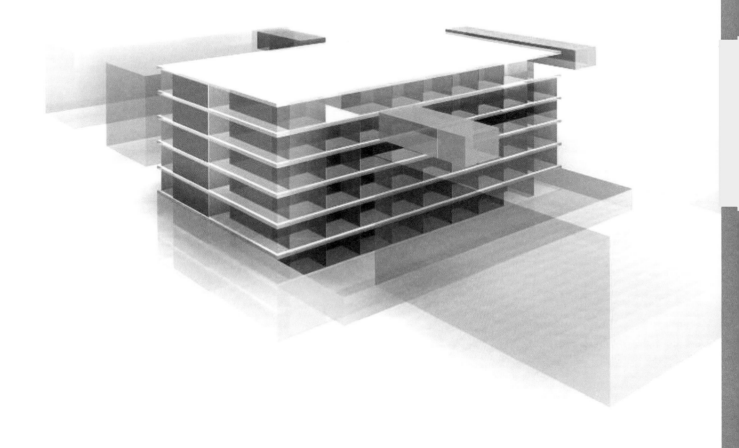

100
"Switching
functions like
drawers in
furniture"
„Funktionen wie
Schubladen
in einem Möbel
tauschen"

3 Space
Raum → 106–145

How is the working environment changing in the field of research? What has changed with respect to scientists' demands from their constructed environment? Research and laboratory buildings are tailored towards a highly complex, precise spatial programme. Form follows function. However, we now know that communication plays an important role in research. Impromptu conversations can encourage unplanned synergies and inspire spontaneous ideas. These "spaces of opportunity" may not necessarily be laboratories or offices, i.e. rooms with specifically defined functions. Instead, intermediate spaces – corridors, staircases and communal areas – give a building its actual identity, going beyond the necessities of the spatial programme.

This chapter presents examples of such spaces of opportunity, investigating the question of how spaces influence the production of knowledge.

Wie verändert sich die Arbeitswelt in der Forschung? Wie hat sich der Anspruch der Wissenschaftlerinnen und Wissenschaftler an ihre gebaute Umgebung verändert? Forschungs- und Laborgebäude sind auf ein hochkomplexes und präzises Raumprogramm abgestimmt. Die Funktion bestimmt die Form. Jedoch wissen wir inzwischen, dass auch Kommunikation ein wichtiger Bestandteil der Forschung ist. Das Gespräch aus dem Augenblick heraus kann ungeplante Synergien befördern und spontane Ideen hervorbringen. Diese „Möglichkeitsräume" sind nicht unbedingt Labore oder Büros, Räume, die auf eine bestimmte Funktion festgelegt sind. Vielmehr sind es die Zwischenräume – die Flure, Treppenhäuser und Aufenthaltsbereiche – die dem Gebäude über die Pflicht des Raumprogramms hinaus die eigentliche Identität verleihen.

Die folgenden Seiten zeigen Beispiele dieser Möglichkeitsräume und befassen sich mit der Frage, welchen Einfluss Raum auf die Produktion von Wissen hat.

3.1 New working environments for research

STEFAN BEHNISCH

Laboratory buildings are mostly planned on the basis of purely technical relationships. The focus lies on work processes and installations – which is why many laboratory buildings look more like a constructed functional and spatial diagram. However, such an approach falls short of the requirements of modern research. Scientists spend a large part of their working lives at their workplaces in laboratories and associated offices. They depend on good communication and quality of stay, as well as interdisciplinary and collegial exchange. Above all, however, they are reliant on an atmosphere that expresses a high degree of identification and makes them proud of their building. A working environment that equally motivates and attracts ambitious colleagues is also beneficial.

Our office has designed and constructed laboratory buildings for renowned universities and research facilities in the USA, Canada and Europe: for instance the Terence Donnelly Centre for Cellular and Biomolecular Research in Downtown Toronto →101-104 and most recently the School of Engineering and Applied Sciences for Harvard University in Cambridge. →105-109 The latter, a 55,000 square-metre building is situated on the new Harvard Campus in Boston's Allston district, to the south of the Harvard Business School. From the outset, the users, clients and we architects found it important to create a highly communicative, flexible building. The School of Engineering comprises many different departments, both for teaching and research, requiring wet labs, computation labs, imaging, office spaces and testing areas. Interdisciplinary work and interdepartmental communication should especially be encouraged – and demanded. In addition to functional areas, which do indeed appear to be rather technically dominated, many informal areas are aimed at inviting people to have conversations and exchange ideas. Paths should cross, while common entrances and relaxation areas should be a focus in planning. However, in addition to aspects of quality of stay, there was also a desire for the building to radiate strongly towards the surrounding environment: architecture as a symbol of a modern research facility, the new School of Engineering.

Like all other renowned research and teaching institutions, Harvard University is in constant competition for talented employees. Instead of beginning with researchers, the process should also attract especially talented

Laborgebäude werden meist aus rein technischen Zusammenhängen heraus geplant. Im Vordergrund stehen dabei die Arbeitsabläufe und Installationen – daher gleichen viele Laborgebäude eher einem gebauten Funktions- und Raumdiagramm. In den modernen Wissenschaften greift dies zu kurz. Denn Wissenschaftler verbringen einen Großteil ihres Arbeitslebens an ihren Arbeitsplätzen in den Laboren und dazugehörigen Büros. Sie sind angewiesen auf gute Kommunikation und Aufenthaltsqualitäten, auf den interdisziplinären und kollegialen Austausch. Insbesondere jedoch sind sie angewiesen auf eine Atmosphäre, die einen hohen Identifikationsgrad vermittelt und es ihnen erlaubt, stolz zu sein auf ihr Gebäude. Von Vorteil ist eine Arbeitsumgebung, die ebenso ambitionierte Kolleginnen und Kollegen zu motivieren und anzuziehen weiß.

Unser Büro hat bereits Laborgebäude für bekannte Universitäten und Forschungseinrichtungen in den USA, Kanada und Europa entworfen und realisiert. So zum Beispiel das Terence Donnelly Centre for Cellular and Biomolecular Research in Downtown Toronto →101-104 oder jüngst die School of Engineering and Applied Sciences für die Harvard University in Cambridge. →105-109 Dieses 55.000 Quadratmeter große Gebäude liegt auf dem neuen Harvard Campus im Bostoner Stadtteil Allston, südlich der Harvard Business School. Von Beginn an war es Nutzern, Auftraggebern und uns Architekten ein Anliegen, ein hoch kommunikatives und flexibles Gebäude zu schaffen. Die School of Engineering beherbergt viele unterschiedliche Abteilungen, sowohl für die Lehre als auch die Forschung, die Nasslabore, Computational Labs, Imaging aber auch Büroflächen und Testflächen benötigen. Gerade die interdisziplinäre Arbeit und die fachübergreifende Kommunikation sollten gefördert, ja gefordert werden. Neben den Funktionsbereichen, die oft tatsächlich recht technisch dominiert erscheinen, sollten viele informelle Bereiche zum Gespräch und Austausch einladen. Wege sollten sich kreuzen, gemeinsame Zugänge und Aufenthaltsbereiche im Vordergrund der Planung stehen. Doch neben den hohen Aufenthaltsqualitäten war gewünscht, dass das Gebäude auch nach außen eine besondere Ausstrahlung zeigt. Architektur als Sinnbild für eine moderne Forschungseinrichtung, die neue School of Engineering.

Die Harvard University steht wie alle anderen renommierten Forschungs- und Lehreinrichtungen im ständigen Wettbewerb um Talente. Dies fängt nicht erst bei den Forschenden an, sondern bereits beim Anwerben von besonders talentierten Studierenden, den Forschenden von morgen. Auch wetteifern die Hochschulen mit in der Umgebung angesiedelten

students, tomorrow's researchers. Universities also compete for attention with the companies based in the local area and their research departments. This is especially noticeable in regions around elite universities such as Harvard, MIT, Yale or Stanford. So in this case, it was important to design a building with a symbolic power that could ensure a high degree of identification and can represent modern teaching and research in Harvard.

A few years earlier, we planned a new administration building on Kendall Square in Cambridge for the Genzyme Corporation, → 122 a globally operative American biotech company. It was the first commercial LEED Platinum building in the USA. The CEO wanted us to design a highly communicative, very sustainable building, while also being architecturally outstanding. He regarded good architecture as a major advantage, especially with respect to recruiting. In a subsequent study, Genzyme found that the architecture was an important identifying factor for the well-trained and demanding employees. Not only the recruiting was more successful, but the company also recorded measurably fewer sick days, longer periods of employment at the company and generally higher productivity. The CEO at the time explained that – in view of 80 percent personnel costs and only around eight percent costs for the workspaces with respect to sales – this represents a major economic success, which had compensated for the additional costs of such a building in only two years.

We all know that research and teaching are in a process of constant transformation. During the planning procedure for a biology laboratory, our office carried out what is known as a shadow study. For several weeks, we monitored the researchers carrying out their daily work, attempting to find out which elements of a traditional laboratory work well and are often used, as well as grasping the actual distribution of tasks within such a laboratory. We discovered that the most elaborate and expensive areas were used relatively rarely, while other areas, such as formal and informal meeting places, documentation zones and office workplaces, were well frequented. Meetings were held less in the intended meeting rooms and much more often informally, for instance in the canteen, break rooms or tea kitchen. So we concluded that places that were not explicitly mentioned in the spatial programme also appeared to be especially valuable to the users. We also noticed that some newly constructed laboratories only actually work because scientists are flexible people who come to terms very well with the given surroundings. But what conclusions should we draw from that as we continue to plan modern laboratory buildings?

Unternehmen samt ihren Forschungsabteilungen um Aufmerksamkeit. Insbesondere in den Gegenden rund um Eliteuniversitäten wie Harvard, MIT, Yale oder Stanford ist dies deutlich wahrzunehmen. Somit war es hier von Bedeutung ein Gebäude zu entwerfen, das Symbolkraft hat, für ein hohes Maß an Identifikation sorgt und das für die moderne Lehre und Forschung in Harvard stehen kann.

So hatten wir einige Jahre zuvor für die Genzyme Corporation → 122 ein amerikanisches, weltweit agierendes Biotechnologieunternehmen, ein neues Verwaltungsgebäude am Kendall Square in Cambridge geplant. Es war das erste kommerzielle LEED-Platinum Gebäude in den USA. Der CEO wünschte sich von uns ein hoch kommunikatives, sehr nachhaltiges Gebäude, das auch architektonisch herausragend sein sollte. Er sah in guter Architektur einen großen Vorteil, insbesondere beim Recruiting. In einer nachfolgenden Studie stellte Genzyme fest, dass die Architektur einen wichtigen Identifikationsfaktor für die gut ausgebildeten und anspruchsvollen Mitarbeiterinnen und Mitarbeiter darstellte. Nicht nur das Recruiting war erfolgreicher, man verzeichnete auch weniger Krankheitstage, eine längere Verweildauer im Unternehmen und es war generell eine höhere Produktivität messbar. Der damalige CEO erläuterte, dass – ausgehend von 80 Prozent Personalkosten und nur etwa acht Prozent Raumkosten in Bezug auf den Umsatz – dieses einen großen, wirtschaftlichen Erfolg bedeutete, der die Mehrkosten eines solchen Gebäudes bereits nach zwei Jahren gerechtfertigt hatte.

Nun ist uns allen bewusst, dass Forschung und Lehre in einem ständigen Wandel begriffen sind. Anlässlich der Planung für ein Biologielabor hatte unser Büro eine sogenannte Shadowstudy erstellt. Wir waren Wissenschaftlerinnen und Wissenschaftlern über mehrere Wochen bei ihrer täglichen Arbeit gefolgt und hatten versucht herauszufinden, welche Elemente eines traditionellen Labors gut funktionieren, oft genutzt werden und wie tatsächlich die Arbeitsverteilung innerhalb eines solchen Labors aussieht. Wir konnten feststellen, dass die aufwändigsten und teuersten Flächen relativ selten genutzt werden, während andere Bereiche wie formelle und informelle Treffpunkte, die Dokumentationszonen oder Büroarbeitsplätze häufig frequentiert werden. Besprechungen fanden weniger in den dafür vorgesehenen Besprechungsräumen statt als vielmehr informell beispielsweise in Kantine, Pausenzone oder Teeküche. Daraus konnten wir schließen, dass auch gerade jene Angebote, die nicht explizit in Raumprogrammen erwähnt werden, von besonderem Wert für die Nutzer schienen. Auch bemerkten wir, dass einige der neu gebauten Labore tatsächlich nur funktionierten, weil Wissenschaftler flexible Menschen sind, die sich in vorgegebenen Umgebungen sehr gut zurechtfinden. Doch welche Schlüsse lassen sich daraus für die weitere Planung von modernen Laborgebäuden ziehen? Die geforderten technischen Vorgaben müssen

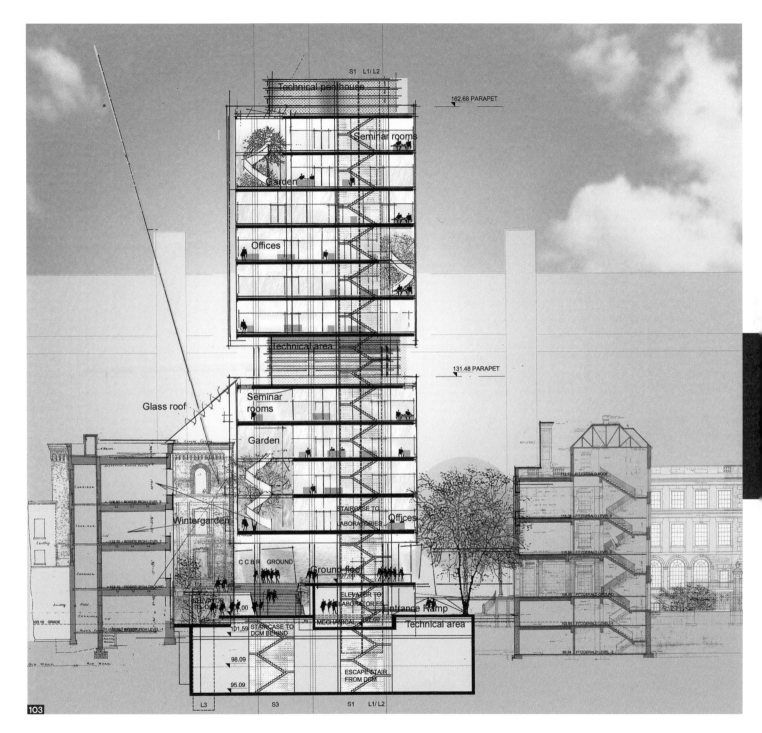

Technical penthouse

S1 L1/ L2

162.68 PARAPET

Seminar rooms

Garden

Offices

Technical area

131.48 PARAPET

Glass roof

Seminar rooms

Garden

Wintergarden

Offices

STAIRCASE TO LABORATORIES

Ground floor

CCBR GROUND

ELEVATOR TO LABORATORIES

ELEVATOR TO DCM

Entrance Ramp

MECHANICAL

Technical area

STAIRCASE TO DCM BEHIND

ESCAPE STAIR FROM DCM

L3   S3   S1   L1/ L2

103

103
Sectional view,
Terence Donnelly
Centre
Querschnitt, Terence
Donnelly Centre

104
Conservatory,
Terence Donnelly
Centre
Wintergarten, Terence
Donnelly Centre

Naturally, they must adhere to and fulfil the defined technical specifications – that is the basic premise. However, the more challenging task is at least as important: to create distinctive characteristics, shape identity and ensure the elements in a building that will motivate the people who work, teach or learn there. In that sense, not only the inward appearance of architecture, but also its outward image is very important for feeling comfortable. The latter creates an address, an identity-building characteristic.

In 2019, we won the competition for the new building for the Max Planck Institute for Medical Research in Heidelberg. →110–113 Its focus was also to design rooms that enable interdisciplinary work. Physicists, chemists and biologists research together on medical themes – during its 90-year history, the famous institute has produced five Nobel Prize winners. During a period of reorientation, it plans to supplement the four existing, experimental departments with additional research groups. The current location, a preservation-listed building constructed in 1928, can no longer fulfil the demands of forward-looking work and its communication demands. The new building should not only compensate for the limitations and compromises of today's use, but also provide a considerable improvement.

The property in a prominent location on the southern edge of the university grounds, directly by the River Neckar, is the first stage of a new innovation campus. A high-rise development is required that represents the science location and refers to its modern research. Outwardly, the building should use contemporary architecture to communicate not only with the neighbouring historical buildings, but also with its surroundings. Due to its exposed location, the institute will be visible from afar and assume a high profile on the urban landscape. So we designed a building with a light, hovering character, rising with an inviting gesture, while defining the image of a transparent research landscape through its open, see-through character. Providing 12 floors and around 6,000 square metres of usable space, it will offer plenty of room for fundamental research on an elite level. The spatial programme comprises highly installed laboratory areas, the necessary auxiliary spaces and the technical rooms, as well as offices, seminar rooms, meeting rooms, workshops and a cafeteria. Towards the west, the building has a calmer appearance and responds to the line of the neighbouring development, while towards the south, it is more playful and multifaceted.

The spatial reference achieved by the design is important. With its terraced design on the first three levels, it manages a topographically defined, gentle transition from the Neckar landscape to the institute, from open space

natürlich eingehalten und erfüllt werden – das ist die Pflicht. Die Kür jedoch ist mindestens genauso wichtig. Denn diese schafft die Unterscheidungsmerkmale, sie gestaltet Identität und sorgt für eben jene Elemente in einem Gebäude, die die Menschen, die künftig darin arbeiten, lehren oder lernen, motivieren. So ist die Architektur nicht nur nach Innen sondern auch in der äußeren Erscheinung von großer Bedeutung für das Wohlbefinden. Sie kreiert eine Adresse, ein identitätsstiftendes Merkmal.

Wir haben im Jahr 2019 den Wettbewerb für das neue Gebäude des Max-Planck-Instituts für Medizinische Forschung in Heidelberg gewonnen. →110–113 Auch hier stand primär im Vordergrund Räume zu entwerfen, die interdisziplinäres Arbeiten ermöglichen. Physiker, Chemiker und Biologen forschen gemeinsam an medizinischen Themen – das traditionsreiche Institut hat in seiner 90-jährigen Geschichte bereits fünf Nobelpreisträger hervorgebracht. In einer Phase der Neuorientierung will es die vier bestehenden, experimentell arbeitenden Abteilungen um zusätzliche Forschungsgruppen ergänzen. Der derzeitige Standort, ein denkmalgeschützter Bestandsbau aus dem Jahr 1928, kann den Anforderungen an ein zukunftsorientiertes Arbeiten mit kommunikativen Aspekten nicht mehr gerecht werden. Das neue Haus soll die Einschränkungen und Kompromisse der jetzigen Nutzung nicht nur kompensieren, sondern vielmehr erheblich verbessern.

Das Grundstück in prominenter Lage am südlichen Rande des Universitätsgeländes, direkt am Neckar, wird den Auftakt zum neu entstehenden Innovationscampus bilden. Gewünscht ist hier ein Hochhaus, das den Wissenschaftsstandort repräsentiert und auf seine moderne Forschung verweist. Nach außen soll das Haus mittels einer zeitgenössischen Architektur nicht nur mit dem benachbarten, historischen Gebäude kommunizieren, sondern auch mit seiner Umgebung. Aufgrund seiner exponierten Lage wird das Institut von weithin sichtbar sein und eine markante Stellung im Stadtbild einnehmen. So haben wir ein Haus entworfen, das sich hier leicht und schwebend, mit einladender Geste erhebt und das mit seinem offenen, transparenten Charakter das Bild einer gläsernen Forschungslandschaft prägt. Auf 12 Geschossen und etwa 6000 Quadratmetern Nutzfläche wird es seinen Nutzerinnen und Nutzern zukünftig viel Raum für Grundlagenforschung auf Spitzenniveau bieten. Das Raumprogramm umfasst neben hochinstallierten Laborflächen, notwendigen Auxiliarflächen und den Technikbereichen auch Büroräume, Seminar- und Besprechungsräume, Werkstätten sowie eine Cafeteria. Nach Westen hin tritt der Baukörper ruhiger in Erscheinung und nimmt die Gebäudeflucht des Nachbarhauses auf, während er sich nach Osten hin verspielter und facettenreicher zeigt.

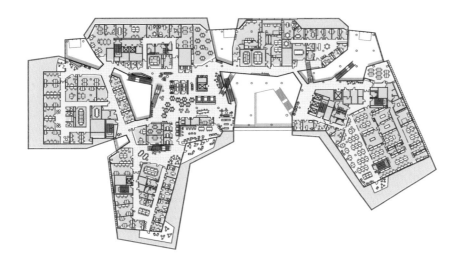

105–106
Ground and
1st floor plans,
Harvard University
Science and
Engineering
Complex, Allston,
Behnisch Architekten,
completed in 2021
Grundrisse
Erdgeschoss und 1.
Obergeschoss,
Harvard University
Science and
Engineering
Complex, Allston,
Behnisch Architekten,
fertiggestellt 2021

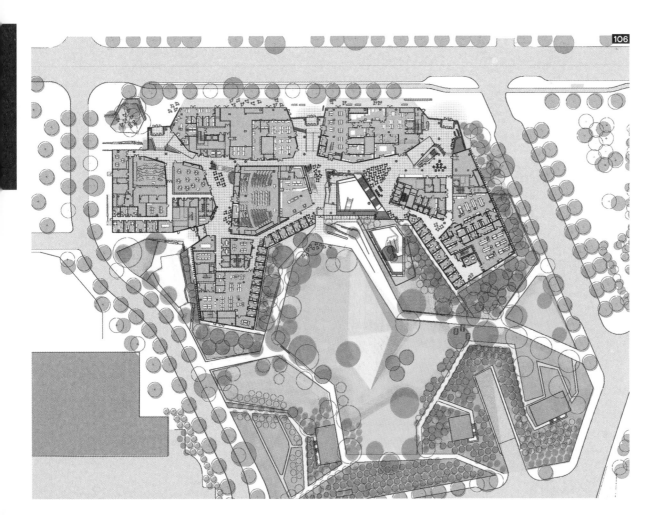

106

107–108
Schematic sketch,
office and
laboratory areas,
Harvard University
Science and
Engineering
Complex
Schemaschnitte
Bürobereich und
Laborbereich des
Harvard University
Science and
Engineering Complex

109
The park grounds
and rooftop terrace
are accessible
to students and
teachers
Parkanlage und
Dachterrassen
stehen Studierenden
und Lehrenden zur
Verfügung

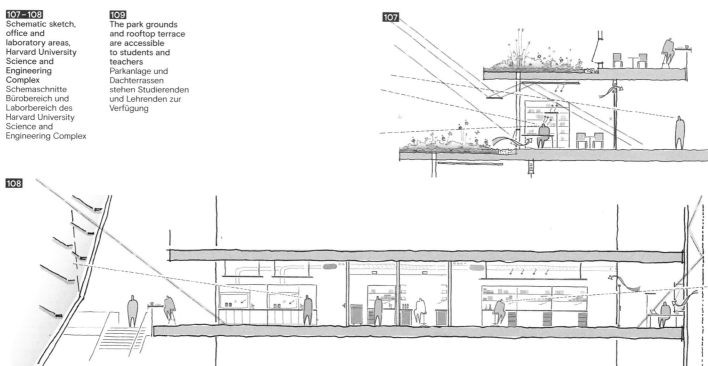

to constructed development. The numerous projections form balconies and terraces. A recessed façade on the fifth floor not only enables a fine adjustment to the proportions, but also provides the institute with a versatile rooftop garden. Prof. Stefan Hell, Institute Director and Jury Chairman, praised the many areas available for exchanging ideas and interaction between researchers, making research tangible: "The office proposed a building typology that offers freedom and transparency towards the outside world. That helps our institute to continue to hire the best employees." (See also 3.2 EXCURSUS We need extremely good architecture!) Inside as well, the range of spaces and the organisation of levels ensure an inspiring research environment. The laboratories appear as clearly perceptible, functional units and are pooled in a rectangular building core that conforms to the ideal interior grid. They are surrounded by varied, lively spatial situations that enhance the research landscape with diverse relaxation and communication zones, as well as employee offices. The large, freely arranged spaces offer a high degree of flexibility. Depending on requirements, either communicative work or zones for individual, highly concentrated research activities are possible. On every floor, generous terraces create a reference to the outside world. Vertical networks are organised via two-storey spaces connected by free-standing stairs. On the first floor, a cafeteria with an outdoor area allows employees and guests to spend time there, while the bridge connects it to the existing building. There are plenty of other meeting and relaxation areas with a high quality of stay. The concept for the open-air areas is also aimed at strengthening the location's identity and encouraging interdisciplinary exchange. The proximity of the plot and its connection to the river play an important role, radiating into the entire campus. A sustainable energy concept uses synergies, for example for heat recovery from laboratories and servers, as well as activating the building envelope with photovoltaic systems.

Thus, this project is exemplary in showing how unmistakable, magical locations can be developed, above all with the help of a large number of individual, locally specific factors. Lively concepts with communicative aspects and unique, concise architecture are necessary to motivate research – and perhaps find the next Nobel Prize winner.

Von Bedeutung ist der räumliche Bezug, der mit dem Entwurf gelingt. Auf den ersten drei Ebenen terrassenförmig gestaltet, schafft er einen landschaftlich geprägten, „weichen" Übergang von der Neckarlandschaft zum Institut, vom Freiraum zum Gebauten. Zahlreiche Auskragungen formen Balkone und Terrassen. Ein Rücksprung der Fassade im fünften Obergeschoss sorgt nicht nur für eine Feinjustierung der Proportionen, sondern schenkt dem Institut auch einen vielseitig nutzbaren Dachgarten. Prof. Stefan Hell, Direktor des Instituts und Vorsitzender des Preisgerichts, urteilt, dass für Austausch und Interaktion zwischen den Wissenschaftlerinnen und Wissenschaftlern viele Flächen bereitstehen, dass Forschung hier greifbar wird: „Das Büro hat eine Gebäudetypologie vorgeschlagen, die nach außen viel Freiheit und Einsicht transportiert. Das hilft uns, weiterhin die besten Mitarbeiter für unser Institut zu gewinnen." Auch im Inneren sorgt das Angebot an Räumen und die Organisation der Ebenen für eine inspirierende Forschungsumgebung. Die Labore sind in einem rechtwinkligen, dem idealen Ausbauraster entsprechenden Gebäudekern gebündelt und treten als eindeutig wahrnehmbare Funktionseinheit in Erscheinung. Doch umspielt werden sie von abwechslungsreichen, lebendigen Raumsituationen, die mit unterschiedlichen Aufenthalts- und Kommunikationszonen sowie Mitarbeiterbüros die Forschungslandschaft bereichern. Als frei gestaltbare, zusammenhängende Großräume bieten sie ein hohes Maß an Flexibilität. Je nach Bedarf kann kommunikativ gearbeitet oder für individuelle, hochkonzentrierte Forschungstätigkeiten weiter zoniert werden. Auf jedem Geschoss schaffen großzügige Terrassen einen Freiraumbezug. Die vertikale Vernetzung ist über zweigeschossige Lufträume, die über Freitreppen verbunden sind, organisiert. Im ersten Obergeschoss lädt eine Cafeteria mit Außenbereich Mitarbeiter und Gäste zum Verweilen, eine Brücke sorgt hier auch für eine Anbindung zum Bestandsbau. Auch im Außenraum finden sich viele Treff- und Verweilpunkte mit hoher Aufenthaltsqualität. Das Freiraumkonzept zielt ebenfalls darauf ab, die Identität des Ortes zu stärken und den interdisziplinären Austausch zu fördern. Die Nähe des Grundstücks und seine Anbindung zum Fluss spielen eine bedeutende Rolle und strahlen auf den gesamten Campus ab. Ein nachhaltiges Energiekonzept nutzt Synergien, so zum Beispiel Wärmerückgewinnung der Abwärme aus Laboren und von Servern oder auch die Aktivierung der Gebäudehülle durch Photovoltaik.

So zeigt dieses Projekt beispielhaft, dass sich unverwechselbare, magische Orte vor allem auch mithilfe einer Vielzahl an individuellen, ortsspezifischen Faktoren entwickeln lassen. Lebendige Konzepte mit kommunikativen Aspekten und eine eindeutige, prägnante Architektur sind notwendig, um Forschung zu beflügeln – und somit womöglich die nächsten Nobelpreisträger hervorzubringen.

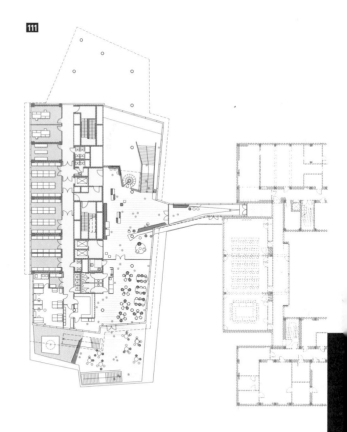

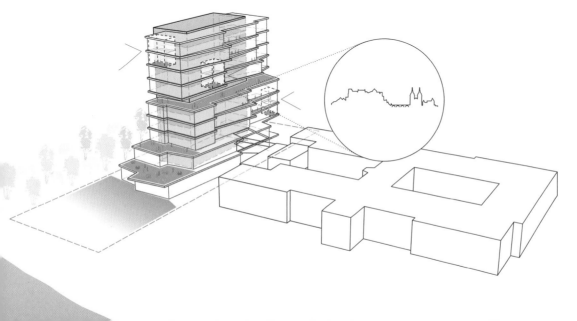

110 – 111
Max Planck Institute for Medical Research, floor plans, 1st floor with connections to the existing building, and 2nd floor, Heidelberg, Behnisch Architekten, since 2021
Max-Planck-Institut für medizinische Forschung, Grundrisse 1. OG mit Anbindung an den Bestand und 2. OG, Heidelberg, Behnisch Architekten, seit 2021

112
Balconies and rooftop terraces afford views of the old town and the River Neckar
Von Balkonen und Dachterrassen blickt man auf Altstadt und Neckar

STEFAN HELL

We need extremely good architecture!

Wir brauchen sehr gute Architektur!

On July 11, 2019, as part of the competition for the new building of the Max Planck Institute for Medical Research in Heidelberg, the Nobel Prize Winner and Institute Director Prof. Stefan Hell presented his demands from architects in a keynote lecture. The text printed here is a translated extract from the lecture and reflects the perspective of a scientist.

(…) The building that we expect must be functional. You have already spoken to some of the people in the individual departments and heard their technical requirements. But what I would like to call for now, which is very important to me, is: we also want very, very good architecture!

Why good architecture? I am speaking from personal experience. The building and its architecture determine a scientist's daily life. Ideally, good architecture, a good research building, has a magical attraction for young scientists. Their decision to work at this institution at all is also influenced by the building's architecture and the way it is designed.

Anlässlich des Wettbewerbs Neubau des Max-Planck-Institut für medizinische Forschung in Heidelberg formulierte Nobelpreisträger und Institutsleiter Prof. Stefan Hell am 11. Juli 2019 seine Forderungen an die Architekten in einem Impulsvortrag. Der hier abgedruckte Text ist ein Auszug dieses Vortrags und reflektiert die Perspektive eines Wissenschaftlers.

(…) Das Gebäude, das wir erwarten, muss funktional sein. Zum Teil haben Sie schon mit Leuten aus den einzelnen Abteilungen gesprochen und haben gehört, was technisch erforderlich ist. Aber, das Plädoyer, das ich jetzt aussprechen möchte und das mir auch wirklich wichtig ist, lautet: wir wollen auch eine sehr, sehr gute Architektur!

Warum eine gute Architektur? Ich spreche hier aus persönlicher Erfahrung. Das Gebäude und seine Architektur bestimmen den Alltag des Wissenschaftlers mit. Eine gute Architektur, ein gutes Forschungsgebäude zieht junge Wissenschaftler oder Wissenschaftlerinnen idealerweise magisch an. Ihre Entscheidung, überhaupt an diesem Institut zu arbeiten, wird auch beeinflusst von der Architektur des Gebäudes und wie diese ausgestaltet ist.

I can give you an example from my own life. In 1993, I went to Turku in Finland. My decision to go there was influenced by the building where I could work at the time. It was brand new and just completed. Without wanting to judge it: to give you an idea of the building, it was rather like a glass palace. A Finnish colleague said it would more than suffice for the Finnish headquarters of Deutsche Bank. It had glass elevators that were very inviting. In the mornings, taking the lift up to the 4th floor and working there was a truly uplifting experience. Naturally, that has a motivating effect. If you are happy to arrive there in the morning, you stay there a little longer and feel privileged to be a researcher carrying out your everyday work. Feeling good and the excitement it inspires also makes you more creative. Ultimately, in that building, I developed the groundwork that later won me the Nobel Prize.

Feeling good, creativity and quality of stay are all important aspects that such a building must communicate. Because researchers don't have a nine-to-five job. Being a researcher is a calling. You enter the world of science because you enjoy doing it. The institute should therefore be atmospherically "uplifting" for everyone working there.

Consider also: most scientists make their fundamental discoveries when they are young. When you are still young, you generally live in modest circumstances, rather than a fancy villa or apartment. If you then come to a marvellous building, you are all the happier to be there, because it is more colourful, modern and communicative than in your neighbourhood at home. These mostly unspoken effects should not be underestimated. I expect the building to fulfil precisely that role. Remember: not all scientists are "nerds" for whom everything around them is irrelevant. There are an increasing number of scientists who want to be functionally and also emotionally engaged with the building.

As you know, the building should be a high-rise development, as the prior urban planning competition found. Imagine we want to hire an employee – and naturally we want to hire the best people in the world. The Max-Planck-Gesellschaft – especially this institution – is a player in the Champions League of science. Our laboratories have the same status and renown as laboratories in Harvard, Stanford and the like. Postdocs who apply to Harvard, Stanford and elsewhere also apply here to sound out their professional prospects and working conditions. If I want to attract those people, if I want them to come to Germany, here to Heidelberg, I have to offer them something special. These people are applying to the best laboratories in the world.

Ich kann Ihnen hierzu ein Beispiel aus meinem eigenen Leben geben. Ich ging 1993 nach Turku in Finnland. Meine Entscheidung dorthin zu gehen war mit beeinflusst von dem Gebäude, in dem ich damals arbeiten konnte. Das Gebäude war funkelnagelneu und gerade erst fertig geworden. Ohne jetzt eine Wertung aussprechen zu wollen: es war – damit Sie sich das vorstellen können – eine Art Glaspalast. Ein finnischer Kollege sagte, es würde der Repräsentanz der Deutschen Bank in Finnland zur Ehre gereichen. Es hatte Aufzüge aus Glas, die sehr einladend waren. Wenn man mit einem solchen Aufzug morgens nach oben fuhr, war es ein wirklich erhebendes Gefühl, im 4. Stock arbeiten zu dürfen. Und das beflügelt natürlich. Wenn man sich freut, morgens dahinzukommen, bleibt man etwas länger und man fühlt sich in seinem Alltag als Forscher privilegiert. Wohlfühlen und die Spannung, die das Gebäude ausdrückt, führen auch dazu, dass man kreativer ist. Letztendlich habe ich da die Grundlagen für die Arbeiten geschaffen, die mir später den Nobelpreis eingebracht haben.

Wohlfühlen, Kreativität und Verweildauer, das sind wichtige Aspekte, die ein solches Gebäude transportieren muss. Denn als Wissenschaftler macht man keinen Nine-to-five-job. Wissenschaftler ist man aus Berufung. Man geht in die Wissenschaft, weil man es gerne macht. Das Institut sollte also für alle, die da arbeiten, atmosphärisch „erhebend" sein.

Bedenken Sie auch: die meisten Wissenschaftler machen ihre fundamentalen Entdeckungen, wenn sie jung sind. Wenn man noch jung ist, wohnt man ja meistens auch nicht in einer tollen Villa oder Wohnung, sondern eher bescheiden. Wenn man dann morgens in ein tolles Gebäude kommt, freut man sich umso mehr dort zu sein, weil es dort mitunter farbenfroher, lebendiger, moderner und kommunikativer zugeht als in dem Viertel zu Hause. Diese meistens unausgesprochen bleibenden Effekte darf man nicht unterschätzen. Ich erwarte, dass das Gebäude genau diese Rolle erfüllt. Bedenken Sie: es gibt nicht nur „Nerds" unter den Wissenschaftlern, für die alles um sie herum egal ist, sondern immer mehr auch solche Wissenschaftler, die vom Gebäude nicht nur funktional, sondern auch emotional angesprochen werden wollen.

Wie Sie wissen, soll das Gebäude – und das hat der städtebauliche Vorwettbewerb ergeben – ein Hochpunkt werden. Stellen Sie sich einmal vor, wir möchten einen Mitarbeiter oder eine Mitarbeiterin anwerben – und wir wollen natürlich die besten Leute der Welt anwerben. Die Max-Planck-Gesellschaft – und dieses Institut erst recht – spielt in der Champions League der Wissenschaft. Unsere Labore sind vom Status und Renommee auf dem gleichen Level wie die Labore in Harvard, Stanford usw. Die Postdocs, die sich in Harvard, Stanford oder sonst irgendwo bewerben, bewerben sich auch hier, um ihre beruflichen Chancen und Arbeitsbedingungen auszuloten. Wenn ich die Person kriegen will, wenn ich sie nach Deutschland bekommen will, hier nach Heidelberg, dann muss ich ihr

113
Competition
presentation, Max
Planck Institute for
Medical Research,
Heidelberg, Behnisch
Architekten, 2021
Wettbewerbs-
visualisierung des
Max-Planck-Instituts
für medizinische
Forschung,
Heidelberg, Behnisch
Architekten, 2021

You can imagine it visually: if you enter a building, then ride up to the 10th or 11th floor and see Heidelberg "at your feet", the city that attracts millions of tourists every year, then if you are an applicant, you feel as if you're being offered something special. Something that doesn't otherwise exist. As a potential employer, that gives me a very considerable bonus point. And it is very important that we don't squander that bonus point. Not many locations have that visual reference, that unique panorama overlooking the old town and the castle. Hundreds of thousands of people a year spend their money to come here, to see it. People who apply here can have that on a daily basis. That has to be incorporated into the building.

The Neuenheimer Feld is one of the largest research campuses in Europe and certainly one of the most prominent in the world. But: if you cross the River Neckar, you will hardly see a building with any symbolic expression. In concrete terms: when researchers organise a science congress here at the Neuenheimer Feld and design a poster for the event – what do you think they normally present on the poster? The castle and the Neckar. They are undoubtedly beautiful. But they don't stand for science and definitely not for the future. We need a building that, even from afar, radiates "the scientific Heidelberg of the 21st century". We have the opportunity – here at the pole position of this campus – to construct such a building. And that is precisely what we expect.

We also have an older building here. It already played a pioneering role in 1930 – also architecturally – and it is therefore preservation-listed. But the new building's design must not be overly influenced by the old building. The opposite also applies. Both buildings should complement each other. As an architect, you have to communicate the feeling that new and old elements go together. In the end, you need to manage the architectural feat of making them look as though they belong together. The architectural brief makes enough points in this respect.

Only few institutes in Germany stand to such an extent for breakthroughs in science as the building in which we find ourselves today. It should therefore be noted that the new building should become something of an icon, a symbol of science, a symbol of advancing to the middle of the 21st century. We now have that unique opportunity. This is the quintessential location to do precisely that. So create something amazing here!

schon was bieten. Denn diese Leute bewerben sich in den besten Laboren der Welt.

Sie können es sich ja plastisch ausmalen: wenn man in ein Gebäude kommt, dann in den 10. oder in den 11. Stock hochfährt und einem dabei Heidelberg „zu Füßen" liegt, die Stadt, die jedes Jahr Millionen von Touristen anlockt, dann fühlt man als Bewerber, dass einem etwas Besonderes angeboten wird. Etwas, was es sonst so nicht gibt. Da habe ich als potentieller Arbeitgeber schon einmal einen ganz großen Pluspunkt. Und genau dieser Pluspunkt darf hier nicht verspielt werden. Es gibt nicht viele Standorte, die diesen Blickbezug, dieses einmalige Panorama auf Altstadt und Schloss bieten. Hunderttausende Leute im Jahr geben Geld aus, um hierher zu kommen, um es zu sehen. Das kann die Person, die sich hier bewirbt, dann täglich haben. Das muss in das Gebäude einbezogen werden.

Das Neuenheimer Feld ist einer der größten Forschungscampusse in Europa und sicher einer der prominentesten weltweit. Aber: wenn Sie über den Neckar kommen, dann werden Sie kaum ein Gebäude wahrnehmen, das eine Symbolsprache spricht. Um das zu konkretisieren: Wenn Naturwissenschaftler hier im Neuenheimer Feld einen wissenschaftlichen Kongress veranstalten und ein Werbeposter dafür machen - was glauben Sie, was auf dem Poster normalerweise zu sehen ist? Das Schloss und der Neckar. Die sind sehr ansehnlich ohne Frage. Doch sie stehen nicht für Wissenschaft und definitiv nicht für Zukunft. Wir brauchen ein Gebäude, das schon aus der Entfernung ausstrahlt „Das ist das Heidelberg der Wissenschaft im 21. Jahrhundert". Wir haben jetzt die Gelegenheit – hier in der Poleposition dieses Campus – ein solches Gebäude zu schaffen. Und genau das ist es, was wir erwarten.

Wir haben hier auch ein altes Gebäude. Es hat 1930 auch schon eine Vorreiterrolle gespielt – auch eine architektonische Vorreiterrolle – und es steht ja deshalb auch unter Denkmalschutz. Aber das neue Gebäude darf in seiner Ausgestaltung nicht zu sehr von dem alten Gebäude in Anspruch genommen werden. Das Gleiche gilt auch umgekehrt. Die beiden Gebäude sollen sich ergänzen. Als Architekt muss man das Gefühl transportieren, dass Neu und Alt zusammengehören. Letztendlich sollte man das architektonische Kunststück hinbekommen, dass es zusammengehörend wirkt. Dafür gibt es auch in der Beschreibung hinreichend Stichpunkte.

Es gibt nur wenige Institute in Deutschland, die so sehr für Durchbrüche in der Wissenschaft stehen, wie dieses Gebäude, in dem wir uns hier befinden. Es ist daher erwägenswert, mit dem neuen Gebäude so etwas wie ein „Icon" zu schaffen, ein Symbol für die Wissenschaft, ein Symbol für den Aufbruch in die Mitte des 21. Jahrhunderts. Diese einmalige Gelegenheit wäre hier gegeben und dies hier ist die „Location" schlechthin, genau das zu tun. Also: schaffen Sie hier etwas Tolles!

"Remember: not all scientists are 'nerds' for whom everything around them is irrelevant. There are an increasing number of scientists who want to be functionally and also emotionally engaged with the building." Stefan Hell

„Bedenken Sie: es gibt nicht nur ‚Nerds' unter den Wissenschaftlern, für die alles um sie herum egal ist, sondern immer mehr auch solche Wissenschaftler, die vom Gebäude nicht nur funktional, sondern auch emotional angesprochen werden wollen." Stefan Hell

3.3 Corridor chat

"Research takes place on the staircase, not in the laboratory." There is much truth in that often-quoted thought: communication is the key to excellent research.

"Nobody thinks on their own," as the physicist and science author Stefan Klein writes. He claims that creative thoughts unfold between people, rather than behind closed doors. Focused work, completely concentrating on a problem, is naturally important, but new ideas, treading off the conceptual beaten track, can only function if there is impetus from outside and people communicate with each other.

However, communication does not always take orderly, planned paths. Above all, informal communication – the fast transfer of information, bypassing organisation charts and hierarchies – is not only an important element of knowledge transfer in public authorities and companies, but also in research and education.

We therefore believe that the atmosphere of the spaces in which those spontaneous, unexpected encounters take place is of central importance. Communication – and especially informal communication – takes place where people enjoy spending time, where the space is not just a walkway, a dark corridor or a bare room. Instead, it should invite people to linger for a conversation outside their official routines.

Get out of the labs and onto the staircase! The following sequence of images presents a number of these "spaces of opportunity", where perhaps the ideas of the future are lingering.

1
Klein, S.: "Keiner denkt für sich allein", ZEIT Magazin, N°10, 4.3.2021

3.3 Flurfunk

„Forschen findet nicht im Labor, sondern im Treppenhaus statt" – es liegt viel Wahrheitsgehalt in diesem viel zitierten Gedanken: Kommunikation ist der Schlüssel zu exzellenter Forschung.

„Keiner denkt für sich allein", schreibt auch der Physiker und Wissenschaftsautor Stefan Klein[1]. Kreative Gedanken, sagt er, entfalten sich zwischen Menschen, nicht hinter verschlossenen Türen. So wichtig das konzentrierte Arbeiten, das völlige Fokussieren auf ein Problem auch sein mag, neue Denkanstöße, das Ausbrechen von den ausgetretenen Wegen des Denkens, kann nur funktionieren, wenn Impulse von außen kommen und Menschen untereinander kommunizieren.

Kommunikation jedoch verläuft nicht immer nur in geordneten und geplanten Bahnen. Gerade die informelle Kommunikation – der schnelle Informationstransfer vorbei an Organigrammen und Hierarchien – ist nicht nur in Behörden und Unternehmen ein wichtiger Bestandteil des Wissenstransfers, sondern auch in Forschung und Bildung.

Die Atmosphäre des Raumes, in dem diese spontanen und unverhofften Begegnungen stattfinden, halten wir dabei für zentral. Kommunikation – und besonders informelle Kommunikation – findet dort statt, wo Menschen sich gerne aufhalten, wo der Raum nicht nur ein Durchgangsraum ist, ein dunkler Flur oder ein kahles Zimmer, sondern ein Ort, der zum Verweilen einlädt, um abseits der offiziellen Wege zu plaudern.

Raus aus den Laboren, rein in die Treppenhäuser! Die folgende Bilderreihe zeigt einige dieser „Möglichkeitsräume" in denen vielleicht die Ideen der Zukunft mäandern.

1
Klein, S.: Keiner denkt für sich allein, ZEIT Magazin, N°10, 4.3.2021

Helmholtz
Institute Ulm,
Nikl & Partner
Architekten, 2014
Helmholtz-Institut
der Universität Ulm,
Nickl & Partner
Architekten, 2014

114

116 – 117
LAVES Veterinary
Institute Oldenburg,
Nickl & Partner
Architekten, 2014
LAVES Veterinär-
institut Oldenburg,
Nickl & Partner
Architekten, 2014

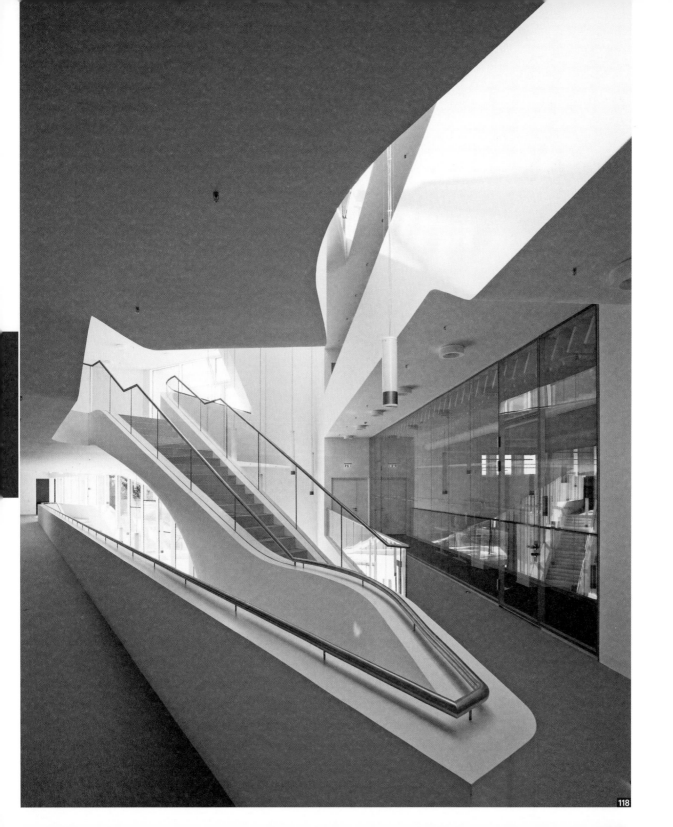

118
Center for Virtual
Engineering ZVE,
Fraunhofer Institute,
Stuttgart,
UNStudio, 2012
Zentrum für Virtuelles
Engineering ZVE,
Fraunhofer-Institut,
Stuttgart,
UNStudio, 2012

119
Novartis laboratory
building, Basel, David
Chipperfield
Architects, 2010
Novartis Laborge-
bäude, Basel, David
Chipperfield
Architects, 2010

120
Tangen Polytechnic,
Kristiansand, 3XN,
2009
Tangen Polytechnic,
Kristiansand, 3XN,
2009

Hörsaal 2

121
Communication
and Information
Centre KIZ,
University of Erfurt,
Nickl & Partner
Architekten, 2016
Kommunikations-
und Informations-
zentrum KIZ der
Universität Erfurt,
Nickl & Partner
Architekten, 2016

122
Genzyme Center,
Cambridge, MA,
Behnisch Architekten,
2004
Genzyme Center,
Cambridge, MA,
Behnisch Architekten,
2004

123
BSS research
building,
ETH Zurich in Basel,
Nickl & Partner
Architekten,
building site in
January 2022
BSS-Forschungs-
gebäude der
ETH Zürich in Basel,
Nickl & Partner
Architekten,
Baustelle im
Januar 2022

124
ISMO Institute,
Sciences Moléculaires
d'Orsay, KAAN
Architecten, 2018
ISMO Institut des
Sciences Moléculaires
d'Orsay, KAAN
Architecten, 2018

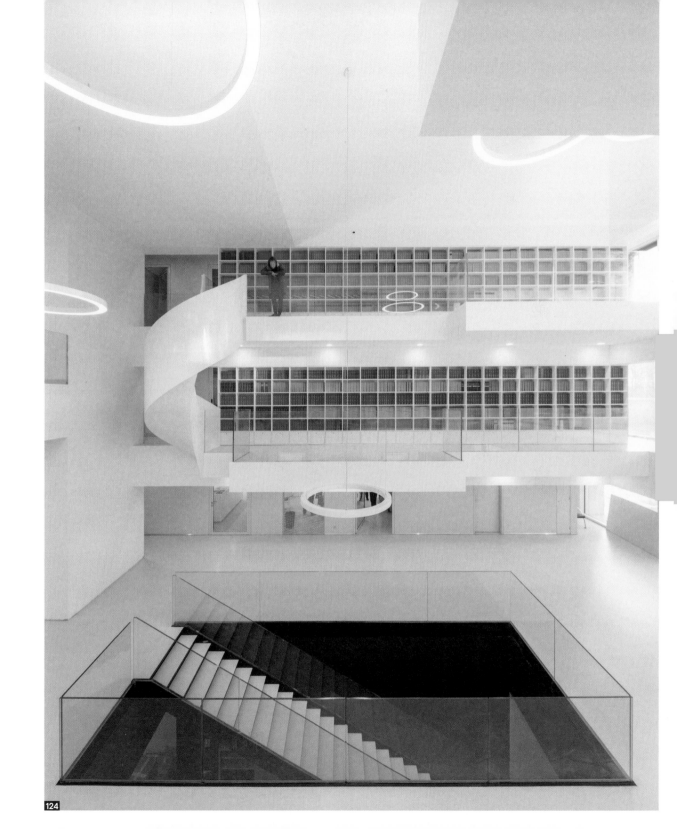

125
Integrative Research
Institute for the
Sciences IRIS
Adlershof, Berlin,
Nickl & Partner
Architekten, 2020
Integratives
Forschungsinstitut
für die Wissen-
schaften IRIS
Adlershof, Berlin,
Nickl & Partner
Architekten, 2020

126
Laboratory for
Automotive
Engineering, Ostfalia
University of Applied
Sciences, Wolfsburg,
Nickl & Partner
Architekten, 2017
Labor für Fahrzeug-
technik, Ostfalia
Hochschule
Wolfsburg, Nickl &
Partner Architekten,
2017

Experimental Zone

SÉVERINE MARGUIN +
HENRIKE RABE +
FRIEDRICH SCHMIDGALL

Experimentalzone

Spaces for collaborative knowledge production[1]

Versatile, flexible, open – ever more companies present their workplaces as "the office of the future" or "innovation spaces". There is a long tradition in office architecture to research space as a driving force behind creativity and innovation: studies include the "office landscape" of the Quickborn team,[2] the classification of workspaces by Francis Duffy and DEGW[3;4] and "Office Urbanism" by Hitoshi Abe.[5] The field of architecture for research facilities seems to be untouched by these developments and has not been questioned, developed further and experimented upon to the same extent, although the university is the epitome of knowledge generation and innovation. Today it faces new challenges through the paradigm of interdisciplinarity. The latest discourse on the Media Lab[6;7] and the design studio[8;9] highlights the current fascination for interdisciplinary, creative knowledge production among researchers. However, the question of designing spaces continues to be overlooked: what influence do spaces have on knowledge production and which spaces and spatial qualities do we need to develop new knowledge – especially at intersections between disciplines?

Räume der kollaborativen Wissensproduktion[1]

Vielfältig, flexibel, offen – immer mehr Unternehmen stellen ihre Arbeitsplätze als „Büro der Zukunft" oder als „Innovationsraum" dar. In der Büroarchitektur gibt es eine lange Tradition, Raum als Motor von Kreativität und Innovation gestalterisch zu erforschen: von der "Bürolandschaft" des Quickborner Teams[2], über die Typisierung von Arbeitsräumen von Francis Duffy und DEGW[3;4] bis zum "Office Urbanism" von Hitoshi Abe[5]. Scheinbar unberührt von diesen Entwicklungen wird die Wissenschaftsarchitektur noch nicht im gleichen Maße hinterfragt, weiterentwickelt und mit ihr experimentiert, obwohl die Universität der Ort der Wissensgenerierung und Innovation schlechthin ist, und sie heute aufgrund des Paradigmas der Interdisziplinarität vor neuen Herausforderungen steht. Zwar machen die neuesten Diskurse um das Media Lab[6;7] oder das Gestalterstudio[8;9] eine Faszination der WissenschaftlerInnen für eine interdisziplinäre und kreative Wissensproduktion deutlich. Die Frage nach der Gestaltung ihrer Räume wird jedoch weiterhin vernachlässigt: Welchen Einfluss hat Raum auf die Wissensproduktion? Und welche Räume und Raumqualitäten brauchen wir, um neues Wissen – insbesondere an der Schnittstelle zwischen den Disziplinen – zu entwickeln?

To investigate that question empirically, our research project "ArchitecturalExperiments", which is part of the excellence cluster "Image. Knowledge. Design. An interdisciplinary Laboratory" at the Humboldt Universität, has developed a new method to research and design spaces. To do so, we created an "Experimental Zone", an open space with a size of 350 m^2 for 40 researchers from human and natural sciences, as well as designing disciplines. Roughly every two months over a period of three years, it is redesigned and converted. → 127 A total of 18 experimental settings were implemented and observed in this way. This experimental, design-based field research entailed a variety of methodological challenges: above all, the question of intervention, as well as the aspect of reflexivity. To take those challenges into account, we carried out our field research in a co-laborative way (with a hyphen).[10] Instead of research on participants, we researched with them. We used a mixed-methods approach in recording data, with tools from sociology (including participatory observation and mental-map interviews) and methods used in architecture (including sketches to record the status quo and simulation using Space Syntax), as well as developing new interdisciplinary methods such as the colour coding of auto-photography and the cartography of movement and interaction. → 128 – 131

The study led to the development of the term "collaborative habitats" with respect to a synecological system for interdisciplinary knowledge production, which supports interdisciplinary collaboration and synergies between researchers. The "collaborative habitat" is largely based on creating and maintaining a collective identity. This is an expected development. However, the study also revealed the spatial implications and consequences they entailed, which we summarised in the form of five statements:

1. Interdisciplinary collaboration is enhanced by **physical co-presence**, which, above all when combined with a high visibility, enables the gradual convergence of disciplines and thereby achieves acculturation processes and new collaboration. The study also confirmed the relevance of face-to-face interaction for knowledge production, especially with respect to the informal exchange of information and chance encounters. So-called "connectors" are decisive since they enhance exchange between teams and create a close network between researchers. Since the Open Space enables co-presence, high visibility and interaction, it is regarded as a typology that encourages interdisciplinarity. One central challenge is designing a balance between the required high visibility and researchers' visual privacy needs, because

Um diese Fragen empirisch zu untersuchen, haben wir in unserem Forschungsprojekt ArchitekturenExperimente am Exzellenzcluster Bild Wissen Gestaltung. Ein Interdisziplinäres Labor der Humboldt-Universität zu Berlin eine neuartige Methode für die Erforschung und Gestaltung von Raum entwickelt. Dabei wurde die Experimentalzone, ein Open Space von 350m^2 für 40 Forschende aus den Geistes- und Naturwissenschaften sowie aus den Gestaltungsdisziplinen geschaffen und dieser etwa alle zwei Monate über einen Zeitraum von drei Jahren hinweg neu gestaltet und umgebaut. → 127 Insgesamt 18 Experimentalsettings wurden so durchgeführt und beobachtet. Diese experimentelle gestaltungsbasierte Feldforschung brachte unterschiedliche methodologische Herausforderungen mit sich: insbesondere die Frage der Intervention, aber auch die Frage der Reflexivität. Um den Herausforderungen Rechnung zu tragen, haben wir die Feldforschung „ko-laborativ" mit Bindestrich durchgeführt[10] und haben nicht über sondern mit den Teilnehmenden geforscht. Bei der Datenerhebung haben wir einen Mixed-Methods-Ansatz verfolgt: wir haben Instrumente aus der Sozialforschung (u. a. teilnehmende Beobachtung, Autofotografie, Mental-Map-Interviews) mit Methoden aus der Architektur (u. a. zeichnerische Bestandsaufnahme, Simulation mit Space Syntax) kombiniert, aber auch neue interdisziplinäre Methoden wie z. B. die Farbcodierung der Autofotografie oder die Kartografie der Bewegungen und Interaktionen entwickelt. → 128 – 131

Die Untersuchung führte zur Entwicklung des Begriffs des „kollaborativen Habitats", eines synökologischen Systems für die interdisziplinäre Wissensproduktion, das interdisziplinäre Kollaborationen und Synergien zwischen Forschenden fördert. Das „kollaborative Habitat" basiert im Wesentlichen auf dem Entstehen und der Pflege einer kollektiven Identität. Dies ist ein erwartetes Ergebnis. Was die Studie jedoch ergeben hat, sind die damit verbundenen räumlichen Implikationen und Konsequenzen, die wir in Form von fünf Statements zusammengefasst haben:

1. Interdisziplinäre Kollaboration wird durch **physische Kopräsenz** begünstigt, die insbesondere im Zusammenhang mit einer hohen Sichtbarkeit eine allmähliche Annäherung der Disziplinen ermöglicht und damit Akkulturationsprozesse sowie das Entstehen neuer Kollaborationen begünstigt. Die Studie bestätigt zudem die Relevanz von Face-to-Face-Interaktionen für die Wissensproduktion, insbesondere in Bezug auf den informellen Austausch und Zufallsbegegnungen. Entscheidend sind sogenannte „KonnektorInnen", da sie den Austausch zwischen den Teams und eine enge Vernetzung der Forschenden vorantreiben. Da der Open Space sowohl Kopräsenz, eine hohe Sichtbarkeits auch Interaktionen erlaubt, stellt er sich als interdisziplinaritätsfördernde Typologie dar. Eine zentrale Herausforderung ist die Gestaltung einer

127

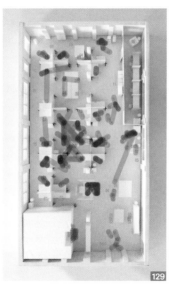

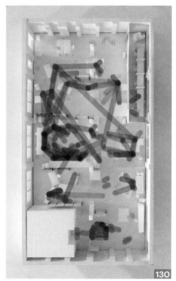

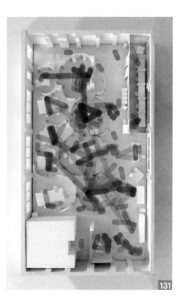

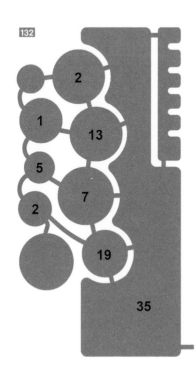

128–131
Cartography of
interaction,
experimental
settings 10, 11, 15
and 16.
Kartografie der
Interaktionen,
Experimentalsettings
10, 11, 15 und 16.

132
Number of brief and
informal interactions
per spatial zone,
connectivity analysis
of experimental
setting 16.
Anzahl der flüchtigen
und informellen
Interaktionen pro
Raumbereich,
Connectivity-Analyse
des Experimental-
settings 16.

the study shows that above all, a combination of low visibility and low connectivity can have a strongly undermining effect on informal interaction.

2. Co-presence requires a **high diversity of various fields**, since the interdisciplinary production of knowledge is characterised by heterogeneous and partly incompatible practices such as writing, collecting and programming. At the same time, contrary to the paradigm of the innovative knowledge employee and the workplace's high level of flexibility, the majority of studied researchers require a firm anchoring that enables fast access to their group and therefore encourages dynamic development in their field of research. They positioned objects to create individual, but also group territories, offering both protection in the Open Space and a certain visual and auditory privacy. Two strategies can further facilitate the implementation of incompatible practices: firstly, different areas can be created within the Open Space itself, e.g. so-called mesh topology provides zones for interaction and others that support focused study. → 132 Secondly – unlike traditional knowledge architecture, where most group activities (e.g. meetings and seminars) are carried out in isolated rooms – shielded withdrawal areas allow people to work in a focused manner.

3. Going beyond the visibility of researchers described in the first statement, we were able to observe the effects of a further step, namely **making research content itself visible**: researchers are passively confronted by third-party work themes and methods if the work is visualised outside the computer, e.g. using highly visible analogue and digital media. Such gradual encounters support the convergence of disciplines and encourage new collaboration. Driven by designers, such open demonstration of one's own work initially encountered scepticism from human and natural scientists, but they gradually became more open to this way of working.

4. The analysis also showed that the fundamental preconditions for creating collaborative spaces are a **smooth transition between individual and collaborative practices**, as well as a common perspective on media. For spatial design, that means achieving a direct spatial proximity between the individual workplaces. It is notable that the "group territories" formed by the participants themselves achieved precisely that: they created a great proximity between the workplaces. Furthermore, analysis showed that constellations in which researchers sit beside each other or – surprisingly – back-to-back, are particularly advantageous since they allow people to view media on screens or notebooks together.

Balance zwischen der erforderlichen hohen Sichtbarkeit und dem Bedürfnis der Forschenden nach visueller Privatsphäre. Denn die Studie zeigt, dass insbesondere eine Kombination aus einer niedrigen Sichtbarkeit und einer geringen Konnektivität die informellen Interaktionen stark hemmen kann.

2. Die Kopräsenz bedarf einer **hohen Vielfalt an unterschiedlichen Bereichen**, denn die interdisziplinäre Wissensproduktion zeichnet sich durch heterogene und zum Teil inkompatible Praktiken wie Schreiben, Entwerfen, Sammeln oder Programmieren aus. Zugleich benötigt die Mehrzahl der untersuchten Forschenden – im Gegensatz zum Leitbild des innovativen Wissensarbeitenden und der hohen Flexibilisierung des Arbeitsplatzes – eine feste Verankerung, die einen schnellen Abruf ihrer Assemblagen und damit eine dynamische Entfaltung ihrer Räume des Forschens begünstigt. Durch die Platzierung von Objekten schaffen sie sich individuelle, aber auch Gruppenterritorien, die Schutz im Open Space sowie eine gewisse visuelle und auditive Privatsphäre bieten. Zwei Strategien können die Durchführung inkompatibler Praktiken weiter erleichtern: Erstens können innerhalb des Open Space selbst unterschiedliche Bereiche geschaffen werden, z.B. bilden sich in einer sogenannten Mesh-Topologie sowohl interaktions- als auch konzentrationsfördernde Zonen. → 132 Zweitens ermöglichen – im Gegensatz zur traditionellen Wissenschaftsarchitektur, in der meist Gruppenpraktiken (z.B. Besprechung oder Seminar) räumlich isoliert werden – abgeschirmte Rückzugsorte die Durchführung konzentrierter Praktiken.

3. Über die im ersten Statement beschriebene Sichtbarkeit der Forschenden hinaus konnten wir die Auswirkungen eines weiteren Schrittes beobachten, nämlich der **Sichtbarmachung der Forschungsinhalte** selbst: Wird die Arbeit außerhalb des Computers visualisiert, z.B. mit Hilfe gut sichtbarer analoger und digitaler Medien, werden die ForscherInnen passiv mit fremden Arbeitsthemen und -methoden konfrontiert. Solch ein graduelles Aufeinandertreffen fördert eine Ann herung zwischen den Disziplinen und die Entstehung neuer Kollaborationen. Vorangetrieben von den GestalterInnen stieß die Offenlegung der eigenen Arbeit zunächst auf Skepsis bei den Geistes- und NaturwissenschaftlerInnen, die sich diesem Arbeitsstil jedoch nach und nach öffneten.

4. Die Analyse ergab zudem, dass die Grundvoraussetzungen für die Entstehung kollaborativer Räume ein **nahtloser Übergang zwischen individuellen und kollaborativen Praktiken** sowie der gemeinsame Blick in Medien sind. Für die Raumgestaltung bedeutet dies, dass eine unmittelbare räumliche Nähe zwischen den Einzelarbeitsplätzen förderlich ist.

5. Finally, a **participatory design approach** contributes to forming a "collaborative habitat". During the study, participants developed a collective identity and a communal sense that was particularly stimulated by an event culture, content visibility and public exposure. At the same time, the "co-laborative" study strengthened participants' reflection on the spatial conditions of their work and their own workplace. Both aspects led them to increasingly appropriate the space and feel familiar, inspired and safe within it. Since this is the underlying condition for new interdisciplinary connections, we propose the thesis that a participatory approach contributes to the formation of a "collaborative habitat".

In addition to researching the characteristics of the "collaborative habitat", the study makes both a theoretical and a methodological contribution to spatial research: theoretically, we have developed a spatial stance that grasps relative and agent-related models together. Based on empirical evidence, we question the dichotomy between the physical and the virtual, instead proposing the concept of physical-virtual space in terms of an integrative continuum. In doing so, we have applied the reflections of Stefan Beck on interleaving analogue and digital media[11] to a spatial perspective and analysed what that means for implementing research practice. Methodologically, the development of a new, interdisciplinary approach makes a key contribution: experimental, design-based field research makes it possible to study at the intersection between design and observation, as well as between hypothesis-guided and exploratory methods, while developed interdisciplinary research methods enable us to reveal hitherto hidden qualities and connections with respect to space.

Bemerkenswert ist, dass die von den Teilnehmenden selbst gebildeten Gruppenterritorien genau das boten: Sie schufen eine hohe Nähe zwischen den Arbeitsplätzen. Darüber hinaus hat die Analyse gezeigt, dass Konstellationen, in denen Forschende nebeneinander sitzen oder – entgegen unser Erwartung – mit dem Rücken zueinander, besonders vorteilhaft sind, da sie den gemeinsamen Blick auf Medien wie Bildschirme oder Notizbücher unterstützen.

5. Zuletzt trägt ein **partizipativer Gestaltungsansatz** zur Bildung eines „kollaborativen Habitats" bei. Im Laufe der Untersuchung entwickelten die Teilnehmenden eine kollektive Identität und ein Zugehörigkeitsgefühl, die vor allem durch eine Eventisierung, eine Sichtbarmachung der Inhalte und öffentliche Exponiertheit stimuliert wurden. Gleichzeitig stärkte die „ko-laborative" Untersuchung die Reflexivität der Teilnehmenden in Bezug auf die räumlichen Bedingungen ihrer Arbeit und ihren eigenen Arbeitsplatz. Beides führte dazu, dass sie sich den Raum zunehmend aneigneten und sich vertraut, inspiriert und sicher fühlten. Da dies eine Voraussetzung für neue interdisziplinäre Verbindungen ist, stellen wir die Hypothese auf, dass ein partizipativer Ansatz zur Bildung eines „kollaborativen Habitats" beiträgt.

Neben der Erforschung der Charakteristiken des „kollaborativen Habitats" liefert die Untersuchung sowohl einen theoretischen als auch einen methodischen Beitrag zur Raumforschung: Theoretisch haben wir eine Position zum Raum entwickelt, die relative und agentifizierte Modelle zusammendenkt. Basierend auf der Empirie stellen wir die Dichotomie zwischen physisch und virtuell in Frage und schlagen das Konzept des physisch-virtuellen Raums im Sinne eines integrativen Kontinuums vor. Wir haben damit die Reflektionen von Stefan Beck über die Verflechtung analoger und digitaler Medien[11] in eine räumliche Perspektive überführt und analysiert, was dies für die Durchführung von Forschungspraktiken bedeutet. Methodisch stellt die Entwicklung eines neuen interdisziplinären Ansatzes einen zentralen Beitrag dar: Die experimentelle gestaltungsbasierte Feldforschung macht es möglich, an der Schnittstelle zwischen Gestaltung und Beobachtung sowie zwischen hypothesengeleitetem und explorativem Vorgehen zu forschen, während es die entwickelten interdisziplinären Untersuchungsmethoden erlauben, bisher verborgene Eigenschaften und Zusammenhänge von Raum aufzudecken.

1
This article is based on: Séverine Marguin, Henrike Rabe and Friedrich Schmidgall, Experimental Zone. An Interdisciplinary Investigation on the Spaces and Practices of Collaborative Research, Park Books, 2019.

Literature

2
Kockelkorn, Anne. 2008. "Bürolandschaft – Eine vergessene Reformstrategie der deutschen Nachkriegsmoderne." ARCH+, No. 186/187: p. 6–7. Niewöhner, Jörg.

3
Duffy, Francis. 1997. The New Office. London: Conran Octopus.

4
Harrison, Andrew, Paul Wheeler and Carolyn Whitehead (Eds.). 2004. The Distributed Workplace. Sustainable Work Environments. London; New York: Spon Press.

5
Nobuyuki, Yoshida. 2003. Office Urbanism. The Japan Architect 50. Tokyo: Shinkenchiku.

6
Plohmann, Angela (Ed.). 2012. A Blueprint for a Lab of the Future. Eindhoven: Baltan Laboratories.

7
Emerson, Lori, Jussi Parikka and Darren Wershler, no date, "What is a Media Lab? Situated Practices in Media Studies." Accessed on May 16, 2019. http://whatisamedialab.com.

8
Yaneva, Albena. 2009. The Making of a Building: A Pragmatist Approach to Architecture. Oxford; New York: Peter Lang.

9
Farias, Ignacio and Alex Wilkie (Eds.). 2016. Studio, studies: operations, topologies and displacements. London; New York: Routledge, Taylor & Francis Group.

10
Niewöhner, Jörg. 2016. "Co-laborative Anthropology: Crafting Reflexivities Experimentally." Accessed on May 28, 2019: https://edoc.hu-berlin.de/handle/18452/19241.

11
Beck, Stefan. 2015. "Von Praxistheorie 1.0 zu 3.0 – oder: wie analoge und digitale Praxen relationiert werden sollten." Presented at the conference "Digitale Praxen", Goethe Universität, Frankfurt am Main. Accessed on May 15, 2019. https://hu-berlin.academia.edu/StefanBeck/Talks.

1
Der Beitrag basiert auf: Séverine Marguin, Henrike Rabe und Friedrich Schmidgall, Experimental Zone. An Interdisciplinary Investigation on the Spaces and Practices of Collaborative Research , Park Books, 2019.

Literatur

2
Kockelkorn, Anne. 2008. „Bürolandschaft – Eine vergessene Reformstrategie der deutschen Nachkriegsmoderne". ARCH+, Nr. 186/187: 6–7. Niewöhner, Jörg.

3
Duffy, Francis. 1997. The New Office. London: Conran Octopus.

4
Harrison, Andrew, Paul Wheeler, und Carolyn Whitehead, Hrsg. 2004. The Distributed Workplace. Sustainable Work Environments . London; New York: Spon Press.

5
Nobuyuki, Yoshida. 2003. Office Urbanism. The Japan Architect 50. Tokio: Shinkenchiku.

6
Plohmann, Angela, Hrsg. 2012. A Blueprint for a Lab of the Future. Eindhoven: Baltan Laboratories.

7
Emerson, Lori, Jussi Parikka, und Darren Wershler. o. J. „What is a Media Lab? Situated Practices in Media Studies". Zugegriffen 16. Mai 2019. http://whatisamedialab.com.

8
Yaneva, Albena. 2009. The Making of a Building: A Pragmatist Approach to Architecture. Oxford; New York: Peter Lang.

9
Farias, Ignacio, und Alex Wilkie, Hrsg. 2016. Studio studies: operations, topologies and displacements. London ; New York: Routledge, Taylor & Francis Group.

10
Niewöhner, Jörg. 2016. "Co-laborative Anthropology: Crafting Reflexivities Experimentally." Zugegriffen 28. Mai 2019: https://edoc.hu-berlin.de/handle/18452/19241.

11
Beck, Stefan. 2015. "Von Praxistheorie 1.0 zu 3.0 – oder: wie analoge und digitale Praxen relationiert werden sollten." vorgetragen bei der Konferenz "Digitale Praxen", Goethe Universität, Frankfurt am Main. Zugegriffen 15. Mai 2019. https://hu-berlin.academia.edu/StefanBeck/Talks.

4 Identity
Identität → 146–223

"Laboratory spaces are as individual as the people who work in them," as Susanne Pohl and Stefanie Kliemt explain in this volume's fourth section on designing various laboratory types (Ch. 4.3). In doing so, they reflect on the fact that, despite the great standardisation of laboratory units due to guidelines and regulations, the individual character of each laboratory and research building must always be discovered and created anew.

Which goals does research pursue in such spaces? Which processes and experiments are carried out there? Which groups work together? And what esprit, which philosophy do they stand for?

Such open questions represent a scope of action that architects can use to give the building an identity. It is manifested in the façade, which can either be open or closed, transparent or solid. It is also expressed in the laboratories' materiality, organisation and equipment. Furthermore, intuitive movement through these spaces, experiencing the path through a building, also serves to consolidate the building's identity.

The interior and exterior identities of laboratory and research buildings are described in detail in the following examples.

„Laborbereiche sind so individuell, wie die Menschen, die in ihnen arbeiten", schreiben Susanne Pohl und Stefanie Kliemt in diesem vierten Buchteil über die Ausgestaltung verschiedener Labortypen (Kap. 4.3). Sie bringen damit zum Ausdruck, dass bei aller Standardisierung der Laboreinbauten durch Richtlinien und Regelwerke, der individuelle Charakter eines jeden Labor- und Forschungsgebäudes immer wieder neu gefunden und geschaffen werden muss.

Welche Ziele verfolgt die Forschung? Welche Prozesse und Experimente werden hier durchgeführt? Welche Gruppen arbeiten zusammen? Und für welchen Esprit, welche Gesinnung stehen sie?

Diese offenen Fragen stellen den Handlungsspielraum dar, den Architekten nutzen können, um dem Gebäude eine Identität zu verleihen. Sie manifestiert sich in der Fassade, die offen oder geschlossen, transparent oder massiv sein kann. Sie manifestiert sich auch in Materialität, Anordnung und Ausstattung der Labore. Auch das intuitive Durchschreiten dieser Räume, das Erleben des Weges durch ein Gebäude, ist Teil dieser Identitätsfindung.

Die inneren und äußeren Identitäten von Labor- und Forschungsgebäuden sollen in den folgenden Beiträgen näher beleuchtet werden.

4.1 Research showcases

A tour of the Basel science campus operated by the Swiss pharmaceutical company Novartis is like walking through a permanent exhibition on the who's who of architecture. Gehry, Moneo, Sanaa, and Herzog & de Meuron, to name just a few, have all left their mark on Vittorio Lampugnani's urban master plan. The research facilities reside behind façades of all colours and materials, plenty of cool glass and shimmering metal, as well as green creepers. Depending on their design, the buildings embody the innovative spirit, prestige or environmental awareness of their respective users.

The façade of a research or laboratory building must be able to do many things. It is not only a symbol of excellence and a calling card for the research or science facility. It must also fulfil concrete, practical tasks defined by the work, research and recreation rooms behind it. Sometimes, the façade assumes an autonomous appearance and becomes a metaphor or name-giver of an entire facility. For instance, the buildings for the FU Berlin, known as the "Rostlaube" and "Silberlaube", unintentionally gained their name from their façade designs. The system designed by Jean Prouvé is based on the idea that the Corten steel alloy would develop a stable, maintenance-free corrosion layer.

Identity

A building is often only perceived in terms of its façade, since it not only makes the first, but also leaves the longest impression with respect to the building's character. A research or science facility can do much for its image using the exterior appearance of its buildings – both for its employees and outsiders. One prominent example is the SC Johnson building in Racine, Wisconsin, which was constructed in 1950 by none other than Frank Lloyd Wright. In the midst of low-rise administrative buildings, the narrow "research tower" is a real eye-catcher. It exudes simple elegance with its façade bands of glass and clinker brick, as well as its rounded edges. At the same time, it offers researchers a workplace in the sunshine in the laboratory environment that Wright called the "Helio-Lab", elevating their work beyond simple office tasks. It is impossible to overlook the fact that the company is particularly proud of its research and development. (Ch. 2.2) → 065-069

However, exterior design can go even further. It can express a commitment to the location or the content-based alignment of the institute or laboratory, thereby making an important contribution to employees' identification with the workplace or research facility. The Masdar Institute in Abu Dhabi is a a good example of this approach.

4.1 Vitrinen der Forschung

Ein Rundgang über den Wissenschaftscampus in Basel des Schweizer Pharmunternehmens Novartis ist wie ein Wandelgang durch eine ständige Ausstellung großer Namen der Architektur. Gehry, Moneo, Sanaa, Herzog & de Meuron, um nur einige zu nennen, haben ihren Gestaltungswillen hier auf dem Stadtgrundriss aus der Feder Vittorio Lampugnanis dokumentiert. Die Forschungseinrichtungen residieren hinter Fassaden aller Farben und Materialien, viel kühles Glas und schimmerndes Metall, aber auch grüne Ranken sind zu sehen. So verkörpern die Bauten, je nach Gestaltung, Innovationsgeist, Prestige oder Umweltbewusstsein ihrer jeweiligen Nutzer.

Die Fassade eines Forschungs- oder Laborbaus muss vieles können. Sie ist nicht nur Sinnbild für Exzellenz und Aushängeschild einer Forschungs- oder Wissenschaftseinrichtung. Es müssen auch handfeste praktische Aufgaben erfüllt werden, welche durch die dahinter befindlichen Räume des Arbeitens, Forschens oder Erholens definiert werden. Und manchmal verselbstständigt sich das Bild der Fassade und wird zum Sinnbild oder Namenspate einer ganzen Einrichtung. So verdanken die Gebäude der FU Berlin ihre Namen, Rostlaube und Silberlaube, wohl nicht ganz beabsichtigt dem Fassadendesign. Das elementierte Fassadensystem, für das Jean Prouvé verantwortlich zeichnete, basierte auf der Vorstellung dass sich auf der Stahllegierung Corten, eine stabile und wartungsfreie Korrosionsschicht entwickeln sollte.

Identität

Ein Gebäude wird schnell allein auf seine Fassade reduziert. Sie hinterlässt beim Betrachter nicht nur den ersten, sondern auch den prägendsten Eindruck. Eine Forschungs- oder Wissenschaftseinrichtung kann über die äußere Gestaltung ihrer Gebäude viel für ihr Ansehen tun. Sowohl bei den Mitarbeitenden wie auch bei Außenstehenden. Ein prominentes Beispiel ist das SC Johnson Gebäude in Racine, Wisconsin, welches 1950 von keinem geringeren als Frank Lloyd Wright fertiggestellt wurde. Inmitten flacher Verwaltungsgebäude ragt ein schlanker „Research Tower" empor und zieht alle Blicke auf sich. Mit seiner Fassade von Bändern aus Glas und Klinker und den abgerundeten Ecken ist er von bestechend simpler Eleganz. Gleichzeitig bietet er den Forschern in den, von Wright als „Helio-Lab" bezeichneten, Laboren einen Arbeitsplatz an der Sonne und erhebt ihr Schaffen gleichsam über das schnöde Wirken in den Büros. Hier war nicht zu übersehen, dass Forschung und Entwicklung der Stolz der Firma waren. (Kap. 2.2) → 065-069

Doch äußere Gestaltung kann mehr. Sie kann auch eine Verbundenheit zum Standort oder zur inhaltlichen Ausrichtung eines Instituts oder Labors schaffen und so einen wichtigen Beitrag dazu leisten, was man Identifizierung mit seinem Arbeits- oder

Foster + Partners designed the façade of the complex using the example of traditional Arab architecture, with a type of projecting oriels in the area of the residential wings: their fibre-glass concrete walls are perforated in delicate patterns to provide protection from the prevalent high temperatures. Regional reddish sand was added to colour the concrete. By contrast, inflatable polymer cushions were integrated into the façades of the actual laboratory areas, making it possible to guide the sunlight into the walkways of the building complex without passing on the heat radiation. In this way, the measures contribute to the facility's overall concept of sustainable and energy-efficient architecture, which is largely based on solar energy, as well as reducing water and electricity consumption. →134–136

One does not always find such extreme conditions when engaging with the location's qualities, although the natural or cultural specifics of a place can still give the building a special character. For instance, in studies for the new building of the HUB de l'énergie at the Université de Picardie Jules Verne in Amiens, we investigated the urban district's past as a former dyeing quarter. In the 18th century, Amiens became economically important due to its textile industry. The cityscape and above all the location of the institute in the district of Saint Leu are characterised by numerous canals developed from branches of the Somme. Water and textiles therefore inspired the façade design of the HUB, which consists of a delicately woven second skin, its vertical glass and metal lamellae celebrating all the nuances of light reflection on the canals of Amiens. →137

By contrast, the Grenoble science campus was inspired by the nearby ice- and snow-capped mountain peaks, motivating us to use a shimmering turquoise-blue glass façade for the IBS² Institute of Structural Biology, which gives the building its unmistakeable character. →138

However, in addition to internalising the surroundings in the building, the façade can also be used to express the research task to the outside world. Our competition entry for the Translational Medicine Building of Beijing Union Medical College Hospital (PUMCH), we developed a three-dimensionally folded secondary façade that was based on the twisted double-helix of DNA. The façade thereby not only acts as a visual shield and blind, but also highlights the institute's high-tech nature, while offering its users – in this case students at the PUMCH – a projection area onto which their research and future field of operations are symbolically perpetuated. →139–140

The Institut Imagine by Atelier Jean Nouvel in Paris similarly communicates its mission to the general public. The glass façades of the institute for genetic diseases,

Forschungsplatz nennen möchte. Das Masdar Institute in Abu Dhabi ist ein schönes Beispiel für diese Herangehensweise. Foster + Partners entwarfen die Fassaden des Komplexes nach dem Vorbild traditioneller arabischer Architektur mit einer Art vorstehendem Erker im Bereich der Wohntrakte, dessen mit feinen Mustern durchbrochene Glasfaserbetonwände vor den hohen Temperaturen schützen. Der Beton wurde mit dem rötlichen Sand der Region durchfärbt. In die Fassaden der eigentlichen Laborräume hingegen wurden aufblasbare polymere Kissen integriert, welche das Sonnenlicht in die Gassen des Gebäudekomplexes lenken, ohne die Hitzestrahlung weiterzugeben. Sie tragen so zu dem Gesamtkonzept nachhaltiger und energieeffizienter Architektur der Anlage bei, welche weitgehend auf Solarenergie, sowie auf Reduzierung von Wasser- und Stromverbrauch setzt. →134–136

Bei der Auseinandersetzung mit den Gegebenheiten des Standortes trifft man nicht immer auf solch extreme Konditionen, jedoch können die natürlichen oder kulturellen Besonderheiten eines Ortes dem Gebäude einen besonderen Charakter verleihen. In der Auseinandersetzung mit dem Neubau für den HUB de l'énergie der Université de Picardie Jules Verne in Amiens beispielsweise erkundeten wir die Vergangenheit des Stadtquartiers als ehemaliges Färberviertel. Amiens wurde im 18. Jahrhundert besonders durch seine Textilindustrie wirtschaftlich bedeutsam. Das Stadtbild und vor allem der Standort des Instituts im Stadtteil Saint Leu sind von zahlreichen kanalisierten Seitenarmen der Somme geprägt. Wasser und Textilien inspirierten schließlich die Fassadengestaltung des HUB, eine filigran gewebte zweite Haut, welche in ihren vertikalen Glas- und Metalllamellen alle Nuancen der Lichtreflektionen auf Amiens Kanälen widerzuspiegeln scheint. →137

Auf dem Wissenschaftscampus Grenoble hingegen waren es die nahen eis- und schneebedeckten Berggipfel, die uns zu einer türkis-blau changierenden Glasfassade für das Institut für Strukturbiologie IBS² inspirierten und die dem Gebäude einen unverwechselbaren Charakter verleiht. →138

Statt die Umgebung im Gebäude zu verinnerlichen, kann aber über die Fassade auch der Forschungsauftrag nach außen getragen werden. Für den Wettbewerbsbeitrag des Translational Medicine Building des Peking Union Medical College Hospital (PUMCH) entwickelten wir eine dreidimensional gefaltete Sekundärfassade, welcher eine in sich gedrehte DNA-Doppelhelix zum Vorbild gedient hatte. Die Fassade wird somit nicht nur Sicht- und Blendschutz, sondern unterstreicht auch den High-Tech-Charakter des Instituts und bietet den Nutzern – in diesem Fall den Studierenden des PUMCH – eine Projektionsfläche, auf der sie ihre Forschung und ihr zukünftiges Tätigkeitfeld symbolhaft verewigt sehen. →139–140

Das Institut Imagine von Atelier Jean Nouvel in Paris trägt auf ähnliche Weise seine Mission an die Öffentlichkeit heran. Die Glasfassaden des an einer

Water as a source of inspiration. The canals of the tanners' quarter define the location of the HUB de l' énergie in Amiens, Nickl & Partner Architekten, 2014
Inspirationsquelle Wasser. Die Kanäle des Gerberviertels prägen den Standort des HUB de l' énergie in Amiens, Nickl & Partner Architekten, 2014

138
The façade of the
IBS² in Grenoble
recalls icy glaciers
and turquoise-blue
Alpine lakes, Nickl &
Partner Architekten,
2013
Die Fassade des IBS²
in Grenoble lässt an
eisige Gletscher und
türkisblaue Bergseen
denken, Nickl &
Partner Architekten,
2013

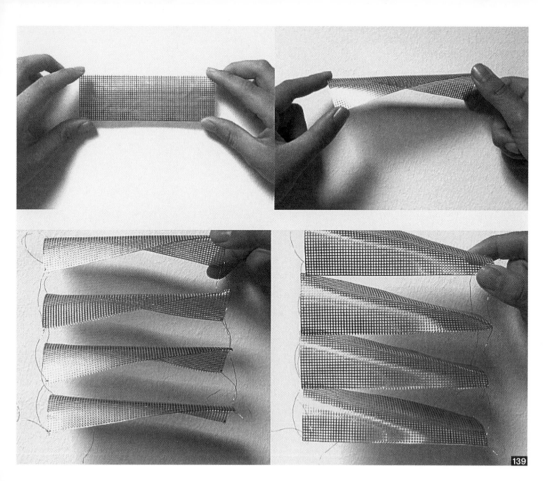

139
The coiled genetic
sequence serves as
inspiration for the
three-dimensional
façade folds
Die in sich verdrehte
Gensequenz ist
Vorbild für die
dreidimensionale
Faltung der Fassaden

140
Illustration of the
PUMCH Translational
Medical Research
Building, Beijing,
Nickl & Partner
Architectural Design
Consulting Ltd.,
competition in 2016
Visualisierung des
PUMCH Translational
Medical Research
Building, Peking,
Nickl & Partner
Architectural Design
Consulting Ltd.,
Wettbewerb 2016

141–142
The theme of genetic
sequences is
presented
graphically on the
façade of the Institut
Imagine in Paris,
Atelier Jean Nouvel
& Valero Gadan
Architectes, 2014
Das Thema
Gensequenzen
wurde in der Fassade
des Institut Imagine
in Paris grafisch
umgesetzt, Atelier
Jean Nouvel & Valero
Gadan Architectes,
2014

which is situated on a prominent street corner, is printed with silhouette-like stripes resembling stylised images of genetic sequences.

Even unknowing passers by will realise that the location is used for research and medicine, with the aim of helping humanity. → 141-142

Flexibility and homogeneity – The second envelope

It should not be forgotten that laboratory and research buildings are structures with high technical demands – also with respect to the façades. Two aspects are particularly relevant. Firstly, the façade should bring together a variety of uses in an overall unity, without limiting the potential of later conversions or shifts in utilisation. The façade design should therefore be based on a flexible grid, with apertures arranged in a way that ideally allows the rooms behind them to be merged, partitioned and converted. Secondly, stable lighting and temperature conditions must be achieved in interior spaces. Although the actual laboratory units are generally air-conditioned, excess heat input should be avoided in order to reduce energy consumption for cooling.

One tried and trusted solution to fulfil the outlined requirements is to construct a primary and a secondary façade. The primary façade forms the actual spatial conclusion and consists of a simple post and mullion construction. The secondary façade, which serves as a blind and provides sun protection, is literally relieved of further tasks. This affords a design freedom that can be used to achieve a homogeneous appearance for the building and its diverse uses, giving it the desired character with an appropriate envelope.

The principle is applied at the Center for Stroke and Dementia Research (CSD) of the LMU Klinikum München. We enveloped the building's simple geometry in a mesh of white-varnished, expanded-metal panels. Only the colour-highlighted entrance area sets itself apart from the stringent design. The façade conceals the secrets of the researchers inside. It is only broken open by the foldable elements that slant upwards in accordance with the time of day or night, as well as the light incidence. → 143-145

A similar method was applied to the laboratory buildings of the Helmholtz Institute in Ulm and the IRIS at the Humboldt-Universität zu Berlin. In both cases, blank, perforated aluminium panels create a characteristic façade image that changes according to the light conditions and the season. While the panels are fixed in front of opaque areas, as well as the laboratory and auxiliary rooms, the elements can be flipped open individually in front of the office windows. → 146-147

prominenten Straßenecke gelegenen Instituts für Generkrankungen ist mit schemenhaften Streifen bedruckt, die an stilisierte Abbildungen von Gensequenzen erinnern.

Auch dem uninformierten Passanten wird an dieser Stelle klar, hier wird im Dienst der Wissenschaft und der Medizin gearbeitet, hier wird Menschen geholfen. → 141-142

Flexibilität & Homogenität – Die zweite Hülle

Nicht zu vergessen, Labor- und Forschungsgebäude sind Bauten mit hohen technischen Anforderungen – auch an die Fassaden. Zweierlei steht dabei im Vordergrund. Zum einen gilt es, mit der Fassade verschiedene Nutzungen in ein großes Ganzes einzufügen, ohne dabei die Möglichkeit zu späteren Umnutzungen oder Nutzungsverschiebungen einzuschränken. Die Fassadengestaltung sollte also auf einem flexiblen Raster beruhen und Öffnungen derart angeordnet sein, dass idealerweise ein Zusammenlegen, Trennen oder Umnutzen der dahinter befindlichen Räume möglich ist. Zum anderen müssen in den Innenräumen stabile Belichtungs- und Temperaturverhältnisse geschaffen werden. Auch wenn die eigentlichen Laboreinheiten in der Regel raumlufttechnisch behandelt werden, sollte übermäßiger Wärmeeintrag vermieden werden, um den Energiebedarf zur Erzeugung von Kälte gering zu halten.

Eine Lösung, die sich bewährt hat, um beiden oben skizzierten Anforderungen gerecht zu werden, ist eine Konstruktion aus Primär- und Sekundärfassade. Die primäre Fassade bildet dabei den eigentlichen Raumabschluss und besteht aus einer einfachen Pfosten-Riegelkonstruktion. Die Sekundärfassade, welche als Blend- und Sonnenschutz dient, ist damit von weiteren Aufgaben regelrecht entbunden. Es entsteht mehr gestalterischer Spielraum, der genutzt werden kann, dem Gebäude und seinen unterschiedlichen Nutzungen eine homogene und dem gewünschten Charakter entsprechende Hülle zu geben.

Am Centrum für Schlaganfall- und Demenzforschung (CSD) des LMU Klinikums München findet dieses Prinzip Anwendung. Wir haben die einfache Geometrie des Gebäudes in ein Netz aus weiß lackierten Streckmetall-Paneelen gehüllt. Lediglich der farblich akzentuierte Eingangsbereich löst sich aus der stringenten Gestaltung. Die Fassade umhüllt die Geheimnisse der Forschenden im Inneren. Sie wird nur durch die klappbaren Elemente durchbrochen, die sich entsprechend der Tages- und Nachtzeit sowie dem Lichteinfall nach oben neigen. → 143-145

Ein ähnliches Konzept wurde für die Laborgebäude des Helmholtz-Instituts Ulm und des IRIS der Humboldt-Universität angewandt. Blanke, gelochten Alupaneelen erzeugen jeweils ein charakteristisches Fassadenbild, das sich entsprechend den Lichtverhältnissen und Jahreszeit verändert.

143 – 145
**Center for Stroke
and Dementia
Research (CSD) at
the LMU Klinikum
München,
Nickl & Partner
Architekten, 2014**
Centrum für
Schlaganfall- und
Demenzforschung
(CSD) des LMU
Klinikums München,
Nickl & Partner
Architekten, 2014

144

145

146–147
Helmholtz Institute in
Ulm, Nickl & Partner
Architekten, 2014
Helmholtz-Institut
Ulm, Nickl & Partner
Architekten, 2014

The metal envelope for the Centro Investigation Biomedica by Vaíllo & Irigaray and Galar in Pamplona is folded three-dimensionally. While appearing as a shimmering, golden protective shield along the two longitudinal sides of the institute, it is perceived as a delicate light filter from inside the building. → **148–150**

Façades with lamellae have the advantage that they also enable good views out of the building, while acting as sunblinds. The light can also be guided into the depth of the building, especially when the lamellae are moveable and can be adapted to the respective position of the sun, as is the case on the campus of the Hochschule Düsseldorf, where the façade cladding is supplemented by horizontal, perforated aluminium lamellae. The diverse functions of the five institute buildings are held together by the uniform façade design to create an overall unity. → **151–152**

In the case of the German Centre for Neuro-degenerative Diseases (DZNE) in Schnarrenberg, Tübingen, the aim was to highlight the free-standing character of the tower-like building. Thus, vertical lamellae were the logical choice. When opened, their frames coated in yellow, orange and red tones add colour accentuation to the otherwise reserved façade colour scheme. → **153–154**

The effect contrasts significantly with the nearby University of Tübingen Institute for Microbiology and Virology, where horizontal slats stress the horizontal nature of the building. → **155**

Curved perforated sheet-metal elements, rather than lamellae, were used by Behnisch Architekten at the Pôle de Recherche sur le Cancer in Lausanne to allow natural light deep into the building interior. The finely structured metal screen recalls white sails or the wings of a seagull. The structure provides protection from the sunshine, while affording unobstructed views of the city from inside. → **156–157**

Research is associated with progress, change and technology. Thus, materials such as glass and metal are popular choices, as well as smooth designs and finely-structured details. Since the Brutalism of the 1970s, planners and building clients appear to have shied away from the massive nature of fair-faced concrete. Nevertheless, recent examples show how research architecture and a massive expression can be combined. The ISMO by Kaan Architecten is characterised by a façade consisting of concrete squares with room-high windows recessed 80 centimetres into the building, forming veritable research showcases. → **158**

Während die Paneele vor opaken Flächen sowie vor den Labor- und Nebenräumen feststehend sind, lassen sich die Elemente vor den Bürofenstern individuell hochfalten. → **146–147**

Zusätzlich dreidimensional gefaltet ist die metallene Haut zudem am Centro Investigation Biomedica von Vaíllo & Irigaray und Galar in Pamplona. Was entlang der beiden Längsseiten des Instituts nach außen als expressiver, golden schimmernder Schutzschild wirkt, wird von Innen als filigraner Licht-filter wahrgenommen. → **148–150**

Fassaden mit Lamellen haben den Vorzug, dass sie ebenfalls einen guten Blick nach außen ermöglichen, jedoch gleichzeitig gegen die Sonne schützen. Zudem wird das Licht in die Tiefe der Räume gelenkt, besonders wenn die Lamellen beweglich sind und dem jeweiligen Sonnenstand angepasst werden können, wie es am Campus der Hochschule Düsseldorf der Fall ist. Dort wird die Fassadenverkleidung durch horizontale, gelochte Aluminium-Lamellen ergänzt. Die vielfältigen Funktionen der fünf Institutsgebäude werden durch die einheitliche Fassadengestaltung zu einem homogenen Ganzen zusammengefasst. → **151–152**

Im Falle des Deutschen Zentrums für Neuro-degenerative Erkrankungen DZNE auf dem Tübinger Schnarrenberg sollte dagegen der Solitärcharakter des turmartigen Gebäudes hervorgehoben werden. Vertikale Lamellen waren hierfür die folgerichtige Wahl. Ihre in Gelb-, Orange- und Rottönen beschichteten Rahmen setzen in offenem Zustand farbige Kontraste zu der ansonsten zurückhaltenden Farbigkeit der Fassade. → **153–154**

Es entsteht ein entschieden anderer Effekt als am nahe gelegenen Institut für Mikrobiologie und Virologie der Universität Tübingen, dessen horizontale Holzlamellen eher die Waagerechte des Gebäudes betonen. → **155**

Gebogene Lochblechelemente statt Lamellen wenden Behnisch Architekten am Pôle de Recherche sur le Cancer in Lausanne an, um das Tageslicht tief ins Gebäudeinnere zu führen. Der filigrane Metall-Screen lässt an weiße Segel oder die Flügel einer Möwe denken. Nach Außen ein effektiver Sonnenschutz, bietet er den Forscherinnen und Forschern von Innen ungehinderte Ausblicke über die Stadt. → **156–157**

Forschung wird mit Fortschritt, Wandel und Technik assoziiert. Gerne wird bei der Materialwahl daher auf Glas oder Metall, auf glattes Design oder filigrane Details gesetzt. Vor der Massivität rohen Betons erscheinen Planer und Bauherren hingegen seit dem Brutalismus der 70er zurückzuschrecken. Dabei zeigen einige jüngere Beispiele, wie sich Forschungsarchitektur und massive Expressivität vereinen lassen. Das ISMO von Kaan Architecten prägt eine Fassade aus Betonquadraten, hinter die raumgroße Fenster um 80 cm zurückspringen. Sie bilden wahre Vitrinen der Forschung. → **158**

148–150
Centro de
Investigación
Biomédica –
Hospital de Navarra,
Pamplona, Vaílló +
Irigaray Architects,
2011

Centro de
Investigación
Biomédica –
Hospital de Navarra,
Pamplona, Vaílló +
Irigaray Architects,
2011

149
Façade section,
ground plan and
elevation, Centro de
Investigación,
Biomédica, Hospital
de Navarra,
Pamplona,
Vaílló + Irigaray
Architects, 2011
Fassadenschnitt,
Grundriss und
Ansicht des Centro
de Investigación
Biomédica, Pamplona
Vaílló + Irigaray
Architects, 2011

1
Aluminium curtain

Folded aluminium
lattice on the
substructure

2
Curtain façade,
opaque

8 mm safety glass,
type: Parsol grey, 12
cm air space, 4 cm
extruded polystyr-
ene, painted grey, 20
cm reinforced
concrete wall,
plasterboard
cladding with 6 cm
mineral wool

3
Curtain façade,
windows

Façade profiles,
Schüco system,
FW50+ 8 mm safety
glass, type: Parsol
grey, exterior 16 mm
air space 5+5
laminated glass,
transparent

1
Aluminium-Vorhang

Gefaltetes
Aluminium-
Gitterwerk auf
Unterkonstruktion

2
Vorhangfassade,
opak

8 mm Sicherheitsglas
Typ Parsol grau
12 cm Luftraum
4 cm extrudiertes
Polystyrol, grau
gestrichen
20 cm Stahl-
betonwand
Gipskartonver-
kleidung mit 6 cm
Steinwolle

3
Vorhangfassade,
Fenster

Fassadenprofile,
Schüco System
FW50+
8 mm Sicherheitsglas
Typ Parsol grau,
außen
16 mm Luftraum
5+5 Verbundglas,
transparent

149

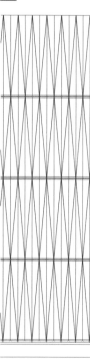

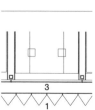

151
University of Applied
Sciences Düsseldorf,
Campus Derendorf,
Nickl & Partner
Architekten, 2018
Hochschule
Düsseldorf, Campus
Derendorf,
Nickl & Partner
Architekten, 2018

Façade section and elevation, University of Applied Sciences Düsseldorf, Campus Derendorf
Fassadenschnitt und Ansicht, Hochschule Düsseldorf, Campus Derendorf

1
Façade structure, windows

OFFICE TYPE
Window proportion: 50%, aluminium window elements with opening elements, double glazed exterior, mobile sun blinds and shutters

2
Façade structure, closed areas

Aluminium elements made of standardised semi-finished products: edged, slatted, anodised
Air layer
16 cm heat insulation
Vapour barrier
Exterior wall
20 cm reinforced concrete

3
Façade structure, window area

SEMINAR TYPE
Window proportion: 70%, room-high aluminium window elements, fixed glazing and opening elements, double glazing
Skylight with opening elements, exterior sun blinds: Rotatable/fixed aluminium slats, perforated, made of standardised semi-finished products
Light-guiding slats in skylight areas with interior mobile sun blind

4
Façade structure, window area

LAB TYPE/PC Pool
Window proportion: 50%
Aluminium windows with opening elements, double glazing and exterior sun blinds: rotatable/fixed aluminium slats made of standardised semi-finished products

5
Folding/sliding door made of sheet steel, insulated

1
Fassadenaufbau, Fenster

TYP BÜRO
Fensteranteil: 50% Aluminium-Fensterelemente mit Öffnungsflügeln 2-Scheiben-Isolierverglasung außenliegender, beweglicher Sonnen- und Blendschutz

2
Fassadenaufbau, geschlossene Bereiche

Aluminiumelemente aus standardisierten Halbzeugen: lamellenartig gekantet, eloxiert
Luftschicht
Wärmedämmung 16 cm
Dampfsperre
Außenwand
Stahlbeton 20 cm

3
Fassadenaufbau, Fensterbereich

TYP Seminar
Fensteranteil: 70% raumhohe Aluminium-Fensterelemente Festverglasung und Öffnungsflügel 2-Scheiben-Isolierverglasung
Oberlicht mit Öffnungsflügeln außenliegender Sonnenschutz: drehbare/fest-stehende Aluminium-lamellen, perforiert aus standardisierten Halbzeugen
Lichtlenklamellen im Oberlichtbereich innenliegender beweglicher Blendschutz

4
Fassadenaufbau, Fensterbereich

TYP Labor/PC Pool
Fensteranteil: 50% Aluminium-Fensterelemente mit Öffnungsflügeln 2-Scheiben-Isolierverglasung außenliegender Sonnenschutz: drehbare/fest-stehende Aluminium-lamellen, perforiert aus standardisierten Halbzeugen

5
Falt-Schiebe-Tor aus Stahlblech, gedämmt

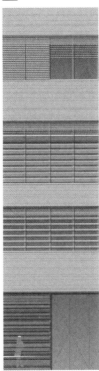

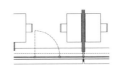

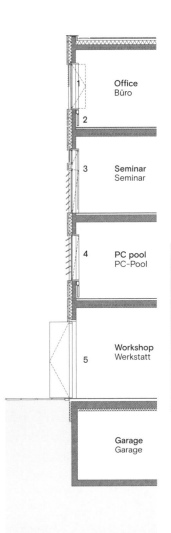

152

1	Office / Büro
2	
3	Seminar / Seminar
4	PC pool / PC-Pool
5	Workshop / Werkstatt
	Garage / Garage

153 – 154
Deutsches Zentrum
für Neurodegenera-
tive Erkrankungen
DZNE, Tübingen,
Nickl & Partner
Architekten, 2013
Deutsches Zentrum
für Neurodegene-
rative Erkrankungen
DZNE, Tübingen,
Nickl & Partner
Architekten, 2013

153
Façade section,
ground elevation
and view, DZNE,
Tübingen
Fassadenschnitt,
Grundriss und
Ansicht, DZNE,
Tübingen

1
Secondary façade

Vertical, edged,
perforated sheet
aluminium slats
acting as partially
openable sun blinds
Maintenance
corridor
Steel structure

2
Primary façade

Balustrades
16 cm reinforced
concrete
20 cm composite
heat insulation
Window mullion-
transom structure
made of light metal
Double glazing
Glass opening
element
Sun blind: interior
textile roller blind

1
Sekundärfassade

vertikale gekantete
perforierte Alu-
miniumblechlamellen,
als Sonnenschutz
teilweise zu öffnen
Wartungsgang
Stahlkonstruktion

2
Primärfassade

Brüstungen
Stahlbeton 16 cm
WDVS 20 cm
Fenster-Pfosten-
Riegelkonstruktion
aus Leichtmetall
2-fach Verglasung
Öffnungsflügel Glas
Blendschutz:
innenliegendes
Textilrollo

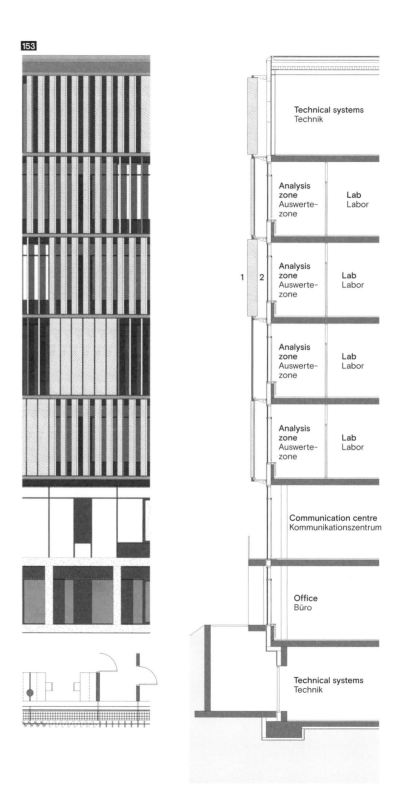

153

1 2

Technical systems
Technik

Analysis
zone
Auswerte-
zone

Lab
Labor

Analysis
zone
Auswerte-
zone

Lab
Labor

Analysis
zone
Auswerte-
zone

Lab
Labor

Analysis
zone
Auswerte-
zone

Lab
Labor

Communication centre
Kommunikationszentrum

Office
Büro

Technical systems
Technik

154

155

155
Institute for
Microbiology and
Virology, University
of Tübingen,
Nickl & Partner
Architekten, 2001
Institut für
Mikrobiologie
und Virologie
der Universität
Tübingen,
Nickl & Partner
Architekten, 2001

156

157

156 – 157
AGORA – Pôle de
Recherche sur le
Cancer, Lausanne,
Behnisch Architek-
ten, 2018
AGORA – Pôle de
Recherche sur le
Cancer, Lausanne,
Behnisch Architek-
ten, 2018

158
ISMO Institute,
Sciences Moléculai-
res d'Orsay, KAAN
Architecten, 2018
ISMO Institut des
Sciences Moléculai-
res d'Orsay, KAAN
Architecten, 2018

159
Ahead of its time:
Zvi Hecker's iconic
façade of the
laboratories of the
Faculty of Mechnical
Engineering,
Technion, Haifa,
1964-1967
Ihrer Zeit voraus:
Zvi Heckers ikonische
Fassade der Labore
der Fakultät für
Maschinenbau,
Technion, Haifa,
1964-1967

Trend – High tech & low tech

There is currently a trend towards higher demands for façades, not just with respect to their function as a calling card for the institution, but also in terms of their energy and thermal qualities, while requiring a low CO_2 footprint and the use of recycled or recyclable materials wherever possible. Façades should be able to "do something". One defining theme is their assessment according to sustainability aspects. Thermal properties can make a key contribution to achieving low or zero energy standards.

At the Research Center ICTA-ICP on the campus of the Universitat Autònoma de Barcelona, a low-cost bioclimatic exterior envelope surrounds the concrete structure. The entire building is structured into three different climatic areas with different demands with respect to thermal comfort levels. Solar radiation and ventilation are regulated by the installation of an industrial greenhouse mechanism that automatically opens and closes flaps on the façades and roof to influence the interior climate in a natural way. → **160**

Façades with greenery are not a new trend, but in view of the increasingly evident effects of climate change, they have attracted renewed attention to integrate them into overall concepts for sun protection, building cooling and energy saving.

Vegetation on façade structures offer protection from heat and sunlight, as well as additional beneficial effects. They improve the air quality, produce oxygen, filter out dust and reduce pollutants. At the Institute for Physics of the Humboldt-Universität zu Berlin, the exterior envelope – except for the north façade – received walkable façade zones for easy maintenance and was equipped with a variety of sun protection systems. The frequented areas enjoy vegetable sun protection. The effects of the evaporation cooling and shading provided by the green façade, forming part of the overall ecological concept, was scientifically assessed, with significant positive results. For instance it could be proven that the work-intensive care for the green façades, which often deters builders from implementing them, is cheaper than maintenance for a motorised exterior sun-protection system. → **161–163**

Additionally, innovative concepts require façades that actively contribute to gaining energy or influencing the microclimate. Integrating photovoltaic elements into the façade structure is a technology-orientated solution and was consistently tested using 170 m² of thin-film photovoltaic modules at the Zentrum für Sonnenenergie- und Wasserstoff-Forschung Baden-Württemberg (ZSW). → **164**

Trend – High Tech & Low Tech

Tendenziell steigen die Anforderungen an Fassaden nicht nur hinsichtlich ihrer Funktion als Aushängeschild der Institution, sondern auch hinsichtlich ihrer energetischen und thermischen Fähigkeiten, bei gleichzeitig niedrigem CO_2-Fußabdruck und möglichst Verwendung von rezyklierten bzw. rezyklierbaren Materialien. Die Fassade sollte „etwas können". Eines der bestimmenden Themen ist die Bewertung nach Nachhaltigkeitsaspekten. Die thermischen Fähigkeiten leisten einen entscheidenden Beitrag zum Erreichen eines Niedrig- bzw. Nullenergiestandards.

Am Research Center ICTA-ICP auf dem Campus der Universitat Autònoma de Barcelona umhüllt eine kostengünstige bioklimatische Außenhaut die Betonkonstruktion. Das gesamte Gebäude ist in drei verschiedene klimatische Bereiche mit unterschiedlichen Ansprüchen an die thermische Behaglichkeit gegliedert. Solarer Eintrag und Belüftung werden durch die Installation eines industriellen Gewächshaus-Mechanismus reguliert, welches Klappen an Fassaden und Dach automatisch öffnet und schließt, um das Innenraumklima auf natürliche Weise zu beeinflussen. → **160** Begrünte Fassaden sind letztlich kein neuer Trend, werden aber angesichts immer stärker spürbarer Auswirkungen des Klimawandels neu diskutiert um sie in Gesamtkonzepte des Sonnenschutzes, der Gebäudekühlung und Energieeinsparung zu integrieren.

Pflanzen bringen in den Fassadenaufbau neben dem Schutz vor Hitze und Sonneneinstrahlung noch weitere günstige Eigenschaften ein. Sie verbessern die Luftqualität, erzeugen Sauerstoff, filtern Staub und Schadstoffe. Am Institut für Physik an der Humboldt-Universität zu Berlin erhielten alle Außenseiten – ausgenommen die Nordfassade – begehbare Fassadenzonen, die als leichte Wartungsstege mit unterschiedlichen Sonnenschutzsystemen versehen sind. Die Verkehrsflächen erhielten einen vegetativen Sonnenschutz. Die Effekte von Verdunstungskälte und Verschattung der Fassadenbegrünung innerhalb des ökologischen Gesamtkonzepts wurden wissenschaftlich evaluiert, mit durchaus positiven Resultaten. Auch konnte dort nachgewiesen werden, dass die aufwändige Pflege von begrünten Fassaden, vor der Bauherren in der Regel zurückschrecken, im Vergleich zu Wartung und Instandhaltung eines motorisierten außenliegenden Sonnenschutzes kostengünstiger ist. → **161–163**

Darüber hinaus gehen innovative Konzepte von einem aktiven Beitrag der Fassaden zur Energiegewinnung oder der Beeinflussung des Mikroklimas aus. Integration von Photovoltaik-Elementen in den Fassadenaufbau ist die technikaffine Lösung und wurde konsequenterweise anhand von 170 m² Dünnschicht-Photovoltaikmodulen am Zentrum für Sonnenenergie- und Wasserstoff-Forschung Baden-Württemberg (ZSW) erprobt. → **164**

160
The Leed Gold
certified Research
Center ICTA-ICP,
Universitat
Autònoma de
Barcelona, H
Arquitectes &
DataAE, 2014
Das mit Leed Gold
zertifizierte Research
Center ICTA-ICP,
Universitat Autònoma
de Barcelona, H
Arquitectes &
DataAE, 2014

161
Illustration of the new lab building, Julius Kühn Institute Berlin, Nickl & Partner Architekten, competition design, 2021
Visualisierung des Neubaus Laborgebäude Julius Kühn-Institut Berlin, Nickl & Partner Architekten, Wettbewerbsentwurf, 2021

162
Section, ground plan and elevation, new lab building, Julius Kühn Institute Berlin
Fassadenschnitt, Grundriss und Ansicht des Neubaus Laborgebäude Julius Kühn-Instituts Berlin

Façade structure

Wood and glass element façade in the office area
Larch-wood ventilation elements
Maintenance corridor
Lattice
Plant troughs
Textile-reinforced concrete including irrigation, rear-anchored to ceilings
Steel-profile connection to support façade loads

Window level

Exterior sun blind
Textile marquee
Fixed triple glazing
Window frames
Wood profiles
Wood opening elements in the office area
Internal sun blind
Textile roller blind and curtain blinds
Façade greenery: wisteria

Fassadenaufbau

Holz-Glas-Element-Fassade im Bürobereich
Lüftungsflügel aus Lärchenholz
Wartungsgang
Gitterrost
Pflanztröge
Textilbeton incl. Bewässerung an Decken rückverankert
Anschluss Stahlprofil zur Aufnahme der Fassadenlasten

Fensterebene

Außenliegender Sonnenschutz
Textilmarkisen
3-fach Isolierverglasung festverglast
Fensterrahmen Holzprofile
Öffnungsflügel Holz im Bürobereich
Interner Blendschutz
Textilrollo und Blendschutz-vorhänge
Fassadenbegrünung Glyzinie

161

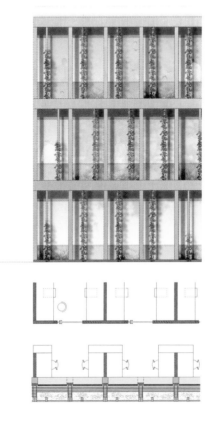

162

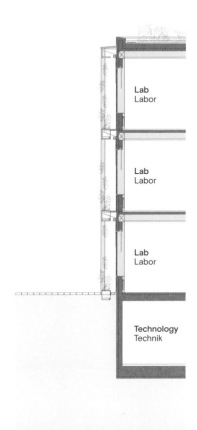

Lab
Labor

Lab
Labor

Lab
Labor

Technology
Technik

163
At the Institute for
Physics, façade
greening was
integrated into the
building cooling
concept, Humboldt
Universität zu Berlin,
Augustin Frank
Architekten, 2003
Am Institut für
Physik wurde die
Fassadenbegrünung
in das Konzept der
Gebäudekühlung
integriert, Humboldt
Universität zu Berlin,
Augustin Frank
Architekten, 2003

164
Approx 170 m² photovoltaic thin-layered elements were integrated into the façade of the Center for Solar Energy and Hydrogen Research Baden-Württemberg (ZSW), Stuttgart, Henning Larsen, 2017
Rund 170 m² Photovoltaik-Dünn-schichtelemente wurden in die Fassade des Zentrums für Sonnenenergie- und Wasserstoff-Forschung Baden-Württemberg (ZSW) integriert, Stuttgart, Henning Larsen, 2017

Innovative façade systems

LUCIO BLANDINI + FLORIAN STARZ + WERNER SOBEK

Innovative
Fassadensysteme

165

180

Examples from research and practice

Architecture not only accommodates research, but can also be the subject of research. Every building can – and should – be regarded as a potential research project that demonstrates methods of resource-saving, climate-neutral and user-friendly construction. The façade plays a key role in this context, since it is the interface between exterior and interior climates, thereby defining the building's basic energy consumption and the degree of climatic comfort inside it.

The following report, resulting from cooperation between the Institute for Lightweight Structures and Conceptual Design (ILEK) at the University of Stuttgart and Werner Sobek AG, investigates which innovative façade systems offer forward-looking, i.e. sustainable, optimisation potential and how such potential can be assessed.

Beispiele aus Forschung und Praxis

Architektur beherbergt nicht nur Forschung, sie kann auch Gegenstand der Forschung sein. Jedes Bauwerk kann – und sollte – als ein potenzielles Forschungsprojekt erachtet werden, welches Wege des ressourcenschonenden, klimaneutralen und nutzerfreundlichen Bauens aufzeigt. Der Fassade kommt in diesem Kontext eine zentrale Bedeutung zu, denn sie ist die Schnittstelle zwischen Außen- und Innenklima und steuert damit grundlegend Energieverbrauch und klimatische Behaglichkeit des Gebäudes.

Der folgende Beitrag, welcher aus einer Kooperation des Instituts für Leichtbau Entwerfen und Konstruieren (ILEK) der Universität Stuttgart und der Werner Sobek AG entstanden ist, geht der Frage nach, welche innovativen Fassadensysteme zukunftsfähige, das heißt nachhaltige Optimierungspotentiale aufweisen und wie diese zu evaluieren sind.

Today more than ever, it is essential that the building sector uses the available resources more sparingly than has been the case in the past: our constructed environment is responsible for more than half the worldwide consumption of resources and produces more than a third of greenhouse-gas emissions.[1] Thus, measures in the building sector can develop enormous leverage to achieve essential environmental policy targets, such as the Paris Agreement. However, this requires a greater innovative spirit and a number of fundamental changes, going beyond ever-stricter normative requirements. Clear goals must be defined, without focusing on specific predefined measures. The authors believe that this goal is most simply described by the Triple Zero® Concept developed by Werner Sobek: our buildings should use no fossil-based energy sources (Zero Fossil Energy), should produce no emissions (Zero Emissions) and should be 100 % reusable in technical or biological cycles (Zero Waste).

This excursus presents selected example façades from a variety of climate zones to demonstrate how the building sector can already use reasonable means to contribute to greater sustainability today. The focus lies on new sun-shading elements, façade-greenery and other approaches that can significantly improve the overall life-cycle assessment of a façade. Creativity is required to implement the necessary change towards new conceptual and working methods: this applies to the entire value-addition chain in the building sector, including planning, construction, operation, refurbishment and demolition. Glass façades will always play an important role in this respect, since it is essential for users to be able to look outside and enjoy sufficient natural light.[2] However, transparent façades made of glass are increasingly being combined with other façade systems to achieve an ideal synthesis with a variety of qualities. Ever more precise and powerful modelling and simulation programs support the planning of such system combinations, thereby contributing to optimisations in the field of façades. Such programs enable early, accurate statements on the expected exterior and interior conditions. The design and construction of the façade can be ideally adjusted according to factors such as solar radiation, internal loads, shading, ventilation and so on. The aim is to achieve the greatest level of comfort while simultaneously ensuring energy-efficiency and reducing greenhouse-gas emissions.

Shading and radiation analyses are among the simplest, but most effective studies. They allow good, early assessment of the expected theoretical thermal loads and possible solar gains. This helps planners to calculate the dimensions of projecting roofs, shading elements and PV modules at an early stage. As planning progresses,

Es ist mehr denn je zwingend erforderlich, dass auch das Bauwesen sorgfältiger mit den verfügbaren Ressourcen umgeht als bisher: Unsere gebaute Umwelt steht für mehr als die Hälfte des weltweiten Ressourcenverbrauchs und für mehr als ein Drittel der Treibhausgasemissionen[1]. Dies zeigt, welche Hebelwirkung Maßnahmen im Bauwesen entfalten können, um essenzielle umweltpolitische Ziele wie beispielsweise das Klimaschutzabkommen von Paris zu erreichen. Damit dies passiert, braucht es aber mehr Innovationsgeist und einige grundlegende Änderungen jenseits der immer strikter werden normativen Anforderungen. Es geht darum, klare Ziele zu definieren und sich nicht allein auf bestimmte vorgefasste Maßnahmen zu fokussieren. Dieses Ziel lässt sich nach Ansicht der Autoren am einfachsten mit dem Triple Zero® Konzept von Werner Sobek beschreiben: Unsere Gebäude sollten keine fossilbasierten Energieträger nutzen (Zero Fossil Energy), sollten keine Emissionen erzeugen (Zero Emissions) und sollten zu 100 % in technische oder biologische Stoffkreisläufe rückführbar sein (Zero Waste).

Der vorliegende Aufsatz zeigt anhand ausgewählter Fassadenbeispiele aus unterschiedlichen Klimazonen, wie das Bauwesen schon heute mit vertretbarem Aufwand einen Beitrag zu mehr Nachhaltigkeit leisten kann. Im Blickpunkt stehen dabei insbesondere neuartige Sonnenschutzelemente, Systeme zur Fassadenbegrünung und andere Ansätze, welche die ganzheitliche Bilanz einer Fassade deutlich verbessern können. Kreativität ist gefragt, um den erforderlichen Wechsel hin zu neuen Denk- und Arbeitsweisen zu realisieren: dies gilt für die gesamte Wertschöpfungskette des Bauwesens, von der Planung über die Fertigung bis zu Betrieb, Sanierung und Rückbau. Glasfassaden werden dabei immer eine wichtige Rolle spielen, denn es bleibt essenziell für die Nutzer, der Blick nach außen richten zu können und hinreichend mit Tageslicht versorgt zu sein[2]. Transparente Fassaden aus Glas werden aber zunehmend mit anderen Fassadensystemen kombiniert, um eine optimale Synthese unterschiedlicher Eigenschaften zu erreichen.

Immer präzisere und leistungsfähigere Modellierung- und Simulationsprogramme unterstützen bei der Planung solcher System-Kombinationen und tragen zur Optimierung des Fassadenbereichs bei. Dank dieser Programme können schon früh präzise Aussagen zu den zu erwartenden externen und internen Bedingungen gemacht werden. Hierdurch können die Gestaltung und die Konstruktion der Fassade optimal auf Faktoren wie solare Einstrahlung, interne Lasten, Verschattung, Lüftung usw. eingestellt werden. Ziel ist es, den höchsten Komfort bei einer gleichzeitigen Steigerung der energetischen Effizienz und Reduzierung der Treibhausgasemissionen zu gewährleisten.

Unser Neues
Haus 2.0, Vienna –
Façade concept
(Chaix & Morel)
and details
(Werner Sobek),
2020
Unser Neues
Haus 2.0, Wien –
Fassadenkonzept
(Chaix & Morel)
und Detaillierung
(Werner Sobek),
2020

more extensive simulations can be applied to support specific considerations. Daylight simulations are among the most frequently used analyses. They assess the lighting conditions and visual quality of a space and are supplemented by thermal simulations to optimise the energetic properties of the façade in connection with internal and external loads. Flow simulations are used for complex studies (for instance double façades).

A future alternative to load-bearing systems in the façade are adaptive systems that help to control aspects such as light transmission, reflection and energy permeability, and to manipulate these in a targeted way. Such systems enable much more dynamic building envelopes.[3] This could lead to a new type of architecture, opening up a new dimension in the interaction between people and spaces. A further benefit is increased resilience against the effects of climate change. 14 institutes at the University of Stuttgart, from the Faculties of Architecture, Civil Engineering, Mechanical Engineering, IT and Aerospace Engineering, have pooled their resources to research such systems and apply them in practical construction. Since 2017, the work has been funded by the Deutsche Forschungsgemeinschaft as part of the special research programme CRC 1244 "Adaptive skins and structures for the built environment of tomorrow".

Innovative façade projects
Three current façade projects and a report from CRC research demonstrate solutions and approaches that are currently regarded as especially promising.

Unser Neues Haus 2.0, Vienna
The Vienna headquarters of the Austrian social insurance association (Hauptverband der österreichischen Sozialversicherungsträger) was modernised in accordance with EnerPHit (passive house) standard and supplemented and extended to include two new structures. Due to the energy and comfort-level demands, and to ensure the desired noise-insulation, the new building envelope consists of a double façade. The architects Chaix & Morel from Paris not only focused on transparency, but also on the building's vertical qualities. →166

The main façade consists of neutral, thermally insulating glazing with exterior sun-shading (Fc value: 9% – 21%), enabling g values between 0.03 and 0.07. The glazing's light transmission is up to 47%. The double façade is a thermally optimised element façade with a back-ventilated baffle pane. Vertically running double pilaster strips serve as load-bearing elements for the baffle pane and as visual elements to highlight the verticality. The pilaster strips were

Zu den einfachsten, aber sehr effektiven Studien zählen Verschattung- und Einstrahlungsanalysen. Diese Art von Studie ermöglicht schon in sehr frühen Entwurfsphasen eine gute Einschätzung der zu erwartenden thermischen Lasten und möglichen solaren Gewinne. Dies hilft den Planern bei der frühzeitigen Dimensionierung von Dachvorsprüngen, Verschattungselementen und PV-Modulen. Mit fortschreitender Planung können dann umfangreichere Simulationen angesetzt werden, die bei spezifischen Fragestellungen unterstützen. Zu den am häufigsten verwendeten Analysen gehört die Tageslichtsimulation. Hierbei werden lichttechnische Eigenschaften und visueller Komfort eines Raums untersucht. Hinzu kommen thermische Simulationen, um die energetischen Eigenschaften der Fassade in Zusammenhang mit den internen und externen Lasten zu optimieren. Strömungssimulationen werden für komplexe Untersuchungen (zum Beispiel bei Doppelfassaden) verwendet.

Eine zukünftige Alternative zu statischen Systemen in der Fassade sind adaptive Systeme, mit Hilfe derer sich Eigenschaften wie Lichttransmission, Reflexion und Energiedurchlässigkeit steuern und gezielt manipulieren lassen. Solche Systeme ermöglichen eine viel dynamischere Gebäudehülle[3]. Dies könnte zur Entstehung einer neuartigen Architektur führen, welche auch eine neue Dimension in der Interaktion zwischen Mensch und Raum eröffnet. Hinzu kommt eine Erhöhung der Resilienz gegenüber den Folgen des Klimawandels. 14 Institute der Universität Stuttgart aus den Fakultäten Architektur, Bauingenieurwesen, Maschinenbau, Informatik und Flugzeugbau haben sich zusammengeschlossen, um solche Systeme zu erforschen und in die baupraktische Anwendung zu bringen. Dies wird seit 2017 von der Deutschen Forschungsgemeinschaft im Rahmen des Sonderforschungsprogramms SFB 1244 „Adaptive Hüllen und Strukturen für die gebaute Umwelt von morgen" gefördert.

Innovative Fassadenprojekte
Drei aktuelle Fassadenprojekte sowie ein Bericht aus der SFB Forschung sollen aufzeigen, welche Lösungen und Ansätze derzeit als besonders interessant angesehen werden.

Unser Neues Haus 2.0, Wien
Die Wiener Zentrale des Hauptverbandes der österreichischen Sozialversicherungsträger wurde nach dem EnerPHit-Standard (Passivhausstandard) modernisiert und durch zwei Neubauten ergänzt und erweitert. Aufgrund der energetischen und Komfortanforderungen sowie zur Gewährleistung des gewünschten Schallschutzes wurde die neue Gebäudehülle als Doppelfassade ausgebildet. Die Architekten Chaix & Morel aus Paris legten dabei nicht nur auf Transparenz Wert, sondern wollten auch die Vertikalität betonen. →166

Bei der Hauptfassade wurde eine neutrale Wärmeschutzverglasung mit außenliegendem Sonnenschutz (Fc-Wert: 9% – 21%) angesetzt, so dass

produced as perforated sheet metal to optimise air circulation: the perforation pattern was based on load-bearing and structural-physical simulations. The balustrade panel is integrated into the façade. A solid masonry façade was not used. The balustrade areas include A1 mineral-fibre insulation with improved WLG 032 heat-conduction group, in order to fulfil structural demands.

During the planning stage, a study was carried out to assess the temperature conditions in the intermediate space between the façade layers, testing different variants. During the study's analysis, it was important to take the methodical limits of the thermo-dynamic building simulation into account (e.g. congestion effects in poorly ventilated areas of the façade's intermediate space could not be calculated). The parametric simulations of the façade sections were each implemented for an entire year, assessing maximum air temperatures in the façade's intermediate space and the maximum temperature of the baffle pane.

Parameters for the analysis were defined properties such as the exterior lamella blinds' level of reflection, the opaque exterior façade surfaces, the size of the apertures for back-ventilation and the physical radiation properties of the baffle pane. The study clearly showed which property had the greatest influence on the façade's performance, thereby enabling calculation of the expected cooling requirements for the interior spaces. Such interactive planning, using the interaction between the façade and the building's technical systems, significantly optimised the design.

The currently ongoing design project for a double façade in Düsseldorf develops this approach even further. Numerical flow simulations (CFD – Computational Fluid Dynamics) provide detailed information on the ideal arrangement of ventilation apertures and the expected temperatures in intermediate façade space. They study the temperature distribution over the height of the façade's intermediate spaces and the average air temperature in the intermediate space under different climatic conditions. In this way, areas with potential stagnant air, i.e. insufficient ventilation, can be identified.

On the one hand, such simulations are important tools with which to optimise the design; on the other hand, they enable innovative solutions in the first place, since they clearly indicate what can be implemented (and what not).

Green façades

Discourse on greenery in the city is becoming increasingly important to urban planners, also due to the evident increase in extreme weather events. Façades can also sensibly combine green and transparent areas. Europe's largest green

g-Werte zwischen 0,03 und 0,07 erreicht werden können. Die Lichttransmission der Verglasung beträgt dabei bis zu 47 %. Die Doppelfassade ist eine thermisch optimierte Elementfassade mit einer hinterlüfteten Prallscheibe.

Vertikal verlaufende Doppellisenen dienen als Tragelemente für die Prallscheibe und als optische Elemente zur Betonung der Vertikalität. Die Lisenen wurden als perforiertes Lochblech ausgeführt, um die Luftzirkulation zu optimieren: Das Perforationsmuster wurde auf Grundlage der statischen und bauphysikalischen Simulationen definiert. Das Brüstungspaneel ist in die Fassade integriert. Auf eine massive gemauerte Brüstung wurde verzichtet. Die Brüstungsbereiche sind mit einer Mineralfaserdämmung A1 mit der verbesserten Wärmeleitgruppe WLG 032 versehen, um die bauphysikalischen Anforderungen zu erfüllen.

In Rahmen der Planung wurde eine Untersuchung zur Einschätzung der Temperaturverhältnisse innerhalb des Fassadenzwischenraumes bei unterschiedlichen Varianten durchgeführt. Bei den Auswertungen der Studie war es wichtig, die methodischen Grenzen der thermisch-dynamischen Gebäudesimulation zu berücksichtigen (z.B. konnten Staueffekte in schlecht belüfteten Bereichen des Fassadenzwischenraumes rechnerisch nicht erfasst werden). Die parametrischen Simulationen eines Fassadenabschnitts wurden jeweils für ein ganzes Jahr durchgeführt. Dabei wurden die maximale Luft-temperatur im Fassadenzwischenraum sowie die maximale Temperatur der Prallscheibe ausgewertet.

Als Parameter für die Analyse wurden Eigenschaften wie der Reflexionsgrad der Lamellenraffstoren und der opaken Außenoberflächen der Fassade, die Größe der Öffnungsflächen für die Hinterlüftung sowie die strahlungsphysikalischen Eigenschaften der Prallscheibe identifiziert. Die Studie zeigte deutlich, welche Eigenschaft den größten Einfluss auf die Performance der Fassade hat. Sie ermöglichte so eine fundierte Berechnung des zu erwartenden Kühlbedarfs der Innenräume. Durch diese interaktive Planung im Zusammenspiel von Fassade und TGA konnte der Entwurf deutlich optimiert werden.

Bei dem aktuell in Arbeit befindlichen Entwurf einer Doppelfassade in Düsseldorf wird dieser Ansatz noch weiterentwickelt. Numerische Strömungssimulationen (CFD – Computational Fluid Dynamics) liefern hier detaillierte Informationen zur optimalen Anordnung der Lüftungsöffnungen und zu den zu erwartenden Temperaturen im Fassadenzwischenraum. Untersucht wird hierbei auch die Temperaturverteilung über die Höhe der Fassadenzwischenräume sowie die durchschnittliche Lufttemperatur im Fassadenzwischenraum in unterschiedlichen klimatischen Situationen. Auf diese Weise können auch die Bereiche mit potentieller Stagnation, also fehlender Durchlüftung und stehender Luft, identifiziert werden.

façade, the K II in Düsseldorf, which includes 8 km of hornbeam vegetation, and the lighthouse project Calwer Passage in Stuttgart, with over 2 km of mixed greenery, are true milestones in this respect. → 167–168

Both projects are the result of collaboration between Ingenhoven Architects and the façade department of Werner Sobek. They combine closed and green façade surfaces with glazed areas and vegetation planted in front of the building. The greenery is a living, renewable "façade skin" that contributes to sustainable façade solutions, not only with respect to heat shielding. It also serves to reduce noise and improve sound insulation; the same applies to visual shielding in front of glazed façades, above all at inner-urban locations. Locally, the shading effect of the plants lowers the surface temperature, which reduces the heat input into the building, thereby sustainably lowering cooling demands.

During heavy rainfall, the greenery and its substrate temporarily store the water volumes; condensation cooling prevents local heat islands and thereby ensures additional comfort levels for densely developed city centres. Furthermore, plants can also reduce local fine-particle levels, bind CO_2 and convert it into oxygen – thereby contributing to CO_2-neutral construction while also providing urban areas with fresh air.

Green façades use natural means to counteract the otherwise observed summer overheating in densely developed areas ("urban heat island" effect). The local microclimate is decisively improved in this way, while people's wellbeing is also increased. Naturally, individual buildings can only contribute to improvements in the urban climate in a limited, local way. However, green façades and roofs at the Calwer Passage and on the K II bring back a piece of nature and biodiversity to the heart of our living environment and can inspire further similar projects.

Wasl Tower, Dubai

The new Al Wasl Tower was planned by UNStudio together with Werner Sobek. The aim was to create a new, sustainable type of high-rise in the context of the Expo 2020. The design's geometry is characterised by rotation. The volume is situated between Sheikh Zayed Road and the 828 m tall Burj Khalifa. The tower accommodates apartments and offices, as well as a 5-star hotel, restaurants and a spa area. → 169–170

A key element of the planning process was the BIM model and the connected parametrically programmed geometry. The measures supported coordination between the project participants and made it easier to react to the different requirements and underlying conditions during the planning process. The façade grid varies

Solche Simulationen sind einerseits wichtige Werkzeuge, die eine Optimierung des Entwurfs erlauben, andererseits ermöglichen sie manche neuartigen Lösungen überhaupt erst, da sie klar aufzeigen, was sich wie realisieren lässt (und was nicht).

Grüne Fassaden

Die Diskussion über das Begrünen der Städte wird für Planer immer wichtiger, auch aufgrund der spürbar zunehmenden Wetterextreme. Auch bei den Fassaden können begrünte sinnvoll mit transparenten Bereichen kombiniert werden. Europas größte Grünfassade – das K II mit 8 km Hainbuchen in Düsseldorf – und das Leuchtturmprojekt Calwer Passage in Stuttgart mit mehr als 2 km Mischkulturen sind hier wirkliche Meilensteine. → 167–168

Beide Projekten sind durch die Zusammenarbeit von Ingenhoven Architects mit der Fassadenabteilung von Werner Sobek entstanden. Sie kombinieren geschlossene und begrünte Fassadenflächen mit verglasten Bereichen und einer vorgelagerten Bepflanzung. Die Begrünung als lebendige und nachwachsende „Fassadenhaut" leistet somit einen Beitrag zu einer nachhaltigen Fassadenlösung, nicht nur in Bezug auf Wärmeschutz. Sie dient auch der Lärmreduktion und dem verbesserten Schallschutz; gleiches gilt für den Sichtschutz vor verglasten Fassaden, vor allem in innerstädtischen Lagen. Lokal werden durch die verschattende Wirkung der Pflanzen die Oberflächentemperaturen verringert; der Wärmeeintrag in das Gebäude wird somit reduziert, die erforderliche Kühlleistung nachhaltig gesenkt.

Bei Starkregen fungieren die Begrünung und der Substrataufbau als Zwischenspeicher für die Wassermassen; die Verdunstungskühlung verhindert lokale Hitzeinseln und sichert so einen Komfortgewinn für dicht bebaute Innenstädte. Darüber hinaus können die Pflanzen auch lokale Feinstaubkonzentrationen reduzieren, CO_2 binden und in Sauerstoff umwandeln – und somit einen Beitrag zum CO_2 neutralen Bauen bei gleichzeitiger Frischluftversorgung urbaner Gebiete leisten.

Grüne Fassaden wirken der ansonsten zu beobachtenden sommerlichen Überhitzung von stark bebautem Gebiet („Urban Heat Island"-Effekt) mit natürlichen Mitteln entgegen. Das Mikroklima vor Ort wird so entscheidend verbessert und das Wohlbefinden erhöht. Einzelne Gebäude können natürlich nur bedingt und lokal zur Verbesserung des Stadtklimas beitragen. Die Begrünung der Fassaden und Dächer bei der Calwer Passage und bei K II bringen aber ein Stück Natur und Biodiversität zurück in die Herzen urbaner Lebensräume und können der Anstoß für weitere solche Projekte sein.

Wasl Tower, Dubai

Der neue Al Wasl Tower wurde von UNStudio zusammen mit Werner Sobek geplant. Ziel war es hierbei, eine neue, nachhaltige Art von Hochhäusern im Kontext der

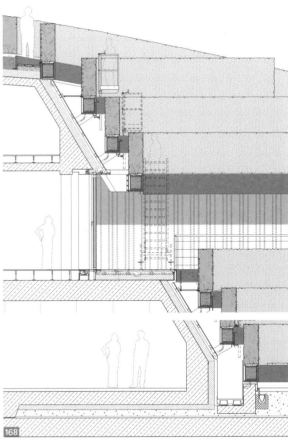

167 – 168
Green façade
with 30,000
hornbeams,
KII, Düsseldorf
Ingenhoven
Architects with
Werner Sobek,
2020
Grünfassade
mit 30.000
Hainbuchen,
KII, Düsseldorf
Ingenhoven
Architects mit
Werner Sobek,
2020

169

170

169–170
**Al Wasl Tower, Dubai,
UNStudio with
Werner Sobek, since
2014**
Al Wasl Tower, Dubai,
UNStudio mit Werner
Sobek, seit 2014

188

depending on the sun's alignment, allowing more than 50 % of the transparent surfaces to face north, affording views of the sea. Overall, the façade uses such measures to provide more colour-neutral and transparent glass surfaces than other comparable buildings in the region.

Especially in the summer months, the sun's radiation is reflected back outwards using ceramic sun-shading elements mounted in a 13° slanted position. They follow the complex geometry of the building floor plan and are also parametrically variable both laterally and longitudinally, thereby providing ideal sun protection. At night, the elements are staged using LED lighting, entering into a relationship with the vibrant city life. The façade lighting uses PV panels on the neighbouring multi-storey car park as a source of energy. Several simulations were carried out to ideally adapt the façade to local environmental conditions through a variety of passive measures. Radiation analyses examined different façade variants during early planning stages with respect to the according sunshine levels. These studies were continuously refined so that ultimately, depending on the alignment, an ideal proportion of opaque and transparent façade areas could be defined. In a second step, the lighting and energetic properties of the glazing were simulated to analyse aspects such as visual and thermal comfort levels. The façade was further optimised by examining the light intensity, the operative temperature and the air temperature; these processes took the light transmission and the g value into account.

Research outlook: Adaptive façades

Based on research by ILEK (Institute for Lightweight Structures and Conceptual Design) in the field of switchable glass,[3] the University of Stuttgart has been researching innovative adaptivity concepts for all aspects of the developed environment since 2017 as part of the CRC 1244 programme, in close interdisciplinary cooperation. Such approaches are largely based on work carried out at ILEK since the 1990s. The adaptivity approach requires a fundamental transformation in the architectural conception of buildings: instead of focusing on the development of individual components, they must be integrated into the overall system. Thus, a 36.5 metre high test tower was constructed on the university campus in Stuttgart-Vaihingen, which will be used in the coming years to test different strategies and technologies.[4] →171

Research and development will use this research building in the field of adaptive load-bearing structures and building envelopes to examine their practical feasibility. Adaptive façades dynamically react to factors such as the sun's radiation, noise, humidity etc. by manipulating the façade

Expo 2020 zu realisieren. Die Geometrie des Entwurfs ist von einer Drehbewegung geprägt. Das Gebäude liegt zwischen der Sheikh Zayed Road und dem 828 m hohen Burj Khalifa. Im Hochhaus finden sich neben Wohnungen und Büros auch ein 5-Sterne-Hotel, Restaurants und ein Spa-Bereich. →169–170

Zentrales Element des Planungsprozess waren das BIM-Modell und die damit verbundene parametrisch programmierte Geometrie. Diese unterstützten die Koordination zwischen den Projektbeteiligten und ermöglichten es, während der Planung besser auf die unterschiedlichen Anforderungen und Rahmenbedingungen reagieren zu können. Das Fassadenraster variiert je nach Sonnenausrichtung, so dass mehr als 50 % der transparenten Flächen Richtung Norden und mit Meerblick ausgerichtet sind. Insgesamt bietet die Fassade durch solche Ansätze mehr farbneutrale und transparente Glasfläche als andere vergleichbare Bauten in der Region.

Die Sonneneinstrahlung wird – insbesondere in den Sommermonaten – durch Sonnenschutzelemente aus Keramik zurück nach außen reflektiert; diese Keramikelemente sind um 13° geneigt. Sie folgen der komplexen Geometrie des Gebäudegrundrisses und sind auch parametrisch in der Breite und Tiefe variabel, so dass sie einen optimalen Sonnenschutz bilden. In der Nacht werden die Elemente durch LED-Beleuchtung inszeniert und nehmen hierdurch Bezug auf das pulsierende Stadtleben. Als Energiequelle für die Fassadenbeleuchtung dienen PV-Paneele, die auf dem benachbarten Parkhaus platziert sind.

Es wurden mehrere Simulationen durchgeführt, um die Fassade durch verschiedene passive Maßnahmen optimal auf die lokalen Umweltbedingungen abzustimmen. Mittels Einstrahlungsanalysen wurden in den frühen Planungsphasen Fassadenvarianten hinsichtlich der jeweils anfallenden Besonnung untersucht. Diese Studien wurden immer weiter verfeinert, so dass schließlich je nach Ausrichtung eine optimale Teilung von opaken und transparenten Fassadenbereichen definiert werden konnte. In einem zweiten Schritt wurden die lichttechnischen und energetischen Eigenschaften der Verglasung simuliert, um Aspekte wie den visuellen und den thermischen Komfort zu analysieren. Durch die Betrachtung der Beleuchtungsstärke, der operativen Temperatur und der Lufttemperatur wurde die Fassade weiter optimiert; hierbei wurden auch die Lichttransmission und der g-Wert berücksichtigt.

Forschungsausblick: Adaptive Fassaden

Aufbauend auf den Forschungen des ILEK (Institut für Leichtbau Entwerfen und Konstruieren) im Bereich der schaltbaren Verglasungen [3] werden an der Universität Stuttgart in Rahmen des SFB 1244 seit 2017 neuartige Adaptivitätskonzepte für alle Bereiche der gebauten Umwelt in enger interdisziplinärer Zusammenarbeit erforscht; diese Ansätze bauen zu einem guten Teil auf die Arbeiten auf, die seit den

171

171
Adaptive
Demonstrator Tower
at the University
of Stuttgart (ILEK),
2022
Adaptives
Demonstrator-
Hochhaus an der
Universität
Stuttgart (ILEK),
2022

qualities relevant to their structural physics.[5] In the field of components, sandwich structures with activated elements have proved especially promising; these structures have been researched at the Institute for Aircraft Design (IFB) and are currently under further development at ILEK for application in the field of façade construction.[6] The elements, known as PALEOs (plastically annealed lamina emergent origami structures), change the rigidity of a flat semi-finished product to allow robust joints with adjustable resetting without requiring any additional building parts or finishing measures. The potential to integrate this technology in textile façade systems will be researched in the coming years. Textile façades provide a very good basis for integrating various technologies and have therefore long been the subject of research at ILEK.[7]

Another focus of research in the field of adaptive building envelopes lies in thermal storage potential. The lightweight construction method reduces the building mass, which in turn lowers the thermal buffer effect with respect to day-night temperature fluctuation. This effect can be compensated through adaptive envelope elements. The potential for this approach will be investigated further in the coming years in collaboration with the Institute of Engineering Thermodynamics at the DLR and the Institute for System Dynamics at the University of Stuttgart.

In the coming years, the Demonstrator Tower constructed as part of the CRC 1244 programme will offer an ideal experimental platform to test and validate the above approaches and technologies, as well as many other innovative approaches. The increased interaction between people and the building envelope as a result of adaptivity will also be taken into account during the validation stage. In this respect, the focus lies not only on the technical quality of the developed situations, but also on the socio-cultural acceptance of such innovative technologies, which will certainly have a significant effect on our constructed environment in the decades ahead.

Conclusion and outlook

The projects presented in this article demonstrate the variety of sustainable façade solutions that combine a high degree of dedicated resource application and high comfort levels. This variety includes façades conforming to "passive house standards" in Vienna, the use of greenery and the application of parametrically constructed sun-shading elements in the Middle East. In all three cases, the sensible combination and integration of glass and opaque surfaces is important: natural light and open views continue to be essential, since they contribute to the level of comfort and quality of life.

Simulation and modelling technologies enable a

1990er Jahren am ILEK durchgeführt wurden. Der Ansatz der Adaptivität erfordert eine grundlegende Transformation der architektonischen Konzeption von Gebäuden: Es geht dabei nicht nur um die Entwicklung einzelner Komponenten, sondern auch um deren Einbindung in das Gesamtsystem. Auf dem Universitätscampus in Stuttgart-Vaihingen wurden deshalb ein 36,5 m hohes Gebäude errichtet, dass in den kommenden Jahren zum Testen unterschiedlicher Strategien und Technologien verwendet wird[4]. →171

Anhand dieses Versuchsgebäudes werden die Forschungen und Entwicklungen im Bereich adaptiver Tragstrukturen und Gebäudehüllen hinsichtlich ihrer Praxistauglichkeit getestet. Bei adaptiven Fassaden geht es darum, durch eine Manipulation der bauphysikalisch relevanten Fassadeneigenschaften dynamisch auf Einwirkungen wie Sonneneinstrahlung, Schall, Feuchte, etc. zu reagieren[5]. Im Komponentenbereich erweisen sich insbesondere Sandwichstrukturen mit aktivierten Elementen als vielversprechend; diese Strukturen wurden am Institut für Flugzeugbau (IFB) erforscht und werden zurzeit am ILEK für die Anwendung in Fassadenbau weiterentwickelt[6]. Es handelt sich dabei um sogenannte PALEOs (plastically annealed lamina emergent origami structures), welche die Steifigkeit eines flachen Halbzeuges derart verändern, dass ohne jegliche zusätzliche Bauteile oder Fertigungsschritte robuste Gelenke mit einstellbarer Rückstellung entstehen. Das Potential für die Integration dieser Technologie in textile Fassadensysteme soll in den kommenden Jahren erforscht werden. Textile Fassaden bieten eine sehr gute Basis für die Integration von verschiedenen Technologien und werden deshalb schon seit langem am ILEK erforscht[7].

Ein weiterer Fokus der Forschung im Bereich der adaptiven Gebäudehülle liegt auf thermischen Speichermöglichkeiten. Durch die im Leichtbau stark reduzierte Gebäudemasse wird nämlich die thermische Pufferwirkung des Gebäudes gegenüber Tag-Nacht-Schwankungen reduziert. Dieser Effekt kann durch adaptive Hüllelemente ausgeglichen werden. Das Potential dieses Ansatzes soll in den kommenden Jahren in Zusammenarbeit mit dem Institut für Technische Thermodynamik des DLR und dem Institut für Systemdynamik der Universität Stuttgart weiter untersucht werden.

Das im Rahmen des SFB 1244 realisierte Demonstrator-Hochhaus wird in den kommenden Jahren eine ideale Versuchsplattform bieten, um die oben genannten Ansätze und Technologien ebenso wie viele andere Innovationen zu testen und zu validieren. Auch die durch die Adaptivität steigende Interaktion zwischen Mensch und Gebäudehülle wird in die Validierungsphase einbezogen; es geht nämlich nicht nur um die technologische Qualität der entwickelten Lösungen, sondern auch um die soziokulturellen Akzeptanz neuartiger Technologien, die unsere gebaute Umwelt in den kommenden Jahrzehnten sicher entscheidend prägen werden.

precise assessment of the envisaged concepts and their consequences. It should be noted that such simulations are merely tools that do not replace the competence of planners and can only play a supporting role. The complex results of the simulations must be interpreted, plausibility-tested, critically observed and sensibly integrated into the design.

Adaptive façade technologies offer even greater resource efficiency and comfort levels, as confirmed by initial results from the University of Stuttgart's special research field CRC 1244, which was initiated by Werner Sobek. In the coming years, the experiment platform of the 36.5 metre adaptive Demonstrator Tower in Stuttgart will show the effects of adaptivity on our developed environment.

Zusammenfassung und Ausblick

Die im vorliegenden Beitrag präsentierten Projekte zeigen, wie unterschiedlich nachhaltige Fassadenlösungen sein können, die eine bewusste Ressourcenverwendung mit einem hohen Komfort kombinieren. Der Bogen spannt dabei von der Fassade im „Passivhausstandard" in Wien über den Einsatz von begrünten Bereichen bis zur Verwendung von parametrisch konstruierten Sonnenschutzelementen im Nahen Osten. Eine sinnvolle Kombination und Integration von Glas und opaken Flächen ist bei allen drei Beispielen wichtig: Auf natürliches Licht bzw. auf den freien Blick nach Außen soll hierbei nicht verzichtet werden, da dies Komfort und Lebensqualität bedeutet.

Simulations- und Modellierungstechnologien erlauben eine präzise Beurteilung der angedachten Konzepte und der aus ihnen resultierenden Konsequenzen. Dabei zu beachten ist, dass diese Simulationen lediglich Werkzeuge sind, die die Kompetenz des Planers nicht ersetzen, sondern nur unterstützend begleiten können. Die komplexen Ergebnisse der Simulationen müssen interpretiert, plausibilisiert, kritisch beobachtet und sinnstiftend in den Entwurf integriert werden.

Noch mehr Ressourceneffizienz und Komfort wird durch die Verwendung von adaptiven Fassadentechnologien ermöglicht. Dies bestätigen die ersten Ergebnisse des Sonderforschungsbereichs SFB 1244 der Universität Stuttgart, welcher von Werner Sobek initiiert wurde. Die Versuchsplattform des 36,5 hohen adaptiven Demonstrator-Hochhauses in Stuttgart wird in den kommenden Jahren zeigen, welche Auswirkungen die Adaptivität auf unsere gebaute Umwelt haben wird.

1
Sobek, W. (2016) "Ultraleichtbau/ Ultra-Lightweight Construction", GAM.12 Architecture Magazine. Basel: Birkhäuser, p. 156–167.

2
Blandini L., Grasmug W. (2018) "The search for dematerialized building envelopes – the role of glass and steel", Steel Construction 11 (2), Ernst & Sohn, Berlin, p. 140–145.

3
Haase, W. et al. (2017) "Adaptiv schaltbare Verglasungen – Übersicht ausgewählter Systeme", Glasbau 2017. (Weller, B., Tasche, S. (Eds.), Ernst & Sohn, Berlin, p. 1–15.

4
Weidner S. et al. (2018) "The implementation of adaptive elements into an experimental high-rise building", Steel Construction 11 (2), Ernst & Sohn, Berlin, p. 140–117.

5
Harder N. et al. (2019) "Bauphysikalische und ökologische Bewertung adaptiver Fassadenkonstruktion auf Raumebene", Bauphysik 41 (6), Ernst & Sohn, Berlin, p. 1–12.

6
Klett, Y. et al. (2017) "Potential of origami-based shell elements as next-generation envelope components", IEEE Int. Conf. on Advanced Intelligent Mechatronics.

7
Eisenbarth, C. et al. (2019) "Adaptive membrane façades", 14th International Conference on Advanced Building Skins, October 28-29, 2019, Bern.n.

1
Sobek, W. (2016) Ultraleichtbau/ Ultra-Lightweight Construction. In: GAM.12 Architecture Magazine. Basel: Birkhäuser, S. 156 – 167.

2
Blandini L., Grasmug W. (2018) The search for dematerialized building envelopes – the role of glass and steel, Steel Construction 11 (2), Ernst & Sohn, Berlin, S. 140–145.

3
Haase, W. et al. (2017) Adaptiv schaltbare Verglasungen – Übersicht ausgewählter Systeme. Glasbau 2017. (Hrsg. Weller, B., Tasche, S.), Ernst & Sohn, Berlin, S. 1–15.

4
Weidner S. et al. (2018) The implementation of adaptive elements into an experimental high-rise building. Steel Construction 11 (2), Ernst & Sohn, Berlin, S. 140–117.

5
Harder N. et al. (2019) Bauphysikalische und ökologische Bewertung adaptiver Fassadenkonstruktion auf Raumebene. Bauphysik 41 (6), Ernst & Sohn, Berlin, S. 1–12.

6
Klett, Y. et al. (2017) Potential of origami-based shell elements as next-generation envelope components. IEEE Int. Conf. on Advanced Intelligent Mechatronics.

7
Eisenbarth, C. et al (2019) Adaptive membrane façades, in 14th International Conference on Advanced Building Skins, October 28-29, 2019, Bern.

172
A future façade
material? Textile
envelope, design
by the Institute
for Lightweight
Structures and
Conceptual Design
(ILEK), Stuttgart
Fassadenmaterial
der Zukunft? Textile
Hülle, Entwurf
des Instituts für
Leichtbau Entwerfen
und Konstruktion
ILEK, Stuttgart

4.3 Laboratory identities

SUSANNE POHL + STEFANIE KLIEMT

Laboratory areas are as individual as the people who work in them. Thus, their determining factors are the processes, equipment and chemicals used, as well as human organisational, technical and structural aspects that influence the required quality of technical laboratory systems. However, relevant underlying principles that generally define the equipment are outlined below.

In addition to the following main groups, a large number of further types exist, such as filling laboratories with semi- or fully automatic filling systems for chemicals, IT laboratories, food labs (training kitchens, sensory labs), aquaristic laboratory areas for fresh and salt water organisms and laboratories for research in specific professional fields such as propaedeutics in dentistry. Often, strict differentiation between different types is difficult and laboratories develop as hybrid forms through interdisciplinary work between different fields. To ensure that all these concerns are taken into account, expert supervision by an experienced laboratory planner during all project stages is essential, ideally also during the assessment of requirements.

● **Laboratory identities are demonstrated using example projects by Nickl & Partner Architekten.**

4.3 Labor-Identitäten

SUSANNE POHL + STEFANIE KLIEMT

Laborbereiche sind so individuell, wie die Menschen, die in ihnen arbeiten. So bestimmen neben Verfahren, Equipments und eingesetzten Chemikalien auch human-organisatorische, technische und bauliche Einflussfaktoren, in welcher Qualität labortechnische Anlagen benötigt werden. Relevante Grundprinzipien, die aber in der Regel ausstattungsprägend sind, sollen im folgenden Beitrag behandelt werden.

Neben den hier vorgestellten Hauptgruppen gibt es viele weitere Typen wie zum Beispiel Abfülllabore mit teil- oder vollautomatisierten Abfüllanlagen für Chemikalien, IT-Labore, Lebensmittellabore (Lehrküchen, Sensoriklabore), aquaristische Laborbereiche für Süß-/Salzwasserlebewesen oder Labore zur Berufsfelderkundung wie zum Beispiel zahnärztliche Propädeutik. Häufig ist eine strenge Abgrenzung der Typen schwierig und Labore bilden dann hybride Mischformen aus interdisziplinär agierenden Bereichen ab. Um all diesen Belangen Rechnung zu tragen, ist eine fachkundige Begleitung des Projektes über alle Projektphasen und sinnvollerweise auch während der Bedarfsermittlung durch einen erfahrenen Laborplaner notwendig.

● Die Laboridentitäten werden mit Projektbeispielen von Nickl & Partner Architekten illustriert.

173

173
Hands-on mentality:
Laboratory area
with gloveboxes
at the Helmholtz
Institute Ulm
for Electrochemical
Energy Storage
Hands-on-Mentalität,
Laborbereich mit
Gloveboxen im
Helmholtz-Institut
Ulm für Elektro-
chemische
Energiespeicherung

Wet chemistry laboratories

These laboratories are usually characterised by classic laboratory elements such as laboratory sinks, tables and fume cupboards. The quality and any variability of the equipment and surfaces must be adapted to the applied wet chemistry process, also with respect to the design of the laboratory fume cupboards. In addition to tabletop fume cupboards, low-level and walkable fume cupboards are used depending on the size of the apparatus operated in the fume cupboards. Framing auxiliary functions such as laboratory areas for chemicals, pressurised gas cylinders and laboratory materials are synergetically integrated into the laboratory areas or defined as individual spaces. Special functional areas (such as hydrofluoric acid laboratories and weighing chambers) are often organised separately to provide the special spatial conditions and equipment they require. Wet chemistry teaching and educational laboratories often have very different infrastructures from wet chemistry research laboratories and must be considered separately, for instance to ensure the required overview for the teaching and supervision personnel. The building technology supplies to these areas and the structural quality of flooring, for example, should also be considered individually depending on the use.

● HIU Ulm

The Helmholtz Institute Ulm researches new methods of chemical energy storage.

Large spaces that can be partitioned as required into several labs are situated to the west at the façades of the forecourt and inner courtyards. The open structure makes it possible to react simply and flexibly to the individual requirements of future research groups.

The above-ground levels accommodate chemical and physical laboratories. These form a block that is surrounded by the associated offices. Special laboratories and building technology are situated on the basement level. → 174–177

Nasschemisch-präparative Labore

Diese Labore werden zumeist von bekannten klassischen Laborelementen wie Laborspülen, Labortischen und Laborabzügen geprägt. Die Qualität und etwaige Variabilität der Ausstattungen und Oberflächen muss den angewendeten nasschemischen Verfahren angepasst werden, ebenso wie die Ausgestaltung der Laborabzüge. Neben Tischabzügen kommen auch Tiefabzüge oder begehbare Abzüge zum Einsatz, je nach Bauartgröße der in den Laborabzügen betriebenen Apparaturen. Umrahmende Auxiliarbedarfe wie Lagerbereiche für Chemikalien, Druckgasflaschen oder Labormaterial werden in die Laborflächen synergetisch integriert oder als Einzelräume abgebildet. Sonderfunktionsflächen (zum Beispiel Flusssäurelabor, Wägeraum) erfahren häufig räumliche Ausgliederung, um den dort benötigten besonderen Raum- und Ausstattungsbedingungen Rechnung zu tragen. Nasschemische Lehr- oder Schülerlabore unterscheiden sich häufig infrastrukturell stark von nasschemischen Forschungslaboren und müssen zum Beispiel bezüglich der benötigten Übersicht für das Lehr- und Aufsichtspersonal gesondert betrachtet werden. Die haustechnische Versorgung der Bereiche und die bauliche Qualität von zum Beispiel Fußböden, ist ebenfalls nutzungsbezogen zu differenzieren.

● HIU Ulm

Im Helmholtz-Institut Ulm werden neue Wege der elektrochemischen Energiespeicherung erforscht.

An den Außen- und Innenhoffassaden im Westen liegen Großräume, die nach Bedarf in mehrere Labore unterteilt werden können. Die offene Struktur ist in der Lage, mit geringem Aufwand auf die individuellen Anforderungen künftiger Forschergruppen flexibel zu reagieren.

In den oberirdischen Geschossen sind chemische und physikalische Labore untergebracht. Diese bilden einen Block, der von den zugehörigen Büros umfasst wird. Im Untergeschoss befinden sich Speziallabore und die Gebäudetechnik. → 174–177

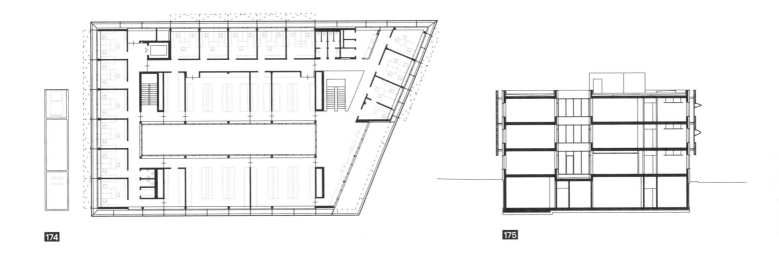

174

175

176

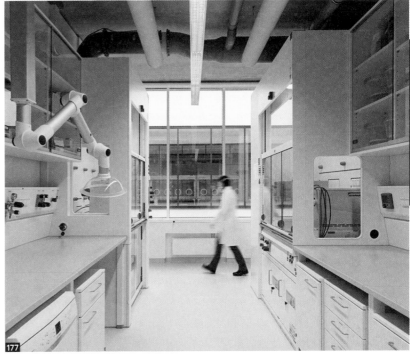

177

Biology and / or genetic laboratories

The quality of equipment for biology and/or genetic laboratories strongly depends on their categorisation. Such laboratory areas are classed in four protection or safety levels (from S1 laboratory to S4 laboratory), depending on the biological or genetic hazard potential in accordance with Bio-StoffV/GenTSV. Up to level 2, disinfection sinks, laboratory tables and microbiological safety workbenches characterise the laboratory environment, which are framed by device functions such as centrifuging, refrigeration, autoclaving/media production or washing kitchens. Often, special laboratory areas, for instance for cell culturing or histology, are located apart from these standardised laboratory structures, in order to prevent contamination issues. With respect to the required easy cleaning and disinfection, additional facings for the technical laboratory facilities, structural suspended ceilings or security gates can already be relevant to safety level 2. It is advisable to involve the responsible authorities at an early stage during the planning process, in order to discuss their requirements and integrate these into the planning steps. Laboratory areas in higher safety levels have much stricter requirements with respect to equipment, in-house technology and the building itself. In addition to access to security gates for personnel and materials, themes such as structural tightness, multi-level technical security systems, for instance for the ventilation or wastewater handling, and special personal protective equipment (PPE), such as a closed protective coverall with an external air supply, should be taken into account.

● CSD München

The Centre for Stroke and Dementia Research on the campus of the Clinic of the Ludwig Maximilian University Munich in Großhadern accommodates the partner institutes of the National Centre for Neurodegenerative Diseases and the Institute for Stroke and Dementia Research under a single roof. The aim is to apply an integrative research approach to achieve the direct exchange of information in the field of underlying and applied research. The square building is organised around a large inner courtyard. Communicative, open laboratory landscapes offer flexible conditions for research, as well as space for people to interact. Areas for offices, communication and central functional elements are pooled in the north and south. → 178-181

Biologische und/oder gentechnische Labore

Die Ausstattungsqualität biologischer und/oder gentechnischer Labore ist stark von deren Einstufung abhängig. Derartige Laborbereiche sind in vier Schutz- oder Sicherheitsstufen (S1-Labor bis S4-Labor) abhängig vom biologischen oder gentechnischen Gefährdungspotenzial nach BioStoffV/GenTSV einzuteilen. Bis zur Stufe 2 prägen Desinfektionslaborspülen, Labortische oder mikrobiologische Sicherheitswerkbänke die Laborwelt, welche von Gerätefunktionen wie Inkubation, Zentrifugation, Kühlen/Gefrieren, Autoklavieren/Medienherstellung oder Spülküchen umrahmt werden. Häufig werden besondere Laborflächen wie Zellkultur oder Histologie von diesen standardisierten Laborstrukturen ausgegliedert, um Kontaminationsthematiken auszuschließen. Bezüglich der erforderlichen leichten Reinigung und Desinfektion können bereits bei Stufe 2 zusätzliche Verblendungen an den labortechnischen Anlagen, bauliche Unterhangdecken oder Zugangsschleusen relevant werden. Es empfiehlt sich hier im Planungsprozess eine frühzeitige Einbindung der zuständigen Behörden, um deren Anforderungen zu dialogisieren und in den Planungsprozess einzutragen. Laborbereiche in höheren Stufen haben deutlich strengere Anforderungen an Ausstattung, Haustechnik und Bau. Neben Zugängen über Schleusen für Personal bzw. Material müssen auch Themen der baulichen Dichtheit, mehrstufiger technischer Sicherheitssysteme, zum Beispiel der Lüftung oder Abwasserbehandlung, und gesonderter persönlicher Schutzausrüstung (PSA), wie etwa geschlossener Vollschutzanzug mit externer Luftzufuhr bei S4-Laboren, beachtet werden.

● CSD München

Das Centrum für Schlaganfall- und Demenzforschung auf dem Campus des Klinikums der Ludwig-Maximilian-Universität München in Großhadern beherbergt das Partnerinstitut des nationalen Zentrums für Neurodegenerative Erkrankungen und das Institut für Schlaganfall- und Demenzforschung unter einem Dach. Ziel ist es, durch einen integrativen Forschungsansatz einen direkten Austausch von grundlagen- und anwendungsorientierter Forschung zu erreichen. Der quadratische Baukörper ist um einen großzügigen Innenhof organisiert. Kommunikative, offene Laborlandschaften bieten flexible Bedingungen für die Forschung und Raum für Austausch. Bereiche für Büros, Kommunikations- und zentrale Funktionsflächen sind im Norden und Süden zusammengefasst. → 178-181

178–179
Centre for Stroke
and Dementia
Research (CSD) at
the LMU Klinikum
München, Nickl &
Partner Architekten,
2014

Centrum für
Schlaganfall- und
Demenzforschung
(CSD) des LMU
Klinikums München,
Querschnitt und
Grundriss
Laborgeschoss, Nickl
& Partner
Architekten, 2014

180–181
Standard laboratory
and analysis area,
CSD München
Standardlabor und
Auswertebereich des
CSD München

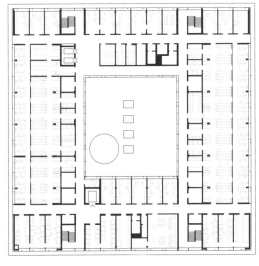

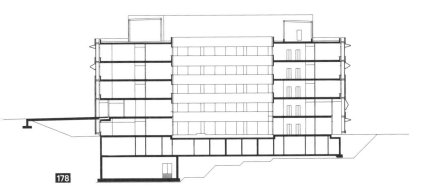

178

179

180

181

182 – 183
HARBOR research
building, ground-
floor sectional view
and plan, Campus
Bahrenfeld, University
of Hamburg,
Nickl & Partner
Architekten, 2020

Forschungsgebäude
HARBOR, Quer-
schnitt und Grundriss
Erdgeschoss,
Campus Bahrenfeld,
Universität Hamburg,
Nickl & Partner
Architekten, 2020

184
Optical laboratory,
HARBOR Hamburg–
Optisches Labor,
HARBOR Hamburg

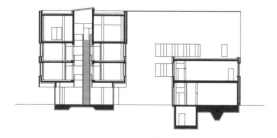

182

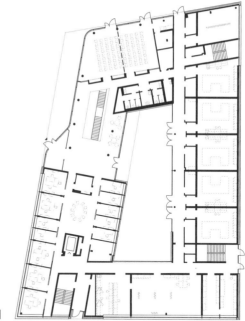

183

184

Physics laboratories / Optics laboratory

These laboratories often no longer have typical lab structures and are dominated by high demands with respect to air-conditioning systems such as temperature and humidity stability, as well as laminar airflow and structural requirements e. g. low vibrations. A system of available media pools has proved to be beneficial for the experiment structures placed in such laboratories (laser tables, optics tables, high-temperature furnaces etc.). Sensibly arranged media pools in such laboratories provide all connections needed by the infrastructure (power, technical gases/high purity gas, helium recirculation, aqueous media, wastewater) from a single source, allowing the users to connect the machinery, which often has large dimensions, in a flexible way. Power rails further enhance flexibility. Depending on the risk assessment or the required standardisation, hand sanitising facilities or individual laboratory extractors and security cupboards for pressurised gas cylinders must be added to the laboratory landscape.

● HARBOR Hamburg

Interdisciplinary teams from the fields of nanophysics, chemistry and structural biology work together at the Hamburg Advanced Research Centre for Bioorganic Chemistry.

The labs for experimental physics on the ground floor are largely used for experiments with light and are equipped with highly sensitive measuring systems, such as the super-resolution microscope (SIM/STED). Thus they are planned without windows and some have reduced vibration properties, while being partitioned from the building's mobility areas by means of a continuous security barrier. This allows the laboratory spaces to be used flexibly as large, connected areas that are completely detached from the required technical facilities. → 182–184

Physikalische Labore / Optische Labore

Derartige Labore weisen häufig keine typischen Labortischstrukturen mehr auf, sondern werden von hohen raumlufttechnischen Anorderungen, wie Temperatur- und Feuchtestabilität bzw. laminare Luftströmung und baulichen Anforderungen, zum Beispiel Schwingungsarmut dominiert. Für die in diesen Laboren platzierten Versuchsaufbauten (Lasertische, optische Tische, Hochtemperaturöfen etc.) hat sich ein System der Bereitstellung von Medienpools bewährt. An diesen im Labor sinnvoll angeordneten Medienpools werden alle infrastrukturell benötigten Anschlüsse (Stromversorgung, technische Gase/Reinstgas, Heliumrückführung, wässrige Medien, Abwasser) gebündelt bereitgestellt, so dass die häufig großen Gerätschaften der Nutzer flexibel angeschlossen werden können. Stromschienen in den Laboren tragen zu weiterer Flexibilität bei. Je nach Gefährdungsbeurteilung oder geforderter Standardisierung müssen Handwaschmöglichkeiten oder vereinzelt Laborabzüge bzw. Sicherheitsschränke für Druckgasflaschen der Laborlandschaft hinzugefügt werden.

● HARBOR Hamburg

Im Hamburg Advanced Research Centre for Bioorganic Chemistry arbeiten interdisziplinäre Teams der Nanophysik, Chemie und Strukturbiologie zusammen.

Die Labore der Experimentalphysik im Erdgeschoss werden großenteils für Experimente mit Licht genutzt und sind mit hochsensibler Messtechnik ausgestattet, etwa einem superauflösenden Mikroskop (SIM/STED). Sie sind daher sowohl fensterlos als auch teilweise schwingungsreduziert geplant und durch eine durchgängige Schleusenzone von den Verkehrsflächen des Gebäudes getrennt. Dadurch können die Laborräume völlig frei von den notwendigen Technikflächen flexibel als große, zusammenhängende Flächen genutzt werden. → 182–184

Technical laboratories /
Scale-up / Testing halls

These laboratory areas serve to apply scientific insight previously gained on a small scale to larger pilot or scale-up facilities. Special areas for setting up equipment are especially required for these usually larger spaces, around which the remaining laboratory structure is arranged. In addition to extractor booths (which can, if necessary, be explosion proof or include integrated fire extinguishers), testing halls can provide suitable spaces to set up such experiment facilities. Laboratory sinks and tables, often combined with workbenches, can supplement the laboratory landscape for preparatory and follow-up activities.

● Process innovation in Bayreuth

Researchers at the Fraunhofer Project Group for Process Innovation in Bayreuth develop and test methods, components and devices, as well as entire machines and systems, in the fields of automotive systems, mechanics, system construction, electronics, microsystems technology, energy, medicine, biotechnology and the process industry. The engineering areas are conceived as column-free as possible to ensure maximum flexibility for future developments. The hall and the office wing organised above it are combined to form an L-shaped building.

To highlight the special nature of the building's interior, the technical centre is as transparent as possible towards the street. Warehouse and technical areas are accommodated in the more closed eastern section. → 185–187

Technische Labore /
Scale-up / Versuchshallen

Diese Laborflächen dienen dem Übertragen von vorher im Kleinmaßstab erworbenen wissenschaftlichen Erkenntnissen auf größere Pilot- oder Scale-up Anlagen. Für diese Anlagen mit zumeist größerer räumlicher Ausdehnung werden besondere Aufstellbereiche benötigt, an denen sich dann die restliche Laborstruktur angliedert. Neben Absaugkabinen (ggf. Ex-geschützt oder mit integrierten Feuerlöschanlagen) schaffen auch Versuchshallen geeignete Aufstellbedingungen für derartige Versuchsanlagen. Für Vor- und Nachbereitungstätigkeiten ergänzen Laborspülen, Labortische oder auch häufig Werkbänke die Laborlandschaft.

● Prozessinnovation Bayreuth

Die Forscherinnen und Forscher der Fraunhofer-Projektgruppe Prozessinnovation in Bayreuth entwickeln und erproben Methoden, Komponenten und Geräte bis hin zu kompletten Maschinen und Anlagen der Branchen Automotive, Maschinen- und Anlagenbau, Elektronik und Mikrosystemtechnik, Energie, Medizin- und Biotechnik und Prozessindustrie. Die Technikflächen sind als stützenfreie Halle konzipiert, die größtmögliche Flexibilität für zukünftige Entwicklungen bietet. Halle und darüber angeordneter Büroriegel verbinden sich zu einem L-förmigen Baukörper.

Zur Straße ist das Technikum so transparent wie möglich gestaltet, um das besondere Innenleben des Gebäudes erlebbar zu machen. Im geschlosseneren östlichen Bereich schließen sich Lager- und Technikflächen an. → 185–187

185–186
Technical centre,
Fraunhofer Project
Group for Process
Innovation, sectional
view and ground
floor plan, Bayreuth,
Nickl & Partner
Architekten, 2015

Technikum der
Fraunhofer-
Projektgruppe
Prozessinnovation,
Querschnitt
und Grundriss
Erdgeschoss,
Bayreuth,
Nickl & Partner
Architekten, 2015

187
Exterior view of the
technical centre hall
Außenansicht der
Technikumshalle

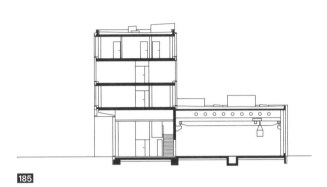

185

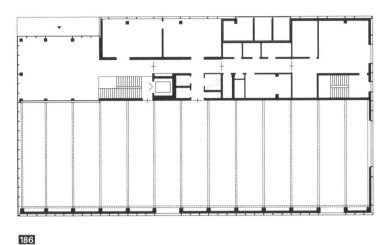

186

187

Basement floor plan,
GMP lab, BSS
research building,
ETH Zurich in Basel,
Nickl & Partner
Architekten, 2022

Grundriss des
GMP-Labors im
Untergeschoss des
BSS-Forschungsge-
bäudes der ETH
Zürich in Basel, Nickl
& Partner
Architekten, 2022

Control system
and security zone,
GMP lab, BSS
research building
Kontrollsystem und
Schleusenbereich
des GMP-Labors,
BSS-Forschungs-
gebäude

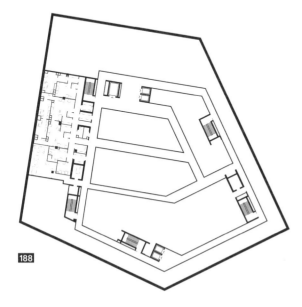

188

189

GMP laboratories

"Good Manufacturing Practices" laboratories, or GMP labs, must be designed according to the required classification (A to D in accordance with the EU GMP guidelines) for user certification. This in turn requires a precise URS (User Requirements Specification), supervision by a GMP consultant and, during the process of planning and implementation, the relevant qualification steps of Design Qualification (DQ), Installation Qualification (IQ), Functional Qualification or Operational Qualification (OQ) and Performance Qualification (PQ). GMP laboratories often contain a very selective stock of instruments (such as isolators, refrigerators and incubators) with a system of framing tables and a media infrastructure inserted into the enveloping cleanroom wall. Personnel and material security gates provide access to GMP areas. Intelligent measuring, controlling and adjusting systems in GMP areas ensure efficient interaction between the required technical components.

● BSS Basel

The new GMP Facility at the ETH Department of Biosystems (DBSSE) on the Schällemätteli Campus is used to produce materials for clinical trials. A broad range of potential products is envisaged, including cell therapy products, vaccines, viral vectors for gene therapy, protein-based biologicals, medical devices and artificially produced tissues.

The GMP Facility comprises three areas, each consisting of a C and a B suite and accessed via separate personal and material security barriers.

Two personal security barriers, separated by gender, lead to a Class D clean-room corridor, from where all three C and B areas area accessed. The corridor leads to the Quality Control Lab, the preparatory area and storage areas. → 188-190

GMP-Labore

„Good Manufacturing Practices"-Labore, kurz GMP-Labore, müssen entsprechend der nutzerseitig benötigten Klassifizierung A bis D gemäß EG-GMP-Leitfaden ausgestaltet werden. Dazu bedarf es einer präzisen nutzerseitigen URS (User Requirements Specification), der Begleitung eines GMP-Beraters und im Prozess der Planung und Realisierung der entsprechenden Qualifizierungsschritte Designqualifikation (DQ), Installationsqualifikation (IQ), funktionale Qualifikation oder „Operational Qualification" (OQ) und Leistungsqualifikation oder „Performance Qualification" (PQ). GMP-Labore beinhalten dabei häufig einen sehr ausgewählten Gerätepark (zum Beispiel Isolatoren, Kühlgeräte, Inkubatoren) mit umrahmenden Tischsystemen und einer in die umfassende Reinraumwand eingelassenen Medieninfrastruktur. Der Zugang zu GMP-Bereichen erfolgt über Personen- und Materialschleusen. Intelligente Mess-, Steuer- und Regelungstechniken sorgen in GMP-Bereichen für ein effizientes Zusammenspiel der erforderlichen technischen Komponenten.

● BSS Basel

Die neue GMP-Facility des ETH-Departement für Biosysteme DBSSE auf dem Campus Schällemätteli wird für die Herstellung von Materialien für klinische Versuche genutzt. Es ist eine breite Palette potenzieller Produkte vorgesehen, die von Zelltherapieprodukten, Impfstoffen, viralen Vektoren für Gentherapien, proteinbasierten Biologika und medizinischen Geräten bis hin zu künstlich hergestellten Geweben reicht.

Die GMP-Facility umfasst drei Bereiche, die jeweils aus einer C- und einer B-Suite bestehen und durch separate Personen- und Material-Schleusen erschlossen werden.

Zwei Personenschleusen, getrennt in männlich und weiblich, führen auf einen Korridor mit Reinraumklasse D, von dem alle drei C- und B-Bereiche erschlossen werden. Von diesem Korridor gehen das Quality Control Lab, der Vorbereitungsbereich sowie Lager ab. → 188-190

Cleanrooms

Clean- and ultra-clean rooms in the fields of optics and laser applications, as well as automotive and microelectronics, operate in so-called ISO Classes 1 to 9 in accordance with DIN EN ISO 14644. Like GMP areas, room-in-room solutions with cleanroom structures and access via personnel and material security gates are standard. Preassembled cleanroom tents or cleanroom cabins can be set up to supplement classic laboratory areas, if some of their space is subject to higher requirements with respect to lower concentrations of airborne particles. For instance Physical Vapour Deposition (PVD) and Chemical Vapour Deposition (CVD) systems can be found in clean- and ultra-clean rooms with equipment for thin-film technologies. They are flanked by systems such as wet processing facilities, cleanroom fume cupboards, additional laminar-flow units or process basins.

● IRIS Adlershof

The Integrative Research Institute for the Sciences IRIS Adlershof at the Humboldt-Universität zu Berlin researches transdisciplinary, innovative, hybrid materials and functional systems with hitherto unachievable optical, electronic, mechanical and chemical properties.

The new laboratory building is flanked by two existing structures. It covers four floors, of which three are aboveground, and accommodates all highly installed laboratories, clean-room areas and also one of the most modern transmission electron microscopes in Europe. The clean-room area is directly connected to the core of the IRIS combined lab, from where it is also visible. → 191–193

Reinräume

Rein- oder Reinsträume der Bereiche Optik- und Laseranwendungen, Automotive oder Mikroelektronik operieren in sogenannten ISO-Klassen 1 bis 9 nach DIN EN ISO 14644. Wie GMP-Bereiche sind auch hier Raum-in-Raum Lösungen mit Reinraumwandkonstruktionen und Zugängen über Personen- und Materialschleusen üblich. Vorkonfektionierte Reinraumzelte oder Reinraumkabinen können in klassischen Laborbereiche ergänzend zur Aufstellung kommen, wenn dort in Teilbereichen höhere Anforderungen an niedrigere Konzentrationen luftgetragener Teilchen bestehen. In Rein- oder Reinsträumen sind zum Beispiel Geräteausstattungen für Dünnschichttechnologien wie beispielsweise „Physical Vapour Deposition" (PVD)–Systeme und „Chemical Vapor Deposition" (CVD)–Systeme zu finden. Diese werden von Ausstattungen wie Nassprozess-Einrichtungen, Reinraumdigestorien, zusätzlichen Laminar-Flow Units oder Prozessbecken flankiert.

● IRIS Adlershof

Das Integrative Research Institute for the Sciences (IRIS) Adlershof der Humboldt-Universität zu Berlin erforscht fächerübergreifend neuartige hybride Materialien und Funktionssysteme mit bisher unzugänglichen optischen, elektronischen, mechanischen und chemischen Eigenschaften.

Der Laborneubau wurde zwischen zwei flankierenden Bestandsgebäuden platziert. Er erstreckt sich über vier Geschosse, von denen drei oberirdisch sind, und beinhaltet sämtliche hochinstallierte Labore, Reinraumbereiche sowie zusätzlich eines der modernsten Transmissionselektronenmikroskope Europas. Der Reinraumbereich schließt direkt an das Herzstück des IRIS – das Verbundlabor – an und ist von dort aus einsehbar. → 191–193

191–192
Integrative
Research Institute
of the Sciences
IRIS Adlershof,
Humboldt-Universität
zu Berlin, sectional
view and ground
floor plan,
Nickl & Partner
Architekten,
2020

Integrative
Research Institute
of the Sciences
IRIS Adlershof der
Humboldt-Universität
zu Berlin, Quer-
schnitt und Grundriss
Erdgeschoss,
Nickl & Partner
Architekten, 2020

193
View from the
clean-room area
into the connected
combined lab,
IRIS Adlershof
Blick vom Reinraum
in das Verbundlabor
des IRIS Adlershof

191

192

Isotope laboratories / Hotlabs

Laboratories where radioactive substances are handled are subject to regulations in accordance with Ordinance on protection against the harmful effects of ionizing radiation (StrlSchV), DIN 25425 and DIN 25422. Depending on the isotopes and processes used, as well as results for radiation protection or radiation-protection monitoring, equipment such as radionuclide fume cupboards with filter technology and shielding is required. Laboratory facilities must therefore often be constructed to cope with heavy loads to ensure they can safely support the required tabletop shielding systems. A pressure-stage concept for the air-conditioning systems, cooling plants for wastewater and monitoring systems to control contamination, as well as further measures (operative dosimeter systems), are additionally relevant to these areas and must be coordinated with the radiation protection officers and the responsible authorities at an early planning stage.

● Special case: Heavy-ion therapy facility HIT Heidelberg

The HIT at the University of Heidelberg accommodates the world's first 360°-rotatable radiation source for ions, a heavy-ion gantry weighing 600 tonnes, with a length of 25 metres and a diameter of 13 metres. Large parts of the radiation area are situated beneath 7 metres of earth, which are smoothly integrated into the existing topography in the form of a grass hill. It accommodates all the radiation systems with ion sources, a linear accelerator and a particle accelerator (synchrotron), where ions are produced and accelerated to around three quarters the speed of light, before reaching the patient.

The three radiation rooms are situated beside it. The entire radiation zone is shielded by 2.5-metre thick walls and ceilings made of reinforced concrete, into which 50 cm steel plates or ribs of reinforced concrete girders have been inserted. Access to this security zone is limited. → 194–196

Isotopenlabore / Hotlab

Labore, in denen mit radioaktiven Stoffen umgegangen wird, unterliegen zusätzlich den Anforderungen der Verordnung zum Schutz vor der schädlichen Wirkung ionisierender Strahlung (StrlSchV), DIN 25425 und DIN 25422. Je nach eingesetzten Isotopen und Verfahren und den daraus resultierenden Ergebnissen zum Strahlenschutz bzw. zur Strahlenschutzüberwachung werden Ausstattungen wie Radionuklidabzüge mit Filtertechnik und Abschirmungen notwendig. Laboreinrichtungen müssen daher häufig in Schwerlastausführung ausgebildet werden, um die erforderlichen Tabletop-Abschirmsysteme sicher tragen zu können. Ein Druckstufenkonzept für die RLT-Anlagen, Abklinganlagen für Abwässer und Überwachungssysteme zur Kontaminationskontrolle sowie weitere Maßnahmen (betriebliche Dosimetriesysteme) sind für diese Bereiche zusätzlich relevant und mit dem Strahlenschutzverantwortlichen und den zuständigen Behörden bereits in frühen Planungsphasen abzustimmen.

● Sonderfall Schwerionen-Therapieanlage HIT Heidelberg

Das Heidelberger Ionenstrahl-Therapiezentrum (HIT) der Universität Heidelberg beherbergt die weltweit erste um 360° rotierbare Bestrahlungsquelle für Ionen, eine 600 Tonnen schwere, 25 m lange und im Durchmesser 13 m große Schwerionen-Gantry. Große Teile des Bestrahlungsbereiches liegen unter einer bis zu 7 m hohen Erdschicht, die als Grashügel fließend in die bestehende Landschaft übergeht. Hier befindet sich die gesamte Bestrahlungstechnik mit Ionenquelle, Linearbeschleuniger und Teilchenbeschleuniger (Synchrotron), in denen die Ionen erzeugt und auf etwa drei Viertel der Lichtgeschwindigkeit beschleunigt werden, bevor sie den Patienten erreichen.

Daran angrenzend liegen die drei Bestrahlungsräume. Der gesamte Bestrahlungsbereich ist aus Gründen des Strahlenschutzes mit bis zu 2,50 m dicken Wänden und Decken aus Stahlbeton umgeben, in die 50 cm dicke Stahlplatten oder Rippen von Stahlbetonunterzügen eingelassen wurden. Er ist zugangsbeschränkt und als Sicherheitsbereich ausgewiesen. → 194–196

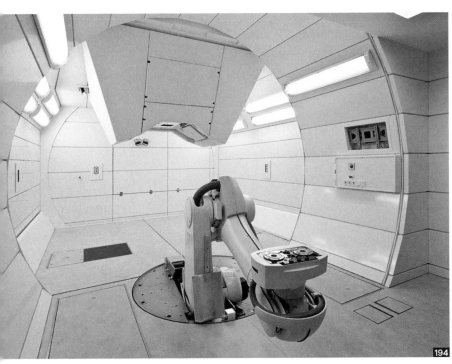

194-196
Heidelberg
ion-radiation
therapy centre HIT,
University of
Heidelberg,
Nickl & Partner
Architekten, 2009
Heidelberger
Ionenstrahl-
Therapiezentrum HIT
der Universität
Heidelberg,
Nickl & Partner
Architekten, 2009

194
Gantry
radiation zone
Gantry-
Bestrahlplatz

195
Control room,
radiation units,
HIT Heidelberg
Kontrollraum
Bestrahlplätze,
HIT Heidelberg

196
HIT gantry
Gantry-HIT

Fab labs / Workshops

For mainly mechanical applications, workshops or fab lab areas supplement classic laboratory landscapes. The transition to the definition of "laboratory" is often fluent in such cases and must be verified with a hazard assessment with respect to the required infrastructure measures and equipment. These rooms contain workbenches, as well as soldering and welding areas with fume extractors and much more. Fab labs are also used for developing ideas and collaborative processes, so they have special demands to accommodate creative tasks.

● IFBW Wolfsburg

The heart of the Institute for Vehicle Construction Wolfsburg is formed by a building-high experiment hall with an integrated drop tower, wind tunnel, four-wheel testing unit and other testing facilities. All associated laboratories and auxiliary rooms are grouped around them.

To achieve a high level of transparency and encourage communication between employees, visual references have been created between the upper levels and the experiment hall.

The hall is equipped with cranes required for operations and receives natural light from the roof. Workshop modules can be flexibly arranged in the hall. Labs, offices, a seminar room and the Virtual Reality Pool are accommodated on the two upper levels. → 197–199

Makerspace / Werkstatt

Für überwiegend mechanische Anwendungen ergänzen Werkstätten oder Makerspacebereiche häufig klassische Laborlandschaften. Der Übergang zur Definition „Labor" ist hier häufig fließend und mit einer Gefährdungsbeurteilung hinsichtlich der benötigten Infrastrukturmaßnahmen und Ausstattungen zu verifizieren. In diesen Räumen finden Werkbänke, aber auch abgesaugte Lötbereiche oder Schweißbereiche und vieles mehr ihre Platzierung. Makerspaceräume sollen außerdem der Ideenfindung dienen und kollaborative Prozesse fördern und haben daher besondere Anforderungen an eine kreative Arbeitsumgebung.

● IFBW Wolfsburg

Das Herzstück des Instituts für Fahrzeugbau Wolfsburg bildet die gebäudehohe Versuchshalle mit integriertem Fallturm, Windkanal, Allradrollenprüfstand und weiteren Prüfständen. Alle dazugehörigen Labore und Dienstzimmer sind um sie herum gruppiert.

Um viel Transparenz zu schaffen und die Kommunikation unter den Mitarbeitern und Studierenden zu fördern, bestehen von den Obergeschossen Blickbezüge in die Versuchshalle.

Diese ist mit den betriebsnotwendigen Kränen ausgestattet und wird über das Dach tagesbelichtet. Innerhalb der Halle können die Werkstattmodule flexibel angeordnet werden. In den beiden Obergeschossen sind Labore, Diensträume, sowie der Seminarraum und der Virtual Reality Pool untergebracht. → 197–199

197–198
Laboratory for
vehicle systems,
IFBW, Ostfalia,
longitudinal
section and
ground floor plan,
Wolfsburg,
Nickl & Partner
Architekten,
2017

Labor für Fahr-
zeugtechnik IFBW,
Ostfalia Hochschule,
Längsschnitt
und Grundriss
Erdgeschoss,
Wolfsburg,
Nickl & Partner
Architekten, 2017

199
Experiment hall,
IFBW Wolfsburg
Blick in die
Versuchshalle des
IFBW Wolfsburg

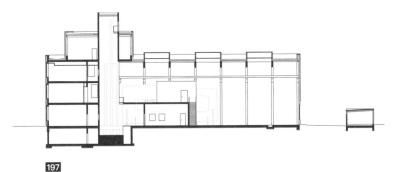

197

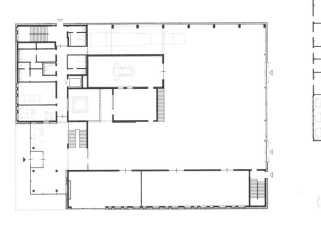

198

199

200–201
Clinical Research
Center CRC,
Hanover, longitudinal
section and first
floor plan,
Nickl & Partner
Architekten, 2014
Clinical Research
Center CRC
Hannover
Längsschnitt und
Grundriss
1. Obergeschoss,
Nickl & Partner
Architekten, 2014

202
Hotel-like test
subject area
Probandenbereich
mit Hotelcharakter

200

201

202

Clinical trial laboratories

Clinical trial laboratories or laboratory-type treatment rooms operate on the system boundary between classic laboratories and medical operations (doctor's practice). In such areas, which are mostly adjacent to public areas of research-laboratory buildings, test persons are allowed to enter and participate in trials and examinations under scientific supervision. The diversity of such examinations is great and tailored towards the profile of the respective field of research. In addition to assessments of cognitive skills, other psychological and physiological performance tests (hearing tests, sight tests, gait analyses and much more) are possible. The technical demands of such areas are significantly lower compared to regular laboratory areas, since generally, no hazardous substances are handled there. Nevertheless, hygienic standards exist in such facilities since the test persons are treated in a similar way to patients in clinics. Thus, small laboratory rows with lab sinks and hand-washing facilities, as well as laboratory bench systems, are standard in such areas.

● CRC Hanover

The Clinical Reasearch Center Hanover combines laboratories, outpatient facilities and test subject accommodation with medical technology centres, magnetic resonance tomography and a highly modern biobank under a single roof. Three research facilities focus on early clinical studies and infection research.

Courtyards, atria and gardens form key themes of the new building. They provide corridors, rooms, waiting areas and gathering places with natural light, while offering leisure and retreat areas for test subjects. Test subjects are accommodated in isolation from the outside world. The quality of stay should resemble that of a hotel. In this way, excellent research can be ensured while providing all-round support for test subjects, including a comfortable stay. → 200-202

Probandenlabore

Probandenlabore oder laborartige Behandlungsräume bewegen sich an der Systemgrenze zwischen klassischem Labor und medizinischem Betrieb (Arztpraxis). In derartigen Bereichen, welche in Forschungslaborgebäuden zumeist an der Grenze zum öffentlichen Bereich platziert werden, erhalten externe Probanden Zutritt und nehmen unter wissenschaftlicher Aufsicht an Studien und Untersuchungen teil. Die Untersuchungsvielfalt ist hierbei mannigfaltig und auf das Profil des jeweiligen Forschungszweiges ausgelegt. Neben Begutachtungen kognitiver Fähigkeiten können auch psychologische und physiologische Leistungstests (Hörtests, Sehtests, Ganganalysen und vieles mehr) möglich sein. Die technischen Anforderungen an derartige Bereiche sind im Vergleich zu regulären Laborbereichen deutlich reduziert, da zumeist kein Umgang mit Gefahrstoffen vorgesehen ist. Dennoch bestehen auch hier hygienische Anforderungen durch den klinikähnlichen Umgang mit den Probanden und daher sind kleinere Laborzeilen mit Laborspülen oder Handwaschmöglichkeiten und Labortischsysteme in diesem Räumen Standard.

● CRC Hannover

Das Clinical Reasearch Center Hannover vereint Labore, Ambulanzbereiche und Probandenunterkünfte, Medizintechnik Magnetresonanztomographen und eine hochmoderne Biobank unter einem Dach. Drei Forschungseinrichtungen befassen sich hier mit frühen klinischen Studien und Infektionsforschung.

Höfe, Atrien und Gärten bilden zentrale Themen des Neubaus. Sie versorgen Flure, Räume, Warte- und Aufenthaltsbereiche mit natürlichem Tageslicht und bieten den Probanden Freizeit- und Rückzugsmöglichkeiten. Die Probanden werden isoliert von der Außenwelt untergebracht. Die Aufenthaltsqualität soll sie an ein Hotel erinnern. So kann neben exzellenter Forschung eine „Rundum"-Versorgung mit hohem Wohnkomfort der Probanden sichergestellt werden. → 200-202

Laboratories in animal experiment facilities

Laboratories in animal-experiment facilities are often on the threshold between scientific operations and classic animal-experiment facilities. Since animal management often requires high hygiene standards, for instance an SPF (specific pathogen-free) environment, their laboratory areas (for behavioural testing, animal operations and dissecting laboratories) are often located separately from the animal management area, also in terms of access. The research employees enter the laboratory areas via security gates, while the laboratory animals are also brought from their holds to the laboratory either via security gates or defined handover points. However, such one-way structures require intelligent systems to maintain the required pressure cascades, thereby ensuring that no contamination can enter the animal management areas. The research laboratories themselves are equipped with technical lab facilities that are subject to high hygiene demands. Such laboratory landscapes are characterised by stainless steel table systems, tailored dissection tables (some with formalin extraction), operating tables and examination devices (animal MRT). All surfaces have high durability requirements with respect to the use of disinfectants.

Labore innerhalb von Versuchstierhaltungen

Labore in Versuchstierhaltungen liegen häufig an der Schnittstelle zwischen wissenschaftlichem Betrieb und klassischer Versuchstierhaltung. Da an Tierhaltungen häufig hohe hygienische Anforderungen bestehen, zum Beispiel SPF (spezifisch pathogenfrei) werden die dort notwendigen Laborbereiche (Verhaltenstest, Tier-OP, Zuschnittlabore) häufig vom Tierhaltungsbereich auch erschließungstechnisch abgegrenzt. Die wissenschaftlichen Mitarbeiter betreten diese Laborbereiche über Personenschleusen und die zu untersuchenden Tiere werden über Schleusen oder definierte Übergabepunkte aus der Tierhaltung zugeführt. Eine derartige einbahnartige Strukturierung benötigt jedoch intelligente Systeme zur Haltung der benötigten Druckkaskaden, damit keine Kontaminationen in die Tierhaltungsbereiche eindringen können. Die wissenschaftlichen Labore selbst sind mit Labortechnischen Anlagen mit hohen hygienischen Anforderungen ausgestattet. Hier prägen Edelstahltischsysteme, Zuschnitttische (teilweise mit Formalinabsaugung), OP-Tische oder Untersuchungsgeräte (Tier-MRT) die Laborlandschaft. Alle Oberflächen haben hohe Anforderungen bezüglich der notwendigen Beständigkeit gegen Desinfektionsmittel.

203

203
Aquaria at the
animal testing centre
Aquarien in der
Versuchstierhaltung

215

ERWIN K. BAUER + KATHARINA HÖLZL

Intuitive signage

for all the senses

Intuitive Signaletik
für alle Sinne

When we need orientation, we look around. We check our field of vision, detect and filter information, estimate distances and, when outdoors, check the position of the sun to determine a cardinal direction. Or we take out our smartphones and open an app to find our position. In a world dominated by visual media, we use the most important of all senses, sight, most of all. However, it has long been clear that we need to combine all our senses to achieve good orientation. If our sight fails, we use hearing or touch all the more intensively. That is also the key to inclusive design, which gives people with reduced perception the chance to continue to live life independently and on equal terms.

Wenn wir uns orientieren wollen, sehen wir uns um. Wir suchen unser Blickfeld ab, erfassen und filtern Informationen, schätzen Entfernungen ab und checken im Freien die Ausrichtung der Sonne, um die Himmelsrichtung festzustellen. Oder wir nehmen unser Smartphone zur Hand und starten eine App, um unsere Position zu bestimmen. In einer Welt, die von visuellen Medien geprägt ist, nutzen wir den wichtigsten aller Sinne, unseren Sehsinn am stärksten. Doch längst ist klar, dass wir für eine gute Orientierung darauf angewiesen sind, alle Sinne zu kombinieren. Schwindet unsere Sehkraft, nutzen wir das Hören oder auch den Tastsinn intensiver. Das ist auch der Schlüssel zu inklusivem Design, das Menschen mit reduzierter Wahrnehmung weiterhin die Möglichkeit gibt, selbständig und gleichberechtigt am Leben teilzunehmen.

In his key psychological work "de anima", Aristotle classified our five senses hierarchically. In accordance with the general assumptions of antiquity, he allocated a dominant role to the remote sense of sight, followed by hearing, smell and the more intimate senses of taste and touch. Indeed, in our western, visually dominated world, the most important senses are sight, followed by hearing. According to a current survey, given the choice, people would rather do without smell, taste and touch compared to sight and hearing. However, that opinion might change if one personally experiences a loss of taste, for instance after contracting COVID-19. It has been shown that smell is the most important sense among specific Aboriginal tribes in Australia, who live as hunter-gatherers. They are able to describe scents much more specifically.

Although our brains use over 40 % of their mass for sight, a fixed evaluation of senses and therefore perception cannot be defined. Certainly, seeing and hearing are our primary tools for spatial orientation. That is also apparent in our language. The German language uses finely distinctive prepositions to describe the positions we adopt. We estimate distances and locate ourselves within our surroundings. Before, behind, over, beside, outer and inner, upper and lower, in between, above and below: we articulate precisely where we are in the space surrounding us. Some of these terms, such as before and after, also address the temporal dimension. They set us in motion. Time and space are therefore directly connected in language.

To navigate through spaces, we must be able to detect them. Our senses help us to perceive them and our language allows us to articulate them. Thus, orientation means being able to think spatially. We can describe spaces verbally, or imagine them in a mind map, a conceptual projection of a plan. In that personal map, each individual saves the specific features of the space that appear to be significant or memorable. That can be a striking colour, the echo of one's own voice, the tactile sensation of one's feet on the floor, the current temperature or a specific odour.

In practice, we also perceive our environment using several senses at the same time. We combine different dimensions to create an overall impression. If one of those senses only partially fails, we intuitively replace it with another. Blind people have above-average hearing or touching skills, thereby competently compensating for the lack of sight. They can navigate through spaces independently if those spaces are designed in a way that supports the senses of hearing and touch.

A fair society enables an autonomous, equally good life for all. For designers, that means focusing on special needs. User-centred design should also follow

Aristoteles reihte in seiner psychologischen Hauptschrift „de anima" unsere fünf Sinne hierarchisch. Entsprechend der allgemeinen Vorstellung der Antike räumte er dem Fernsinn Sehen eine dominante Rolle ein, gefolgt vom Gehör, dem Geruchssinn sowie den Nahsinnen Geschmack und Tasten. Tatsächlich nimmt in der westlichen, visuell geprägten Welt das Sehen die erste und das Hören die zweitwichtigste Stelle ein. Laut einer aktuellen Umfrage könnten Menschen entsprechend eher auf das Riechen, Schmecken oder Tasten verzichten, wenn sie die Wahl hätten. Erlebt man einen Geschmacksverlust persönlich, wie es etwa bei COVID-Patient:innen war, dürfte sich diese Einschätzung aber ändern. Bei bestimmten Naturvölkern in Australien, Jäger-und-Sammler-Kulturen, konnte man feststellen, dass das Riechen bei ihnen der zentralste Sinn ist. Sie konnten wahrgenommene Gerüche deutlich spezifischer beschreiben.

Auch wenn unser Gehirn über 40 % seiner Areale für das Sehen nutzt, kann eine festgeschriebene Wertung der Sinne und damit der Wahrnehmung nicht getroffen werden. Fest steht, dass Sehen und Hören uns vorrangig bei der räumlichen Orientierung helfen. Das lässt sich auch in unserer Sprache nachvollziehen. Im Deutschen beschreiben fein differenzierte Präpositionen unsere Position, die wir einnehmen. Wir schätzen Entfernungen ab und verorten uns in unserer Umgebung. Vor, hinter, über, neben, außer- inner-, ober- und unterhalb, dazwischen, darüber und darunter artikulieren präzise, wo wir uns im Raum befinden. Einige dieser Vorwörter wie davor und danach bilden zugleich die zeitliche Dimension ab, sie versetzen uns in Bewegung. Zeit und Raum sind damit in der Sprache unmittelbar verbunden.

Um durch Räume zu navigieren, müssen wir sie erfassen können. Unsere Sinne helfen uns bei der Wahrnehmung und unsere Sprache, das zu artikulieren. Orientierung bedeutet also, Räume denken zu können. Wir können sie verbal beschreiben, stellen sie uns auch als Mind Map vor – die gedankliche Projektion einer Karte. In dieser persönlichen Karte speichert jeder individuell jene Merkmale des Raumes ab, die ihm als signifikant und merkwürdig im besten Sinne auffallen. Das kann eine auffällige Farbe, der Hall der Stimme, das taktile „Fußgefühl" beim Betreten des Bodens, die aktuelle Temperatur oder auch ein spezieller Geruch sein.

In der Praxis nehmen wir unsere Umwelt zugleich mit mehreren Sinnen wahr. Wir kombinieren unterschiedliche Dimensionen zu einem Gesamteindruck. Fällt einer dieser Sinne auch nur zum Teil aus, ersetzen wir ihn intuitiv durch andere. Blinde Personen hören oder tasten überdurchschnittlich gut und kompensieren damit das fehlende Sehen souverän. Sie können selbständig durch Räume navigieren, wenn diese hör- und tastunterstützend gestaltet sind.

204
Back-lit branding and a scientific illustration of a haemoglobin molecule "marks" the new main entrance and the wall behind the reception of the Max Perutz Labs at the Vienna Biocenter, achieving a clear, emotional effect.
Hinterleuchtetes Branding und eine wissenschaftliche Illustration eines Hämoglobin-Moleküls „markiert" den neuen Haupteingang und die Wand hinter dem Empfangs der Max Perutz Labs am Vienna Biocenter klar und emotional.

205
A helpful tool to change designers' perspectives: glasses can simulate different kinds of visual limitations. They can be hired from associations for the blind and used to test the effect of designs on prototypes.
Ein hilfreiches Tool zum Perspektivenwechsel für Gestalter:innen: Brillen, die visuelle Einschränkungen unterschiedlicher Art simulieren. Man kann sie bei Blindenverbänden leihen und damit die Wirkung von Entwürfen an Prototypen selbst überprüfen.

the "design for all" logic: a solution that can be used equally well by everyone. In signage, that requires prudent planning according to the double- or triple-sense principle. If the "first" sense fails, a second or third sense must receive the information on equal terms: audio output and tactile elements replace the sense of sight, which cannot receive any information. However, not just blind people benefit from this design strategy. People with poor eyesight can use a high-contrast tactile guideline for navigation, without having to touch them. In that respect, it is doubly sensible in terms of design for all.

It is helpful for designers to occasionally wear a blindfold, sit in a wheelchair or integrate people with special needs into the design process as consultants. Such measures not only lead to better design, but are also rewarding human experiences that broaden personal horizons.

Visual design – Seeing

Some fundamental principles of signage help everyone to grasp information more quickly and clearly. In terms of content, the basic premise is reduced information that is clearly structured and therefore also provides an easy overview. Depending on the distance, the text's font, size and contrast are important aspects to ensure good legibility. The connotations of colours can be used to communicate more directly; for instance red can indicate danger. During the design process, it is smart to take limitations such as colour blindness into account. Back-lit carriers of information, for instance those often seen in airports, set themselves more strongly apart from their surroundings; it has been proven that people understand them more quickly. People with poor eyesight are also supported by contrasting colours for the walls and flooring, allowing them to judge the distances and dimensions of a space more easily. → 204–205

Auditive design – Hearing

Blind people use the audio output of their smartphones to help them navigate autonomously in a space. They gather information in advance before visiting a location. Thus, barrier-free prior information on websites, for instance in the form of acoustic descriptions of images or plans, are essential. Once at the location, classic digital tools such as touchscreens with audio output can be used, as is the case at the new campus of the Vienna University of Economics and Business. Info points can send signals with inductive audio loops for people with impaired hearing, which can be directly amplified through their hearing aids – allowing these people to understand the personnel at reception more easily. → 206–207

Eine faire Gesellschaft sichert ein selbstständiges, gleichberechtigt gutes Leben für alle. Für GestalterInnen bedeutet das, den Fokus auf besondere Bedürfnisse zu legen. User-centered-Design sollte zugleich der „Design-for-All-Logik" folgen: eine Lösung, die für alle gleich gut nutzbar ist. In der Signaletik entspricht dem eine umsichtige Planung nach dem 2- bis 3-Sinne-Prinzip. Versagt der „erste" Sinn, muss ein zweiter oder dritter Sinn gleichwertig mit Information versorgt werden: Audioausgabe und taktile Elemente ersetzen den Sehsinn, der keine Information aufnehmen kann. Doch nicht nur blinde Menschen profitieren von dieser Designstrategie. Sehschwache Personen können eine kontrastreiche taktile Leitlinie als visuelle Unterstützung für ihre Navigation nutzen, ohne sie ertasten zu müssen. Im Sinne des Design-for-All ist sie damit doppelt sinnvoll.

Für Gestalter:innen ist es hilfreich, von Zeit zu Zeit eine Augenbinde zu tragen, sich selbst in den Rollstuhl zu setzen oder Menschen mit besonderen Bedürfnissen als Ratgeber:innen in den Designprozess zu integrieren. Das führt nicht nur zu besserem Design, sondern ist auch eine menschliche Bereicherung, die den persönlichen Horizont erweitert.

Visuelle Gestaltung – Sehen

Einige Grundprinzipien in der Signaletik helfen allen, Informationen rascher und eindeutiger zu erfassen. Inhaltliche Grundlage sind reduzierte Informationen, die klar gegliedert und auch deshalb übersichtlich sind. Für die bessere Lesbarkeit sind Schriftwahl, -größe und Kontrast zu beachten, die auch auf die Entfernung abgestimmt sind. Farbe kann mit ihrer Bedeutung wie z.B. Rot als Hinweis für Gefahr Inhalte direkter vermitteln. Dabei ist es smart, in der Gestaltung auf Einschränkungen wie Farbenblindheit Rücksicht zu nehmen. Hinterleuchtete Informationsträger, wie wir sie von Flughäfen kennen, heben sich aus der Umgebung stärker ab und werden nachweislich schneller erfasst. Zusätzlich helfen sehschwachen Personen Maßnahmen wie unterschiedliche Farbgebung von Wand und Boden, Entfernungen und Dimensionen eines Raums besser abzuschätzen. → 204–205

Auditive Gestaltung – Hören

Blinde Menschen nutzen die Sprachausgabe ihres Smartphones zur Unterstützung für die selbständige Navigation im Raum. Sie informieren sich vorab, bevor sie einen Ort besuchen. Deshalb ist die barrierefreie Vorinformation wie etwa über akustische Bild- oder Planbeschreibungen auf Webseiten essenziell. Vor Ort lassen sich dann klassische digitale Tools oder Touchscreens mit Audioausgabe wie am neuen Campus der Wirtschaftsuniversität in Wien nutzen. Bei Infopoints können Signale für hörschwache Personen mit einer induktiven Hörschleife direkt über ihre Hörhilfe verstärkt werden – so verstehen sie Personen beim Empfang deutlich besser. → 206–207

206

206

206
Easy to use: When
users touch the
touchscreen, the text
is read out loud by
the screen reader.
Einfach zu bedienen:
Beim Berühren des
Touch Screens wird
der Text via
Screenreader
vorgelesen

207
Interactive
searching: It is easy
to search for rooms,
people and lectures
and find suitable
route descriptions,
also for blind people,
using the spoken
audio output.
Interaktive Suche:
Räume, Personen
oder Lectures
können einfach
gesucht mit
passender
Wegbeschreibung
gesucht werden,
auch für Blinde
Menschen via
Sprachausgabe

207

6.162
6.162

Projektraum
Project room

Mo 23. Apr 2013   14:40

Now

Grundlagen wissenschaftlichen Arbeitens – aus dem
Bereich Betriebswirtschaft
1064- Frank H.

Text

16:00–17:00 Angewandte sozioökonomische M... 2063
17:00–19:00 Erziehungswissenschaftliche Frag... 3172

rooms.wu.ac.at/LC/1/162

208

209

208
Although the norm for guidelines requires lines moving in perpendicular directions, the organic route of the Campus WU was well received by the Association of the Disabled as a new best-practice example.
Auch wenn die Norm für Leitlinien eine Linienführung im rechten Winkel vorsieht, wurde die Ausnahme des organischen Verlaufs am Campus WU als neues Best-Practice-Beispiel vom Behindertenverband positiv aufgenommen.

209
Tactile plans and inscriptions in tangible pyramid symbols and Braille script help blind people, as well as people with impaired vision, to navigate safely through the new new campus of the Vienna University of Economics and Business.
Taktile Pläne und Beschriftungen in tastbarer Pyramiden- und Brailleschrift helfen den Blinden und auch Seheingeschränkten, sicher durch den neuen Campus der Wirtschaftsuniversität zu navigieren.

Tactile design – Feeling

As soon as one enters a building, the switch from a hard to a soft floor surface helps one "sense" the space. Furthermore, tactile plans and touchable 3D models help blind people to imagine the structure and dimensions of a location. They reach their intended destinations by moving along tactile guidelines, touchable, marked handrails or structural elements which they can navigate using their white canes. The example of the campus of the Vienna University of Economics and Business shows how organic guidelines that are tailored to the architecture make the spatial experience of the outstanding architecture by Zaha Hadid directly tangible. → 208–209

(Multi-)Sensorial design – Smell, taste, feeling the temperature, sensing the draft, …

Although we do not primarily consider these other senses when planning a good orientation system, they have the potential to provide additional support. For instance we perceive a wide range of significant odours when we stroll through the city. Smells are most closely connected to our memories and therefore an important part of mind maps, which we charge with odours. A draft on exiting the underground or a change of temperature marks a new spatial zone that we can appreciate more clearly. For designers, it is decisive that these sensorial experiences are researched in concrete on site, to plan them spatially and consider ways of aiding orientation.

Taktile Gestaltung – Fühlen

Schon beim Betreten eines Gebäudes hilft etwa der Wechsel von einem harten zu einem weichen Bodenbelag beim „Spüren" des Raumes. Blinde werden darüber hinaus durch taktile Pläne oder tastbare 3D-Modelle bei der Vorstellung von Struktur und Dimension eines Ortes unterstützt. Ihre Ziele erreichen sie entlang taktiler Leitlinien, tastbar beschrifteter Handläufe oder baulicher Elemente, die sie mit ihrem Langstock als Führung nutzen. Das Beispiel am Campus der Wirtschaftsuniversität in Wien zeigt, wie organische, an die Architektur angepasste Leitlinien das Raumerlebnis der aussergewöhnlichen Architektur von Zaha Hadid für Blinde unmittelbar spürbar machen. → 208–209

(Multi)Sensorische Gestaltung – Riechen, Schmecken, Temperatur fühlen, Luftzug spüren, …

Auch wenn wir bei einem guten Orientierungssystem nicht in erster Linie an diese anderen Sinne denken, haben sie Potential, das man ergänzend nutzen kann. So nehmen wir vielfältige und signifikante Gerüche wahr, wenn wir etwa durch eine Stadt schlendern. Sie sind am stärksten mit unserer Erinnerung verknüpft und deshalb ein wichtiger Teil der Mind Maps, die wir damit aufladen. Auch ein Luftzug beim Ausgang der U-Bahn oder ein Temperaturwechsel markieren neue räumliche Zonen, die wir uns so besser merken können. Für Gestalter:innen ist es entscheidend, diese Sinneserfahrungen an Orten konkret zu recherchieren, sie räumlich einzuplanen und so als Unterstützung für die Orientierung mitzudenken.

5 Vision

⁵ Challenges & Opportunities

The constant and ongoing transformation in the field of constructing research buildings is outlined in this concluding outlook section. We have chosen a few questions that we find especially relevant with respect to opportunities the future offers.

How will science, research methods, teaching and learning change and what influence will that change have on knowledge-producing locations?

In this context, what will laboratories look like in the future? What research themes will change the construction sector, which is struggling with the challenges of massive resource shortages and climate neutrality? One common aspect that affects all these questions is the ubiquitous digitisation of processes. Thus, the following pages are filled with digital tools and data flows, as well as laboratory and construction robots, sensors and simulations.

5 Herausforderungen & Chancen

Der stetige Wandel, dem das Bauen von Forschungsgebäuden auch in Zukunft unterworfen sein wird, soll in diesem abschließenden Ausblick skizziert werden. Aus dem Möglichkeitsraum, den diese Zukunft vor uns aufspannt, haben wir einige Fragestellungen herausgegriffen, die uns besonders relevant erscheinen.

Wie verändert sich die Wissenschaft, wie verändern sich die Methoden des Forschens, Lehrens und Lernens, und welchen Einfluss haben diese Veränderungen auf die Orte der Wissensproduktion?

Wie sieht vor diesem Hintergrund das Labor der Zukunft aus? Und welche Forschungsthemen werden zukünftig das Bauen verändern, ein Sektor, der massiv mit den Problemen Ressourcenknappheit und Klimaneutralität zu kämpfen hat? Ein gemeinsamer Nenner, der sich unausweichlich als roter Faden durch diese Fragestellungen zieht, ist die allgegenwärtige Digitalisierung von Prozessen. Daher sind diese Seiten von digitalen Helfern und Datenströmen bevölkert, von Labor- und Baurobotern, von Sensoren und Simulationen.

5.1 Science futures

JÖRG RAINER NOENNIG

How digitalisation and the data paradigm will re-shape our places for learning, research and innovation

"Facts are plenty. What is missing – is fantasy."
W. Blochinzew "Some Questions regarding the development of modern physics" (1959)

1. Future science: Big data to knowledge

Big data
One of the most disruptive events in recent science history is the advent of digital technologies, especially the big data paradigm. High throughput devices, omics research and real-time monitoring have thoroughly changed scientific practices. From now, scientific work starts from ever-growing data sets, while it produces large data itself in turn. The current amount of data evidence raised is unprecedented in the history of science. This new condition will thoroughly alter the way how we create knowledge, and how scientific analysis and synthesis is carried out. In retrospect from a somewhat distant future, we will probably estimate the advent of big data as a paradigm shift in scientific thinking.

Scientific paradigms
There have always been key paradigms in science history, e.g. speculative discourse in the scholastic era, empirical observation in the early modern age, or engineering approaches in the industrial age. The science philosopher Thomas Kuhn has described how established paradigms become obsolete when there are serious discrepancies and misfits (incommensurabilities) in the scientific models and explanations, when their explicative power has been exhausted.[1] In such cases, any theory that could explain the matter at hand in a more satisfactory way would then replace the insufficient previous paradigm.

Paradigm shift
The big data paradigm replaces a scientific approach which commonly started from a specific problem statement ("What caused malaria?") and proceeding from there to modelling and hypothesizing potential explanations ("Mosquitos are transmitters").

5.1 Zukunft der Wissenschaft

JÖRG RAINER NOENNIG

Wie Digitalisierung und Datenparadigma unsere Lern-, Forschungs- und Innovationsstandorte verändern werden

„Fakten gibt es immer zur Genüge – was fehlt, ist Fantasie."
W. Blochinzew „Einige Fragen der Entwicklung der modernen Physik" (1959)

1. Zukunft der Wissenschaft: von Big Data zur Erkenntnis

Big Data
In der jüngeren Wissenschaftsgeschichte war das Aufkommen digitaler Technologien, insbesondere des Big Data-Paradigmas, das einschneidende Ereignis. Hochdurchsatzgeräte, „-omics"-Forschung und Echtzeit-Monitoring haben wissenschaftliches Arbeiten umfassend verändert. Sein Ausgangspunkt liegt nunmehr in stetig wachsenden Datensätzen, derweil die Forschung selber auch immer größere Mengen an Daten produziert. Der derzeitige Zuwachs an Datenevidenz ist ein in der Wissenschaftsgeschichte bisher beispielloser Vorgang. Diese neue Bedingung verändert die Art und Weise, wie wir Wissen schaffen und wissenschaftliche Analysen und Synthesen durchführen, grundlegend. Im Rückblick aus einer etwas ferneren Zukunft wird das Aufkommen von Big Data sich wahrscheinlich als Paradigmenwechsel im wissenschaftlichen Denken erweisen.

Wissenschaftliche Paradigmen
In der Geschichte der Wissenschaft hat es schon immer Schlüsselparadigmen gegeben – z.B. den spekulativen Diskurs der Scholastik, die empirische Beobachtung in der Frühen Neuzeit oder die ingenieurtechnischen Ansätze im Zeitalter der Industrialisierung. Der Wissenschaftsphilosoph Thomas Kuhn hat beschrieben, wie etablierte Paradigmen obsolet werden, wenn es zu ernsthaften Diskrepanzen und Fehlpassungen („Inkommensurabilität") in den wissenschaftlichen Modellen und Erklärungen kommt, wenn sich ihre erklärende Kraft erschöpft hat.[1] In solchen Fällen würde jede Theorie das unzureichende, vorhergehende Paradigma ersetzen, die in der Lage ist, die zur Debatte stehende Thematik besser zu erklären.

Paradigmenwechsel
Das Big Data-Paradigmas ersetzt einen wissenschaftlichen Ansatz, der üblicherweise von einer spezifischen Problemstellung ausgehend (Ursache von Malaria?) zur Modellbildung und Aufstellung von Hypothesen für mögliche Erklärungen (Moskitos als Überträger) führte. Daraufhin wurden Beweise durch empirische Datener-

Thereupon it eventually sought evidence by way of empirical data gathering (field study in malaria regions) and validated the assumed solution by experimental testing (clinical study). In short, this paradigm proceeded from problem to idea to data (Fig. 1). In this process, the logical activities of induction (generalising from individual samples) or deduction (specifying from general assumptions) were complemented by the process of abduction. Abduction is essentially the formulation of hypotheses on the basis of explorative thinking and scientific intuition.[2] Here, the scientist's mind creates assumptions, even though there may be no evidence for them yet. We state what we are looking for, but the challenge is to find the right data that confirm the hypothesis. → **210**

Data paradigm

By contrast, the new big data paradigm establishes a scientific practice that starts out from masses of data in order to create problem statements ("We have gathered 10 million urban data sets – now let's see!"). Here, pattern recognition technologies and algorithms search for significant correlations in large data sets which may deserve closer investigation ("There are 20 critical patterns that suggest the spread of diseases being related to garbage disposal spots."). This paradigm proceeds from data to problem statement ("Garbage disposal may affect urban health."). What the problem exactly is may not be known when the search itself begins. Here, scientific hypothesizing and synthetic conclusion turn into an unexpected challenge: we may have plenty of evidence, but no assumptions yet. That way the data paradigm puts an end to the explorative speculative thought, and replaces it with practically infinite experimentation. As it is hard to speculate on big data, a new immanence of research is being established – a condition which bears risk of turning into a scientific echo chamber, or a methodological bubble, in which only those issues can be investigated that are data-based, digitally registered and stored matter-of-fact.

New assistants

Intelligent assistants or AI bots have become indispensable in sectors like health, production, or education. But also in the scientific context, the overwhelming masses of data create a demand for new kinds of assistance. We need helper systems to gain scientific insight and draw conclusions, we need extended guidance, orientation and an overview of the vast information arena. Digital assistants will replace the various types of scientific assistants of the past – the laboratory helpers, technical staffs, secretaries and administrators.

hebung zu finden versucht (Feldstudie in Malariagebieten) und die vermutete Lösung durch experimentelle Erprobung validiert (klinische Studie). Kurz: dieses Paradigma verlief von der Problemstellung über die Ideen- und Hypothesenfindung hin zur Datengewinnung. In diesem Arbeitsverfahren wurden die logischen Aktivitäten der Induktion (Verallgemeinerung individueller Beispiele) oder Deduktion (Spezifizierung allgemeiner Annahmen) durch den Prozess der Abduktion ergänzt. Abduktion meint das Aufstellen von Hypothesen auf der Basis explorativen Denkens und wissenschaftlicher Intuition.[2] Dabei werden Annahmen formuliert, für die möglicherweise noch keine Beweise existieren. Es wird somit möglichst klar definiert, wonach gesucht wird – die Herausforderung bleibt jedoch, die formulierte Hypothese dann auch belegen. → **210**

Datenparadigma

In scharfem Kontrast zu diesem Vorgehen etabliert das neue Big Data-Paradigma eine wissenschaftliche Praxis, die Problemstellungen ausgehend von riesigen Datenmengen formuliert („Wir haben 10 Millionen Datensets zum Städtebau zusammengetragen – schauen wir mal!"). In diesen großen Datensätzen suchen Mustererkennungstechnologien und Algorithmen auffällige Korrelationen, welche eine nähere Untersuchung verdienen („Wir haben 20 kritische Muster, die einen Zusammenhang von Krankheitsausbreitung und der Lage von Mülldeponien vermuten lassen"). Bei diesem Paradigma sind die Daten der Ausgangspunkt, der zur Problemstellung führt („Müllentsorgung kann sich auf die Gesundheit im städtischen Umfeld auswirken"); das konkrete Problem aber ist zu Beginn der eigentlichen Recherche oft noch unklar. Unter diesen Bedingungen verwandeln sich wissenschaftliche Hypothesenentwicklung und synthetische Schlussfolgerung zu einer unerwarteten Herausforderung: wir verfügen vielleicht über einen Überfluss an Beweisen, haben jedoch keine Vermutung. Auf diese Weise zieht das Datenparadigma einen Schlussstrich unter das explorativ-spekulative Denken und ersetzt es mit praktisch unbegrenztem Experimentieren. Da Big Data nur wenig Raum für Spekulation zulässt, etabliert sich eine neue Immanenz von Wissenschaft – eine Gegebenheit, die das Risiko mit sich führt, eine wissenschaftliche Echokammer bzw. methodologische Blase zu etablieren, in der nur jene Fragestellungen erforscht werden, die digital erfasst, technischnüchtern und datenbasiert bearbeitbar sind.

Neue Assistenten

In Bereichen wie dem Gesundheitswesen, oder dem Bildungssektor sind intelligente Assistenten oder KI-Bots nicht mehr wegzudenken. Doch auch im wissenschaftlichen Kontext hat die überwältigende Menge an Daten den Bedarf für neue Arten von Assistenz geschaffen. Neben Helfersystemen zur Generierung

1
From problem to idea
Vom Problem zur Idee

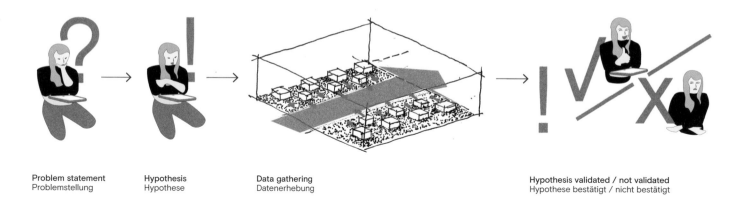

Problem statement
Problemstellung

Hypothesis
Hypothese

Data gathering
Datenerhebung

Hypothesis validated / not validated
Hypothese bestätigt / nicht bestätigt

2
Data paradigm
Datenparadigma

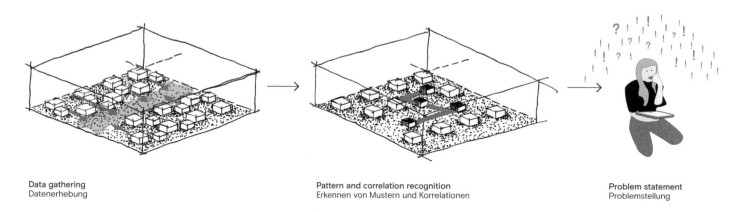

Data gathering
Datenerhebung

Pattern and correlation recognition
Erkennen von Mustern und Korrelationen

Problem statement
Problemstellung

210
**Paradigm shift
of scientific
approaches
towards big data**
Paradigmenwechsel
wissenschaftlicher
Ansätze hin
zu Big Data

In view of the speculative deficit of data-driven research, as described above, we may even need "creative bots" or inspiration machines that help us generate hypotheses, or are able to create hypotheses even on their own.[3]

New intelligences

Not only in the scientific context, natural intelligences and human creativity will be accompanied by several new forms of knowledge, triggered by digital technologies and data-driven methodologies. Artificial intelligence, machine learning and neural network algorithms will enable us to see clearly through large sets of data and make sense of them (given that we are able to train those algorithms properly). They may not only provide help in detecting correlational patterns, but also effectively assist higher-level synthetic activities such as ideation. Furthermore, there will be forms of intelligence that digitally connect large groups and collectives to involve them in research tasks, while broadening the roster of scientific work (citizen science, co-innovation, crowdsourcing). As we are pulling together these natural, artificial, individual, collective forms of knowledge into a hybrid form of intelligence, we need to explore and validate its reliability and validity turn – which in itself becomes a new scientific challenge.

Human-machine interaction

In any case, we will need to learn how to interact and cooperate with these new intelligences and knowledge support systems. Research in Human-Machine Interaction (HMI) investigates the vast array of new technological and intellectual opportunities – which in most cases also have implications for the immediate spatial environment on all scales and levels. New interfaces and interactions (gesture, touch, language) induce new physical and psychological behaviour of individuals as well as of collectives. The following paragraphs outline how future science environments may accommodate such interactions – from the workplace to the city level.

2. Future workplace: The cognitive cockpit

Data interaction

In the near future, researchers will physically interact with large quantities of information in their spatial nearfield; they will work in environments richly augmented with "live" data. The immediate workplace will become a scientific instrument in itself: a spatial device that helps researchers to explore and understand data, provides inspiration and creates insight. However, that is a long way down the line, although certain

wissenschaftlicher Erkenntnis und Schlussfolgerungen, benötigen wir vor allem effektive Anleitung, Orientierung und Überblick in der Weite der Informationslandschaften. Digitale Assistenten werden die unterschiedlichen Arten wissenschaftlicher Assistenz in der Vergangenheit ersetzen – die Laborhelfer, das technische Personal, die Sekretäre und Administratoren. Angesichts des oben beschriebenen spekulativen Defizits datengestützter Forschung, brauchen wir möglicherweise kreative „Bots" oder „inspiration machines", die uns beim Erstellen von Hypothesen behilflich sind – oder die sogar in der Lage sind, auch ohne uns eigene Hypothesen aufzustellen.[3]

Neue Intelligenzen

Nicht nur im wissenschaftlichen Kontext werden, ausgelöst durch Digitaltechnologien und datengetriebene Methodologien, natürliche Intelligenzen und menschliche Kreativität von verschiedenen neuen Intelligenzen flankiert werden. Maschinelles Lernen und neuronale Netzwerkalgorithmen werden uns ermöglichen, den Überblick über große Datensets zu behalten und aus ihnen kluge Ableitungen zu treffen (vorausgesetzt, dass wir in der Lage sind, diese Algorithmen zweckmäßig zu trainieren). Sie könnten nicht nur eine Hilfe beim Erkennen komplexer Muster darstellen, sondern auch eine effektive Unterstützung bei synthetischen Aktivitäten auf hohem geistigen Niveau, etwa bei der Ideenfindung. Zusätzlich wird es Formen von Intelligenz geben, die große Gruppen und Kollektive digital vernetzen, um sie in Forschungsaufgaben einzubeziehen und so den Teilnehmerkreis wissenschaftlicher Arbeit zu erweitern (Citizen Science, Co-Innovation, Crowdsourcing). Und während sich aus der Konvergenz dieser natürlichen und künstlichen, individuellen und kollektiven Wissensformen neue, hybride Intelligenzen entwickeln, müssen wir deren Zuverlässigkeit und Gültigkeit untersuchen und bestätigen – eine vordringliche wissenschaftliche Aufgabe, die unmittelbar vor uns liegt.

Mensch-Maschine-Interaktion

In jedem Fall werden wir die Interaktion und Kooperation mit diesen neuen Intelligenzen und Wissensunterstützungssystemen erlernen müssen. Forschung auf dem Gebiet der Mensch-Maschine-Interaktion (HMI) untersucht dieses weite Feld neuer technologischer und intellektueller Möglichkeiten – welche in den meisten Fällen auch für die unmittelbare räumliche Umgebung direkte Auswirkungen auf allen Ebenen und Dimensionen mit sich führen. Neue Schnittstellen und Interaktionsformen (Gesten, Berührung, Sprache) erzeugen sowohl beim Individuum wie auch im Kollektiv neues physisches und psychisches Verhalten. Die folgenden Absätze versuchen zu skizzieren, wie zukünftige Wissenschaftsumgebungen, vom einzelnen Arbeitsplatz bis hin zur Stadtebene, solchen Interaktionen Rechnung tragen können.

211
Cockpit for integrated urban planning (HCU Digital City Science)
Cockpit für integrierte Stadtplanung (HCU Digital City Science)

212–214
Human activity (left) sensed by IoT (centre) transforms workplaces into adaptive environments.
Aktivität (links) wird durch IoT wahrgenommen (Mitte) und steuert die räumliche Adaption (rechts)

211

212

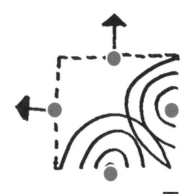

213

214

basic challenges have been pinpointed already. Previous studies on the research processes in data-intensive disciplines such as life sciences, material research and pharmacy have indicated a twofold dilemma that corresponds to the two opposite ends of a conventional research pipeline.[4]

Cognitive overload

Researchers who work in the early phases of scientific projects (where fundamental investigations are carried out and initial ideas are generated) are subject to cognitive overload. At the front-end of the research pipeline, only few scientists usually monitor a high number of experiments and projects. Thus they find themselves in a vast ocean of data and research processes that are hard to overview. The volatility and high-risk nature at this fundamental research phase – where experiments may easily fail and initial concepts may prove wrong – adds psychological pressure.

Communication overkill

At the opposite end of the research project life cycle, where successful results are transferred into practical application, a high number of researchers engage with a few high-profile projects (e.g. the roll-out of a new blockbuster drug). This setting demands high communication and interaction efforts to streamline contributions by multiple actors which need to be carried out on top of the regular scientific work.

Attention places

These two scenarios represent extreme edges of scientific research, yet they form blueprints for common knowledge work in the future. They bear implications for the organisation of work processes and spaces, as they can be translated into design strategies on the basis of psychological concepts of attention. Before long, "attention economy" will be a central concern not only in advertisement and online gaming (where every millisecond and every inch of screen space counts in commercial terms). Also in science, the resource "attention" is a high-value asset. The overflow of data and information (e.g. experiment monitoring, peer communication, tracking scientific publications) poses a fundamental challenge to scientific practice which by nature demands in-depth study, care and thoroughness. Scientific work, more than other fields, demands a clear distinction between relevant and irrelevant information, the selection of data, and concentrated observation and scrutiny. To enable these qualities at the scientific workplace, workplace design must skilfully support and manage attention.

2. Arbeitsplatz der Zukunft: Das kognitive Cockpit

Dateninteraktion

In der nahen Zukunft werden Wissenschaftler in ihrem räumlichen Nahbereich nicht nur physisch mit immensen Mengen von Informationen interagieren, in ihren stark augmentierten Umfeldern werden sie vor allem mit „lebendigen" Daten arbeiten, d.h. mit schnellveränderlichen Echtzeitdaten. Der unmittelbare Arbeitsplatz wird selbst zu einem wissenschaftlichen Werkzeug: eine räumliche Vorrichtung, die Wissenschaftlern beim Untersuchen und Verstehen von Daten, der Inspiration und beim Erkenntnisgewinn aktiv unterstützt. Der Weg dorthin ist noch lang; aber einige grundlegende Probleme wurden bereits erfasst. Studien zum Forschungsprozess in datenintensiven Disziplinen wie der Biowissenschaft, der Materialforschung, oder der Pharmazie haben auf ein doppeltes Dilemma hingewiesen, das den zwei gegenüberliegenden Enden einer konventionellen Forschungspipeline entspricht.[4]

Kognitive Überlast

Forscher, die in Projektfrühphasen wie z.B. der Grundlagenrecherche oder der Konzeptfindung arbeiten, sind mit kognitiver Überbeanspruchung konfrontiert. Am vordersten Ende einer Forschungspipeline leiten in der Regel nur einige wenige Forscher eine hohe Anzahl von Experimenten und Projekten. Die Volatilität und der Hochrisikocharakter zum Zeitpunkt dieser fundamentalen Forschungsphase – wo Experimente leicht fehlschlagen können und sich initiale Konzepte als falsch erweisen können – erzeugen erheblichen psychischen Druck.

Kommunikations-Overkill

Am anderen Ende des Forschungsprojektzyklus, wo erfolgreiche Resultate in praktische Anwendungen übertragen werden, befassen sich in der Regel eine Vielzahl von Forschern mit wenigen high-profile Projekten (z.B. der Markteinführung eines Blockbuster-Medikaments). Die Koordination der Beiträge aller Beteiligten erzeugt immense Kommunikations- und Abstimmungsanforderungen, die meist zusätzlich zu den eigentlichen wissenschaftlichen Aufgaben zu leisten sind.

Orte der Aufmerksamkeit

Diese zwei Szenarien repräsentieren die äußersten Ränder wissenschaftlicher Forschung, können aber dennoch als Blaupause für kollektive Wissensarbeit in der Zukunft dienen. Aus ihnen ergeben sich klare Implikationen für die Organisation von Arbeitsprozessen und Arbeitsplätzen. Auf der Basis psychoergonomischer Konzepte können konkrete Gestaltungsstrategien abgeleitet werden. Die sogenannte Aufmerksamkeitsökonomie ist nicht nur in der Werbung und im Online-Gaming (wo jede Millisekunde und jeder Zoll Bildschirmfläche in kommerzieller Hinsicht zählt) von Bedeutung. Die Ressource „Aufmerksamkeit" wird

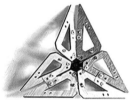

215

opened   semi-opened   closed

215–216
Adaptive surfaces
"Translated
Geometries",
Research team:
Efilena Baseta,
Ece Tankal,
Ramin Shambayati
Institute for
Advanced
Architecture
of Catalonia,
Spain, 2014
Adaptive
Oberflächen
„Translated
Geometries",
Forschungsgruppe:
Efilena Baseta,
Ece Tankal,
Ramin Shambayati,
Institute for
Advanced
Architecture
of Catalonia,
Spanien, 2014

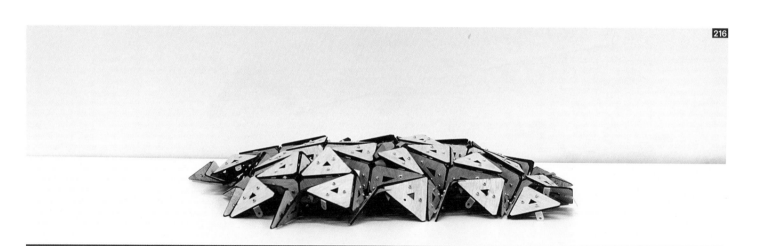

216

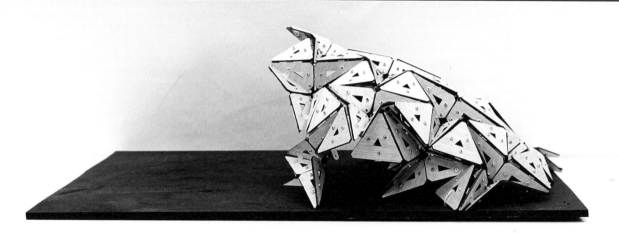

Monitors, dashboards and cockpits

To relieve the cognitive and communication overload, data dashboards and cockpits suggest themselves as future workplace solutions. They purposefully exploit the powers of graphical representation and visual thinking to support complex cognitive tasks such as monitoring and comparing large amounts of data, drawing quick conclusions and deriving reliable actions. Depending on the user and application context, interaction level and available data basis, a typology of basic solutions derives with different levels of complexity:

→ *Monitor* – simple visual displaying of one parameter or data set (e.g. local temperatures on a geographic map)

→ *Dashboard* – arrangement of multiple monitors for the visual comparison and linkage of multiple parameters (e.g. temperature vs. traffic vs. emissions)

→ *Cockpit* – dashboard environment with specific choreography (→ 1. Viewing ongoing experiments → 2. Selecting the critical case → 3. Analysing the case → 4. Reporting the results).

A key demand for the architectural design of workplaces will be the skilful augmentation of conventional work environments (office, lab, work desk etc.) with effective attention support technologies. The spatial character of the physical environment must be synchronised with the functionality of cockpits and dashboard tools. User-orientated design and psychological insight on the user experience (UX) will help scientists focus their attention while interacting with large data sets, as well as with a large number of partners and collaborators, thus preventing a cognitive or communication overload.[5] → **211**

Sensing spaces

Apart from the above-mentioned attention support environments, new sensing technology can turn the workplace itself into an attentive environment. Cyberphysical systems (CPS) and connected devices (Internet of Things, IoT) will establish sensing spatial environments that can perceive and consolidate data from the scientific work as well as from the working scientist. Sensed data on individual and collective activities as well as on physical and cognitive conditions can trigger the adjustment of acoustics, light, shape, visibility and accessibility. Equipped with faculties of algorithmic learning, workplaces will increasingly be able to actively support and facilitate research work. → **212–214**

auch in der Wissenschaft zu einem kostbaren Gut. Der Überfluss an Daten und Informationen z.B. durch Überwachung von Experimenten, Peerkommunikation oder Verfolgung wissenschaftlicher Veröffentlichungen stellt eine fundamentale Herausforderung an die wissenschaftliche Praxis dar – da diese ja grundsätzlich Sorgfalt, Gründlichkeit und vertiefende Betrachtung verlangt. Wissenschaftliches Arbeiten impliziert, mehr noch als andere Bereiche, die klare Unterscheidung relevanter von irrelevanter Information. Datenselektion, konzentrierte Beobachtung und eingehende Überprüfung sind fundamentale wissenschaftliche Praktiken. Um diese Qualitäten am wissenschaftlichen Arbeitsplatz zu ermöglichen, bedarf es eines klugen, aufmerksamkeitsfördernden und -schützenden Arbeitsplatzdesigns.

Monitore, Dashboards, Cockpits

Um kognitive und kommunikative Überlastung abzumildern, bieten sich Dashboards und Cockpits als Lösungen für zukünftige Arbeitsplätze an. Sie nutzen das Potential graphischer Darstellung und visuellen Denkens bei der Unterstützung komplexer kognitiver Aufgaben z.B. beim Monitoring großer Mengen von (Live-) Daten oder dem schnellen und verlässlichen Ableiten von Aussagen und Schlussfolgerungen. Aus Anwendungskontext, Interaktionsbedarf und Datengrundlage ergibt sich eine Typologie grundsätzlicher Lösungen mit unterschiedlichen Komplexitätsgraden:

→ *Monitor* – einfache visuelle Darstellung eines Parameters oder Datensets (z.B. örtliche Temperaturen in einer geografischen Karte)

→ *Dashboard* – Arrangement mehrerer Monitore zum visuellen Vergleich und zur Verknüpfung von Parametern (z.B. Temperaturen vs. Verkehrsfluss vs. Emissionen)

→ *Cockpit* – Dashboard-Umgebung mit spezifischer Nutzungschoreografie bzw. spezifischen Handlungsanweisungen (z.B. → 1. Monitoring laufender Experimente → 2. Selektion eines kritischen Falles → 3. Komplexe Analyse des Falles → 4. Reporting der Ergebnisse).

Eine zentrale Forderung an die architektonische Gestaltung von Arbeitsplätzen wird die adäquate Erweiterung konventioneller Arbeitsumgebungen (Büro, Labor, Arbeitsfläche etc.) durch Technologien zur Aufmerksamkeitsunterstützung sein. Die physische Umgebung muss mit den o.g. Cockpit- und Dashboard-Werkzeugen räumlich synchronisiert werden. Anwenderorientiertes Design und psychologische Erkenntnisse über User Experience (UX) werden Wissenschaftlern dabei helfen, ihre Aufmerksamkeit auf die Interaktion mit großen Datensätzen und einer großen Anzahl von Partnern und Mitarbeitern zu fokussieren, und somit einer kognitiven oder kommunikativen Überlastung vorbeugen.[5] → **211**

Spatial robotics

To some degree, such spatial intelligence is already implemented in environments with electronic control of parameters like colour or intensity of room lighting. Recent experiments with activated spatial surfaces add yet another dimension of interactivity. Automated changes of geometry (e.g. by folding) not only turn physical properties like noise reflection or absorption into adaptive qualities, but also visual and emotional characteristics (e.g. smooth vs angular shapes). Science laboratories as highly regulated and monitored spaces are especially suitable for such spatial robotics. These upcoming technologies will transform spaces themselves into intelligent co-workers that act in real-time. The space actively works in parallel and becomes another kind of co-working space. Here, the space will be the robot, not just the devices moving within it. → 215-216

Scientific work comfort

In addition to the cases described above, scenarios will determine future working environments in science that are based on the precise recording of spatial conditions as well as individual and collective user behaviour. By consolidating the attention levels and the physical condition of researchers with the communication load and information complexity, future work environments will enable new levels in terms of spatial comfort and scientific work performance.

3. Future City: The city as an experiment

Smart city contests

Perhaps the biggest ongoing scientific and technological experiment today are cities themselves. The societal and environmental disruptions of our so-called urban age have triggered large-scale experimenting with the living urban body. Under the banner of Smart City Agendas and Future City Challenges, political, industrial and social actors tinker with the operation systems of urban networks and communities, transforming them into large-scale experimental testbeds, objects for a new kind of science.[6]

Digital City Science

Before all, the ongoing speculative experiments require reflection and forecasting of the impacts of the newly implemented urban technologies and operations. City observatories are being implemented to create evidence about the

Wahrnehmende Räume

Neben den oben genannten Umgebungen zur Aufmerksamkeitsunterstützung kann neue Sensortechnologie den Arbeitsplatz selbst in eine aufmerksame Umgebung verwandeln. Cyberphysische Systeme (CPS) und vernetzte Geräte im Internet der Dinge (Internet of Things, IoT) schaffen zunehmend wahrnehmungsfähige räumliche Umgebungen, die potentiell in der Lage sind, Daten sowohl aus der wissenschaftlichen Arbeit als auch vom arbeitenden Wissenschaftler zu erfassen und zu verarbeiten. So können z.B. individuelle oder gemeinschaftliche Aktivitäten wie auch physische und kognitive Zustände erfasst werden und eine Justierung der Akustik, des Lichts, der Sichtverhältnisse und der Zugänglichkeit auslösen. Durch Verfahren des maschinellen Lernens kommen so ausgestattete digitale Arbeitsplätze zunehmend in die Lage, die Forschungsarbeit aktiv zu unterstützen. → 212-214

Raumrobotik

Zu einem gewissen Grad ist solch eine räumliche Intelligenz schon implementiert. Es existieren Raumsysteme, in denen Parameter wie Farbe oder Intensität der Raumbeleuchtung aktiv gesteuert werden. Neue Experimente mit aktivierten Raumoberflächen fügen noch eine weitere Dimension von Interaktivität hinzu. Eine automatisierte Veränderung der Geometrie (z.B. durch Faltung) kann physikalische Charakteristika wie Schallreflektion oder Absorption nicht nur in adaptive Eigenschaften verwandeln, sondern auch in visuelle und emotionale Qualitäten (Steuerung der Glätte bzw. Facettierung von Oberflächen). Insbesondere Laborumgebungen sind als hochgradig regulierte und kontrollierte Umgebungen für solche Raumrobotik geeignet. Entsprechende Technologien können Räume zu „intelligenten Mitarbeitern" transformieren, die in Echtzeit reagieren. Der Raum arbeitet aktiv mit; das Labor wird zu einer neuen Art Co-Working Space. Hier wird der Raum zum Roboter: nicht nur technische Gerätschaften im Raum, sondern dieser selbst agiert klug und verändert sich zielgerichtet. → 215-216

Wissenschaftliche Arbeit und Komfort

Über die oben beschriebenen Fälle hinaus werden Szenarien die künftigen Arbeitsumgebungen in der Wissenschaft bestimmen, die auf der präzisen Erfassung räumlicher Bedingungen als auch des individuellen und kollektiven Nutzerverhaltens basieren. Im zweckmäßigen Abgleich der entsprechenden Aufmerksamkeitsbedarfe, physischen Verfassungen, Informations- und Kommunikationslasten können Arbeitsumgebungen geschaffen werden, die künftig ein hohes Maß an Komfort wie auch an wissenschaftlicher Leistung ermöglichen.

socio-spatial effects on cities and communities and to anticipate urban futures. They are to monitor and measure, and – as far as data provision and AI power allow – predict the impacts of ongoing experiments such as autonomous driving, digital participation, and crowd sensing. The information models of buildings and cities (BIM / CIM) will be enhanced with vast real-time data streams from sensors and urban-data hubs. The hope is that the comprehensive representation of the physical and informative environments in the form of so-called digital twins enables more precise predictions of urban development and more effective city management. At the same time, however, it replaces the idea of targeted planning and design with a paradigm of digital control and predictability.

Beyond planning

Digitisation will increase the acceleration of the complexity and dynamics of urban systems up to a level that prohibits long-term planning. Real-time monitoring and predictive analysis will become the key activities in urban development and management. Instead of masterplans, there will be continuous experimentation and testing, small and fast steps of trial and error, and quick strategy readjustments. The accelerated collection, monitoring and use of urban data enables new learning cycles that will potentially lead to more flexible, more open-ended strategies for urban development. The growth of Urban Living Labs worldwide is a clear indicator of this development.

Agile development

Data-driven urbanism also impinges on the way buildings are conceived and executed. As an established pattern in history, any leading technology of an age will dictate its procedures and practices to other fields and disciplines. From now on, data science and information technologies will determine the new procedures for architectural design and urban development. In practice, this will usher in an agile and incremental way of planning and building. By iterative cycles, architects and planners will determine requirements in constant contact with end users, while permanently updating spatial and functional programmes. We will communicate with objects and infrastructures directly and acknowledge their condition as a starting point for situation-based design and decision making. We will talk to buildings and cities – and they will talk to us.

Smart City-Wettbewerbe

Das zurzeit wohl größte wissenschaftliche und technische Experiment sind die Städte selbst. Die gesellschaftlichen und ökologischen Brüche unseres sogenannten urbanen Zeitalters haben groß angelegte Experimente an den lebendigen Stadtkörpern ausgelöst. Unter dem Banner von Smart City-Programmen und Zukunftsstadtprojekten greifen politische, industrielle und soziale Akteure tief in die Betriebssysteme der urbanen Systeme und Gemeinschaften ein, transformieren sie in groß angelegte Experimentierfelder. Sie stellen somit die Versuchsobjekte für eine neue Art der Stadtforschung dar.[6]

Digital City Science

Die laufenden spekulativen Experimente benötigen vor allem Reflektion und Vorausschau bezüglich der Auswirkungen neuer digitaler Stadttechnologien. Um Belege für die sozialräumlichen Auswirkungen auf Städte und Kommunen zu sammeln und auf dieser Basis die Zukunft der Städte zu antizipieren, werden Stadtobservatorien implementiert, in denen die Effekte urbaner Experimente wie z.B. autonomes Fahren, digitale Beteiligung oder Crowd Sensing sichtbar werden sollen. Die Informationsmodelle von Gebäuden und Städten (Building/City Information Models) werden zunehmend kurzgeschlossen, ebenso der Datenfluss zwischen Stadtraumsensorik, urbanen Datendrehscheiben und Entscheidungssystemen. Die Hoffnung hierbei ist, dass die umfassende Repräsentation unserer physischen und informativen Umgebungen in Form sogenannter Digitaler Zwillinge präzisere Vorhersagen der urbanen Entwicklung und effektiveres Stadtmanagement ermöglicht. Gleichzeitig aber ersetzen sie jedoch die Idee gezielter Planung und Gestaltung mit einem Paradigma der digitalen Kontrolle und Berechenbarkeit.

Jenseits der Planung

Die Digitalisierung wird die Komplexität und die Dynamik urbaner Systeme in einer Weise beschleunigen, dass langfristige Planungen zunehmend unwahrscheinlich werden. An ihre Stelle treten Echtzeit-Monitoring und statistische Prädiktion als zentrale Praktiken in Stadtentwicklung und -management. Anstelle von Masterplänen tritt eine Praxis des kontinuierlichen Experimentierens und Testens. Urbane Entwicklungskonzepte werden in kleinen und schnellen Schritten sondiert; gegebenenfalls werden die jeweiligen Strategien schnell nachjustiert. Die beschleunigte Erfassung, Monitoring und Nutzung urbaner Daten ermöglicht dabei neue Lernzyklen, die potentiell zu flexibleren, ergebnisoffeneren Strategien der Stadtentwicklung führen können. Das Wachstum von Urban Living Labs weltweit ist ein deutlicher Indikator dieser Entwicklung.

1
Thomas Kuhn:
The Structure of
Scientific Revoluti-
ons. University of
Chicago Press 1962

2
Charles Sanders
Peirce: Illustrations
of the Logic of
Science, Open Court
Publishers 2014

3
For a research group
at TU Dresden/
RWTH Aachen, the
TU Dresden Labora-
tory of Knowledge
Architecture has
conceived an AI-
based "Inspiration
Engine" aimed at
inspiring engineers
and material scien-
tists with creative
impulses from the
visual arts, music,
literature etc.

4
Noennig, J., Richter,
S. (2010) Urbane
Pharmazie?
Über den Abstand
zwischen Pharma-
unternehmen und
Großstadt, in:
Transformation: Vom
Werk im Wedding
zum globalen
Pharmaquartier
(Kulturkreis der
deutschen Wirt-
schaft/BDI, Ed.),
p. 96–111, 2010

5
Fujitsu's Digital
Future Center pre-
sents a convincing
prototype of an
interactive collective
work environment
that can support
high-level scientific
work by skilfully
directing user atten-
tion, monitoring
collective activities
and providing
inspirational
"food for thought".

6
See for example:
The international
Morgenstadt
Initiative of Fraun-
hofer Gesellschaft;
Future City
(Zukunftsstadt)
Competition of the
German Federal
Ministry for Research
and Education;
India's "Smart
Cities Mission" with
100 experimental
city projects.

Agile Entwicklung

Die daten-getriebene Urbanistik wird in die Prozesse eingreifen, mit denen Gebäude konzipiert und ausgeführt werden. Es ist ein etabliertes historisches Muster, dass die führenden Technologien eines Zeitalters ihre Prozesse und Praktiken anderen Feldern und Disziplinen einschreiben. Datenwissenschaft und Informationstechnologien werden neue Abläufe im architektonischen Entwurf und in der Stadtplanung diktieren. Mit ihnen entsteht eine agile und inkrementelle Art des Planens und Bauens, bei der Architekten und Planer im ständigen Kontakt mit den Endnutzern in interaktiven Entwicklungszyklen die Anforderungen ermitteln und diese mit flexiblen Raum- und Funktionsprogrammen umsetzen. Sie werden mit vernetzten Objekten, Infrastrukturen und Gemeinschaften direkt interagieren und diese als Ausgangspunkt situationsbezogener Gestaltungskonzepte und Entscheidungsfindung nutzen. Planer und Architekten werden mit Gebäuden und Städten kommunizieren – und umgekehrt.

1
Thomas Kuhn:
The Structure of
Scientific Revoluti-
ons. University of
Chicago Press 1962

2
Charles Sanders
Peirce: Illustrations
of the Logic of
Science, Open Court
Publishers 2014

3
Das Laboratory of
Knowledge Architec-
ture der TU Dresden
hat für eine For-
schungsgruppe der
TU Dresden / RWTH
Aachen eine KI-ba-
sierte "Inspiration En-
gine" konzipiert, die
Ingenieure und Ma-
terialwissenschaftler
mit kreativen Impul-
sen aus bildender
Kunst, Musik, Litera-
tur etc. inspirieren
soll.

4
Noennig, J., Richter,
S. (2010) Urbane
Pharmazie? Über den
Abstand zwischen
Pharmaunternehmen
und Großstadt, in:
Transformation: Vom
Werk im Wedding
zum globalen Phar-
maquartier (Hg.
Kulturkreis der deut-
schen Wirtschaft/
BDI), S. 96-111, 2010

5
Fujitsus Digital Future
Center ist ein über-
zeugender Prototyp
einer interaktiven,
gemeinschaftlichen
Arbeitsumgebung,
die, durch gekonntes
Lenken der Anwen-
deraufmerksamkeit,
Überwachung ge-
meinsamer Tätigkeit
und das Liefern
von Denkanstößen,
wissenschaftliche
Arbeit auf hohem
Niveau unterstützen
kann.

6
Vgl. internationale
Morgenstadt
Initiative der
Fraunhofer Gesell-
schaft; Zukunfts-
stadt-Wettbewerb
des deutschen
Bundesministeriums
für Bildung
und Forschung;
Indiens "Smart
Cities Mission" mit
100 experimentellen
Stadt Projekten.

217
Adaptive surfaces
"Translated
Geometries"
Adaptive
Oberflächen
„Translated
Geometries"

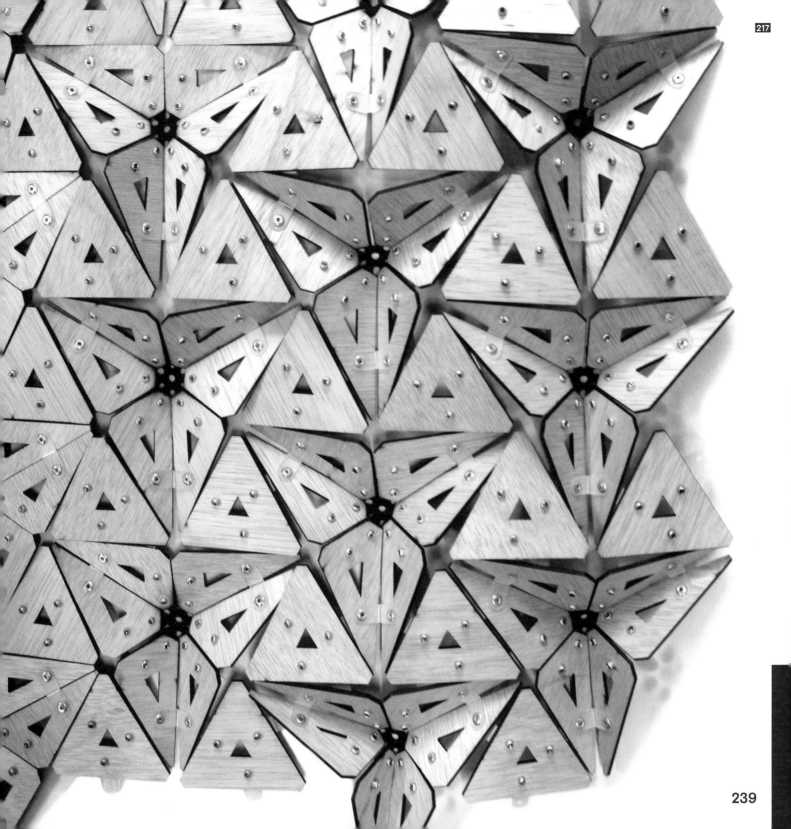

Dialogue

ANDREAS TRAUBE + STEFAN BÖTEL + STEFANIE MATTHYS

Laboratories of the future

Labore der Zukunft

Digitisation has also affected the laboratory world. Robotics and artificial intelligence, simulated research and remote work have long been elements of everyday research. Will these changes also have an influence on spatial planning in the future? Stefan Bötel, architect and Managing Director at Nickl & Partner Architekten in the field of research and university buildings, and Stefanie Matthys, architect and editor of this publication, discuss the lab of tomorrow together with Andreas Traube, Head of the Laboratory Automation and Biomanufacturing Engineering Department at the Fraunhofer Institute for Manufacturing Engineering and Automation (IPA) in Stuttgart.

Stefan Bötel: The image of researchers in white coats, handling their pipettes and test tubes, is firmly anchored in people's minds. Is that notion of a laboratory outdated?

Andreas Traube: Presumably, researchers who sit at their workbenches carrying out long, monotonous activities will soon be a thing of the past. Nevertheless, laboratories will continue to be strongly shaped by people in the future. Instead of working completely robotically, my idea of the labs of tomorrow is a hybrid environment that is shaped by people, digitisation and also automation, working hand in hand as efficiently as possible to generate knowledge and data. The challenge will be to divide tasks between technical systems and people in a way that allows everyone to do what they are best at. Human intuition, inventiveness and the planning of experiments will still be impossible for research robots in the foreseeable future, even though initial approaches to that field have already begun. The monotonous activities, monitoring processes, operative tasks and so on, will increasingly be taken over by machines, or at least assisted by them.

SB: If laboratory work is increasingly carried out by robots or machines, could that mean the future laboratory will be

Die Digitalisierung macht auch vor den Türen des Labors nicht Halt. Robotik und künstliche Intelligenz, simulierte Forschung und Remotearbeit prägen längst den Forscheralltag. Wirken sich diese Veränderungen in Zukunft auch auf die räumliche Planung aus? Stefan Bötel, Architekt und Geschäftsführer für den Bereich Forschungs- und Hochschulbauten bei Nickl & Partner Architekten, und Stefanie Matthys, Architektin und Redakteurin dieser Publikation, diskutieren über das Labor von morgen mit Andreas Traube, Leiter der Abteilung Laborautomatisierung und Bioproduktionstechnik am Fraunhofer-Institut für Produktionstechnik und Automatisierung in Stuttgart.

Stefan Bötel: Das Bild des Forschers in seinem Kittel, der mit Pipetten und Reagenzgläsern hantiert, ist fest in den Köpfen verankert. Gehört dieses Bild des Labors der Vergangenheit an?

Andreas Traube: Der Forscher, der an der Arbeitsbank sitzt und lange, monotone Tätigkeiten ausübt, wird vermutlich bald der Vergangenheit angehören. Dennoch wird das Labor auch in Zukunft stark durch Menschen geprägt sein. Ein Labor der Zukunft ist nach meiner Vorstellung kein Raum, der rein robotisch funktioniert, sondern es ist ein hybrider Workspace, geprägt durch Menschen, durch Digitalisierung und auch durch Automatisierung, die Hand in Hand möglichst effizient Wissen und Daten generieren. Dabei gilt es, eine Aufteilung zwischen Technik und Mensch zu finden, in der jeder das macht, das ihm am meisten liegt. Die menschliche Intuition, der Erfinderreichtum, das Planen von Experimenten, wird noch lange nicht von forschenden Laborrobotern übernommen werden, obwohl auch hier erste Ansätze bereits bestehen. Die monotone Tätigkeit, das Monitoring von Prozessen, das operative Tun, wird mehr und mehr von Maschinen übernommen oder wenigstens assistiert.

SB: Wenn Laborarbeit zunehmend von Robotern oder Maschinen übernommen wird, könnte das Labor der Zukunft dann einfach eine Art Industriehalle sein, eine sehr große, flexible Fläche mit einer langen Leitung zu den Auswerteplätzen? Schon heute arbeiten wir mit sehr großflächigen Laborlandschafen.

241

a simple type of industrial hall, a very large, flexible space with a long line to the analysis workplaces? We already work with very large-scale laboratory landscapes today.

AT: Not all processes that need to be carried out in laboratories will be replaced by machines. However, open workspaces with "human workplaces" as well as "machine workplaces", an open space with media connections from above and below, are naturally the most flexible solution.

SB: Will it still be necessary for researchers to be physically close to all processes in their experiment? One could imagine accommodating machine workplaces in other rooms, perhaps even in other buildings.

AT: You can imagine it like other professional fields. The mathematician no longer sits there with his slide rule. I'm an engineer and no longer use a drawing board, nor do I calculate every machine and every mechanical stability by hand anymore. That's done for me by software or a machine. The same applies to future laboratory processes.

Stefanie Matthys: Could you give us an example of a process with a human-machine interface in a laboratory?

AT: One aspect that is currently being intensively discussed in our field is the use of mobile laboratory robots. Mobile robots used flexibly in the lab are real game changers in some ways. They overcome the separation between an automated and a manual workplace, introducing a hybrid working environment. The robots also extend normal working hours. When employees arrive at the lab at eight in the morning, they might need to start by labelling test tubes for two hours – which is not exactly a cognitively challenging task. A robot can do things like that especially well. It can start at five in the morning and when the employees arrive at the lab, the samples can be used straight away. When the laboratory personnel finishes its working day, the robot can continue working. Laboratory capacities can be expanded by 50 to 70 percent in this way. Such cooperation between technical and human systems achieves a very high added value for the laboratory's efficiency. Incidentally, our mobile lab robot is called Kevin, inspired by the film "Home Alone". → 219–221

SM: Is Kevin like a "buddy" rolling behind the researcher?

AT: Yes, more or less. Naturally, Kevin does his own jobs in parallel with humans in the lab. In addition to such human-machine cooperation, augmented reality (AR) in the form of digital assistance will also play a role in laboratories. Imagine, for instance, a tablet that I can carry through the lab and, as I pass a refrigerator, it tells me, without having to open it, "this refrigerator contains cell culture medium XY"; it could also be an incubator that says it's time to replace the medium.

SB: Do such automated solutions also have the advantage that they don't require a hygienic laboratory

AT: Nicht alle Vorgänge, die im Labor erfolgen müssen, werden durch Maschinen ersetzt werden. Aber für offene Workspaces mit "Menscharbeitsplätzen" genauso wie "Maschinenarbeitsplätzen" ist eine offene Fläche mit Medienversorgung von oben oder unten natürlich am flexibelsten.

SB: Ist dann die körperliche Nähe des Wissenschaftlers zu allen Vorgängen seines Experiments noch erforderlich? Man kann sich vorstellten, die Maschinenarbeitsplätze in anderen Räumen, gegebenenfalls sogar in anderen Gebäuden unterzubringen.

AT: Man kann sich das wie in anderen Berufszweigen vorstellen. Der Mathematiker sitzt nicht mehr mit dem Rechenschieber da. Ich, als Ingenieur, sitze heute nicht mehr vor dem Zeichenbrett und berechne auch nicht mehr jede Maschine und jede mechanische Stabilität von Hand, sondern das erledigt Software oder eine Maschine für mich. Genauso ist es bei Laborprozessen in Zukunft auch.

Stefanie Matthys: Vielleicht könnten Sie uns einen beispielhaften Prozess der Schnittstelle Mensch-Maschine im Labor beschreiben?

AT: Ein Thema, das im Moment in unserem Umfeld intensiv diskutiert wird, ist der Einsatz von mobilen Laborrobotern. Fahrbare Roboter, die flexibel im Labor eingesetzt werden können, sind in gewisser Weise ein echter Game-Changer. Sie überwinden die Separation zwischen automatisiertem und manuellem Arbeitsplatz und bilden den Einstieg in einen hybriden Workspace. Der Roboter erweitert auch die normalen Laborarbeitszeiten. Wenn die Mitarbeiter morgens um acht ins Labor kommen, kann es sein, dass sie erstmal zwei Stunden lang Probenröhrchen beschriften – keine kognitiv sehr anspruchsvolle Tätigkeit. Ein Roboter kann so etwas besonders gut. Er fängt schon morgens um 5 Uhr an und wenn der Mitarbeiter dann ins Labor kommt, können die Proben direkt verwendet werden. Wenn das Laborpersonal irgendwann Feierabend macht, kann der Roboter weiterarbeiten. So kann die Kapazität eines Labors um 50 bis 70 Prozent erweitert werden. Es ist eine Kooperation zwischen technischem und menschlichem System, die einen sehr hohen Mehrwert für die Effizienz des Labors liefert. Unser mobiler Laborroboter heißt übrigens Kevin – „Kevin allein im Labor". → 219–221

SM: Kann man sich Kevin wie einen "Buddy" vorstellen, der hinter dem Forscher her rollt?

AT: Ja, so ungefähr. Kevin macht natürlich seine eigenen Aufgaben parallel zu den Menschen im Labor. Neben einer solchen Mensch-Maschine-Kooperation wird auch Augmented Reality (AR) in Form digitaler Assistenz ins Labor einziehen. Stellen Sie sich zum Beispiel ein Tablet vor, mit dem ich durch das Labor laufe und ich komme dann an einem Kühlschrank vorbei, der mir sagt, ohne dass ich ihn öffnen muss: „In diesem Kühlschrank befindet sich Zellkultur Medium XY", oder der Inkubator sagt: „Hier muss ein Medienwechsel gemacht werden".

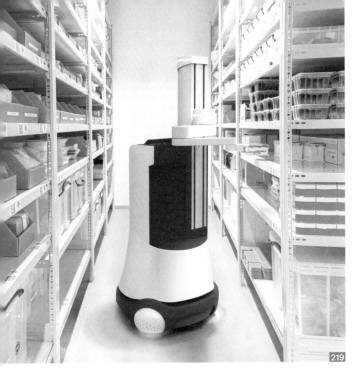

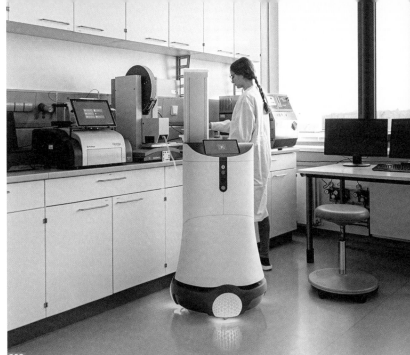

219

220

221

219–221
Kevin, the mobile lab partner and collaborative robot. Kevin can carry out automated tasks by combining manual workplaces and devices in different rooms, on different floors or even in different buildings.
Kevin, der mobile Laborpartner und kollaborative Roboter. Mit Kevin werden automatisierte Arbeitsabläufe ermöglicht durch die Verbindung von manuellen Arbeitsplätzen und Geräten in verschiedenen Räumen, Stockwerken und Gebäuden.

environment? Processes are encapsulated inside the machine, so the surroundings might not require the same hygiene standards.

AT: That's not the case so far. Even when using closed machines, it is still necessary to plan laboratory environments with an appropriate security standard. However, technically, it's conceivable to work with closed systems that would make clean rooms unnecessary in the long term. But particularly in high-security laboratories with S3 and S4 standards, only a very small amount of automation is used: what would happen if such a machine were contaminated with a very dangerous pathogen or highly hazardous substances? How can maintenance or disposal work be carried out on such systems? We also have a considerable interdisciplinary hurdle with respect to laboratory automation. The machines are built by engineers who don't have a great deal of practical experience, while on the other hand, users often lack the technical know how. That's one of the main reasons why technological advances in laboratory environments have not progressed further so far.

SM: How do you approach your planning processes at the Fraunhofer Institute?

AT: We have established a team structure with application experts, mechanical engineers and software developers that cover the full range of interdisciplinarity we need. That creates enormous synergies. You can see similar developments in major pharmaceutical corporations, which have their own automation departments that work closely together with researchers. Today's construction planning very rarely considers which technologies will be used in the buildings in ten or 15 years' time. Thus, we need a flexible approach to enable specific adaptations. In our own laboratory building in Stuttgart, we had to carry out the first conversion measures almost as soon as it had been completed in 2016, because demands had changed considerably in the period from planning to construction.

SB: We often also experience a kind of "kingdom philosophy". Each professor imagines they have a certain available space. By the time the building is finished, the professor is often somewhere completely different. So, we always propose creating larger continuous spaces that can cope with the building's long-term existence and react flexibly. What would you consider a good environment for working in a laboratory?

AT: I believe it is also important to design a friendly working environment in laboratories. There is definitely room for improvement with respect to themes such as ergonomics and user-friendliness. In the lab, we're already happy if there's room for our feet beneath a table.

SB: Haben solch automatisierte Lösungen gegebenenfalls auch den Vorteil, dass sie kein hygienisches Laborumfeld mehr brauchen? Dass Vorgänge innerhalb einer Maschine eingekapselt funktionieren, aber das Umfeld gar nicht mehr den gleichen Hygienestandard haben muss?

AT: Das ist bisher noch nicht der Fall. Selbst bei geschlossenen Maschinen ist es weiterhin notwendig, die Laborumgebung mit einem entsprechenden Sicherheitsstandard zu planen. Rein technisch ist es aber vorstellbar, mit geschlossenen Systemen zu arbeiten, um so perspektivisch auf Reinräume verzichten zu können. Aber gerade in Hochsicherheitslaboren mit S3-, S4-Standard wird bisher ganz wenig Automation eingesetzt. Denn was passiert, wenn so eine Maschine mit einem sehr gefährlichen Erreger oder mit sehr gefährlichen Substanzen kontaminiert wird? Wie kann solch ein System gewartet oder entsorgt werden? Wir haben in der Laborautomation noch eine erhebliche interdisziplinäre Hürde. Die Maschinen werden von Ingenieuren ohne viel Applikationswissen gemacht, gleichzeitig bringen die Anwender oft nicht das technische Wissen mit. Das ist einer der Hauptgründe, weshalb die Technisierung von Laborumfeldern nicht schon weiter ist.

SM: Wie gehen Sie denn am Fraunhofer Institut in Ihrem Planungsprozess vor?

AT: Wir haben eine Teamstruktur mit Applikationsexperten, Maschinenbauern und Softwareentwicklern geschaffen, die diese Interdisziplinarität komplett abbildet. Das schafft enorme Synergien. Das sieht man auch teilweise in großen Pharmaunternehmen, die ihre eigenen Automationsabteilungen haben und dort eng mit Wissenschaftlern arbeiten. In der Bauplanung überlegen heute die wenigsten, welche Technologien dort nach zehn oder 15 Jahren eingesetzt werden. Es braucht daher eine Form von Flexibilisierung, um bestimmte Anpassungen möglich zu machen. Bei unserem eigenen Laborgebäude in Stuttgart mussten wir, kaum war das Gebäude 2016 fertig, bereits den ersten Umbau machen, weil sich die Anforderungen von der Planung bis zur Realisierung stark weiterentwickelt haben.

SB: Wir erleben auch oft ein gewisses "Königreichdenken". Jeder Professor hat die Vorstellung, dass er eine gewisse Fläche zur eigenen Verfügung hat. Häufig ist er dann, wenn das Gebäude fertig ist, schon längst woanders. Deswegen schlagen wir immer vor, größere zusammenhängende Flächen zu schaffen, die im langfristigen Bestehen des Gebäudes flexibel reagieren können. Was wäre denn für Sie eine gute Umgebung, um in einem Labor arbeiten zu können?

AT: Ich glaube, wichtig im Laborumfeld ist, dass auch dort das Arbeitsumfeld freundlich gestaltet ist. Da ist noch deutlich Luft nach oben, was Themen wie Ergonomie und Benutzerfreundlichkeit angeht. Im Labor ist man schon froh, wenn man unter dem Tisch einen Platz für die Füße hat.

In future, we probably won't need to consider the aspect of office work in a laboratory environment. The Covid-19 pandemic changed many things. At our institute, we now offer employees a free choice of workplace within Germany. They only come into the institute if necessary. Perhaps in time, laboratory space will therefore take over such office areas.

SB: That means it's no longer necessary for the thinking work to be carried out near the information-gathering processes. We are also currently observing a trend towards digital labs in the planning process for the Pathology Department of a university clinic. The new building will only accommodate work on digitised images of histological sections. Only the information on the sample is required, not the sample itself.

AT: Yes, in the long-term future, the entire laboratory will take place on microchips, and everything will be fully simulated. But that's not yet relevant to current building planning. At the moment, we are tackling the task of enabling devices or machines to talk to each other and exchange data using standardised interfaces. But the benefits of completely digital laboratory processes will be enormous. A digital representation of what is actually happening in the laboratory can also be accessed at a later date. That means experiments can be carried out repeatedly, allowing us to adjust possible influencing factors.

It's like a digital BIM model in building planning. Wouldn't it be great to simulate the laboratory and its processes in the same way? And we envisage a type of operating system for the laboratory, in the same way as Windows runs on our computers. It could use sensors to record data in a specific environment to feed a digital representation and keep it permanently up to date.

SM: Would the operating system coordinate the planning, operation and further development of a laboratory system with all of its interfaces? There are similar systems in the building sector that are already experimenting with automated processes on the construction site. The same question arises: "How do I manage to transfer my information to the BIM model in a way that allows it to be implemented on the building site?"

SB: We're currently researching such networked processes for major machines in a research building in Aachen, which we're constructing for the RWTH, the Centre for Digitally Networked Production (CdvP). It includes so-called intensive stations that can simulate climatic conditions, severe heat, cold and vibrations in order to assess their effects on a process. That allows us to extract these fluctuating environmental influences.

Das Thema Büroarbeit müssen wir wahrscheinlich in Zukunft nicht mehr im Laborumfeld mitdenken. Die Corona-Pandemie hat da vieles verändert. In unserem Institut stellen wir den Mitarbeitern inzwischen einen frei wählbaren Arbeitsplatz innerhalb von Deutschland zur Verfügung. Nur bei Bedarf kommen sie ans Institut. Vielleicht wird sich die Laborfläche daher die Bürofläche mit der Zeit einverleiben.

SB: Das heißt, man braucht nicht mehr unbedingt die räumliche Nähe der Denkarbeit, zu dem Ort, wo die Prozesse der Informationsbeschaffung stattfinden. Diesen Trend zum digitalen Labor sehen wir aktuell auch in der Planung einer Pathologie für ein Uniklinikum. In dem neuen Gebäude soll nur noch mit digitalisierten Bildern von histologischen Schnitten gearbeitet werden. Es wird nur noch die Information der Probe gebraucht, nicht mehr die Probe selbst.

AT: Ja, in weiter Zukunft wird das ganze Labor auf Mikrochips stattfinden und alles komplett simulierbar sein. Das wird aber für die aktuellen Gebäudeplanungen noch nicht relevant werden. Im Moment kämpfen wir noch damit, Geräte oder Automaten von unterschiedlichen Herstellern miteinander sprechen zu lassen und an standardisierten Schnittstellen Daten miteinander auszutauschen. Aber der Nutzen komplett digitaler Laborprozesse wird enorm sein. Eine digitale Repräsentation dessen, was tatsächlich im Labor vor sich geht, kann ja retrospektiv immer wieder abgerufen werden. Experimente können so mehrfach durchgeführt und mögliche Einflussfaktoren nachjustiert werden.

Das ist wie ein digitales BIM-Modell in der Bauplanung. Wie toll wäre es, darin auch das Labor mit seinen Abläufen zu simulieren? Und unsere Vision ist eine Art Betriebssystem für das Labor, ähnlich wie auf unseren Rechnern Windows läuft. Dieses könnte über Sensoren wiederum Daten aus dem Umfeld des Labors aufnehmen, die das digitale Abbild füttern und permanent aktuell halten.

SM: Ein Betriebssystem also, welches Planung, Betrieb und auch Weiterentwicklungen eines Laborsystems mit all seinen Schnittstellen koordiniert? Auch im Bau gibt es Systeme, die bereits damit experimentieren, Prozesse auf der Baustelle zu automatisieren. Die Frage ist auch dort: „Wie schaffe ich es, meine Informationen aus dem BIM Modell so zu übertragen, dass es auf der Baustelle ausgeführt werden kann?"

SB: In einem Forschungsgebäude in Aachen, das wir für die RWTH bauen, CdvP, werden solche vernetzten Prozesse für große Maschinen erforscht. Dort gibt es sogenannte Intensivstationen, wo man klimatische Umgebungsbedingungen, große Hitze, Kälte, Erschütterungen, simulieren und deren Auswirkungen auf einen Prozess auswerten kann. Was die Möglichkeit eröffnet, diese Schwankungen der Umgebungseinflüsse herauszurechnen.

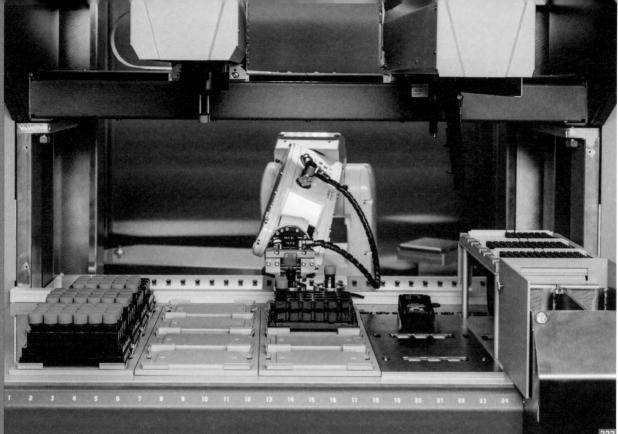

222
Personalised
specialist system
to regulate
pharmaceutical
production
Personalisierte
Sonderanlage für
die regulierte
Pharmaproduktion

223
Merlin Bench, a
modern operating
system for the lab
bench, making
the documentation
of operative steps
more systematic
and recordable
Merlin Bench, ein
modernes Bedien-
system für die
Laborbank, um die
Dokumentation der
Arbeitsschritte
systematischer und
besser zu erfassen

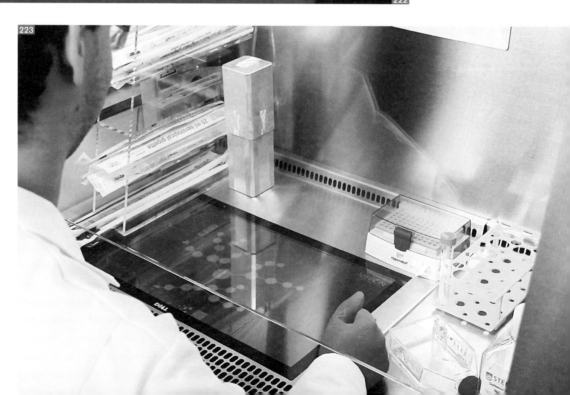

AT: That would help us to apply research results from one location to another. In this context, we see a trend whereby central research hotspots are emerging at university clinics and major research centres. The most technically complicated and expensive machines are concentrated there. One could regard them as laboratory service centres.

SB: And the digitised processes also make the results usable at long distances – even internationally.

SM: Considering all the different types of laboratory – chemistry, physics, biology and so on – do you see an area where these trends towards digitisation and automation are especially strong?

AT: Our focus lies in life sciences and that is where I also see the greatest need. It's the field where the most laboratory research has been required in the past. Many people describe the convergence of technology, information and biology as the next industrial revolution. The boundaries between biology, chemistry and physics are also blurring to an ever-greater extent.

SB: We also notice that in our buildings. More and more hybrid research buildings are being planned, pooling various disciplines under a single roof.

AT: We see the same developments in device technology. Nowadays, we often build devices that already have physical measuring and sensor functions, as well as a little intelligence of their own, in the form of AI, which can be trained.

SM: All the way to the point where experiments no longer need to be carried out and can simply be simulated?

AT: Considering the performance of quantum computers, simulating biology is not that unrealistic. And once you can simulate biology, you can also simulate the experiment.

SM: Is that the point where laboratories are finally replaced by computer centres?

AT: I think, at the end of the day, it won't be the case of one or the other system winning through. Laboratory processes will diversify massively, and you planners will have to build in a way that makes everything possible in future research buildings. Good luck with that! I've been working in the field for 17 years and developments have constantly accelerated, while strategies have steadily diversified. So I don't think we'll ultimately see a major shift and suddenly everything is digital. Instead, there will always be different parallel systems and their number will tend to grow. We must prepare for many changes in laboratories, while their number will also increase in the years ahead.

AT: Das würde die Übertragung von Forschungsergebnissen von einem Standort auf den anderen erleichtern. Vor diesem Hintergrund sehen wir den Trend, dass sich zentrale Forschungshotspots an Universitätskliniken und großen Forschungszentren ansiedeln. Dort konzentrieren sich die technisch aufwändigsten und teuersten Maschinen. Man kann sich das wie Servicezentren in Form von Laborspaces vorstellen.

SB: Und durch die digitalisierten Prozesse ist es dann auch möglich die Ergebnisse über eine größere Distanz – sogar international – nutzbar zu machen.

SM: Bei den verschiedenen Arten von Laboren, chemisch, physikalisch, biologisch, sehen Sie da einen Bereich, wo sich diese Tendenzen in Richtung Digitalisierung und Automation ganz besonders herausarbeiten?

AT: Wir haben unseren Schwerpunkt in den Life Sciences und dort sehe ich auch die größte Notwendigkeit. Es ist der Bereich, in dem klassisch am meisten Laborforschung vorhanden ist. Die Konvergenz von Technologie, Information und Biologie wird von vielen als die nächste industrielle Revolution bezeichnet. Auch die Grenzen zwischen Biologie, Chemie und Physik verschwimmen immer mehr.

SB: Das merken wir ja auch in unseren Bauten. Es werden immer mehr hybride Forschungsgebäude geplant, die verschiedene Fachbereiche unter einem Dach zusammenführen.

AT: Auch in der Gerätetechnologie sehen wir das. Heute bauen wir oft Geräte, die bereits über physikalische Messtechnik und Sensorik verfügen, über eine eigene kleine Intelligenz, in Form von KI, die antrainiert werden kann.

SM: Bis hin zu dem Szenario, dass man Experimente gar nicht mehr real durchführt, sondern nur noch simuliert werden müssen?

AT: Biologie zu simulieren ist, wenn man an die Performance von Quantencomputer denkt, gar nicht so unrealistisch. Und sobald man die Biologie simulieren kann, kann man auch das Experiment simulieren.

SM: Dann wird das Labor endgültig durch das Rechenzentrum ersetzt?

AT: Ich denke, am Ende des Tages wird nicht das eine oder das andere System gewinnen. Die Laborprozesse werden sich massiv diversifizieren und Sie als Planer müssen so bauen, dass alles in zukünftigen Forschungsbauten möglich ist. Viel Spaß dabei! Ich arbeite seit 17 Jahren in diesem Feld und die Entwicklung läuft immer schneller ab die Strategien haben sich immer stärker diversifiziert. Deswegen glaube ich nicht, dass wir am Ende den großen Ruck sehen und dann ist plötzlich alles digital. Stattdessen werden wir immer verschiedene Systeme parallel haben und diese werden tendenziell mehr. Wir müssen uns im Labor auf viel Veränderung einstellen und die Veränderungen werden in den nächsten Jahren auch zunehmen.

Buildings as laboratories for robotics

THOMAS LINNER + MARC SCHMAILZL
KEPA ITURRALDE + THOMAS BOCK

Gebäude als Laboratorien für die Robotik

Architecture is changing in the way we plan, construct, and manage buildings. Digital design methods, advances in robotics and sensor technology, as well as the rising accessibility of interdisciplinary knowledge offer unimagined possibilities. The robot is one of the most important tools in this development, which translates the rapid advances in digitisation to the physical world. In future, construction robots will serve as end points in digital data management and construction chains.

While the articles in this book deal with architecture for research and science, this excursus is intended to take a look in the other direction. In the area of robot-assisted construction methods, the construction site itself becomes a laboratory.

Architektur verändert sich in der Art und Weise wie wir Gebäude planen, bauen und verwalten. Digital-gestützte Entwurfsverfahren, Entwicklungen in der Robotik und Sensortechnologie, wie auch die wachsende Verfügbarkeit von interdisziplinärem Wissen bieten ungeahnte Möglichkeiten. Eines der bedeutendsten Instrumente dieser Möglichkeiten ist der Roboter, welcher die rasanten Entwicklungen des digitalen Zeitalters in die physische Welt übersetzt. In der Zukunft werden Bauroboter als zentrale Endpunkte im digitalen Datenmanagement und in Bauprozessen fungieren.

Während sich die Beiträge in diesem Buch auf die Architektur für Forschung und Wissenschaft beziehen, ist die Intention dieses Exkurses einen Blick in die andere Richtung zu wagen. Bei Bauverfahren mit robotischer Unterstützung wird die Baustelle selbst zum Labor.

Coexistence of architecture and robotics: New thinking in a postmodern world

When thinking about robotics in architecture as a field of research, various references of architectural history and pop culture inevitably appear. The ideas displaying numerous utopian worlds, shaped by an optimism towards progress and machine aesthetics, show technology in a spatially staged manner. Thus, the relationship between architecture and machines or robots, and the associated fascination, date back to the 1960s/70s. That time was characterised by a new way of life: pop, rebellion, science-fiction, new media art and temporary installations were introduced, while radical and visionary ideas about the future of architecture were created. Some of those visionary ideas, combining architecture and robotics already in early decades, were made by "Archigram", a London-based architecture group. This group created visionary ideas which display architecture in collaboration with robots, or as a machine or robot itself. Robotics thereby becomes an integral part of architecture, while buildings become intelligent, adaptive systems. The dystopian ideas of the postmodern world consisted of giant robots that interlink with each other, forming new cities and architectural forms. → 224

Unfortunately, the very speculative ideas of that time were never realised since they were partially too ambitious or economically unrealistic. To be fair, building massive mobile robotic structures, with their own artificial intelligence (AI) was quite an ambitious goal for that time. Nevertheless, the visions and technological utopianism of that time were important to create an initial awareness of the possible future correlation between architecture and robotics. Today, the body of thought created by Archigram is lived and executed in many ways due to the colourful comic artworks and drawings. It laid the foundation for further innovative robotic-architectural, symbiotic ideas. In the following years it resulted in the introduction of construction automation and was executed widely in the industry to optimise manufacturing processes and make buildings more cost-efficient.

New possibilities for architecture through construction robots

The technological utopianism was an incubator for a new robotic development period in the field of architecture and construction. Architecture is a form of expression and a field of work that has always developed in response to technical progress and social needs and is now facing a completely new technological dynamic: comparable to the invention of bricks, concrete, or the central perspective.

Koexistenz von Architektur und Robotik: Neue Denkweisen in einer postmodernen Welt

Betrachtet man die Robotik in der Architektur als Forschungsgebiet, tun sich unweigerlich diverse Referenzen sowohl aus der Architekturgeschichte als auch aus der Popkultur heraus auf. Idealvorstellungen utopischer Welten, geprägt von Fortschrittsoptimismus und Maschinenästhetik, bilden Technologie in einer Art räumlicher Inszenierung ab. Dementsprechend lässt sich die Beziehung zwischen Architektur und Maschinen bzw. Robotern, und auch die damit verbundene Faszination, bis in die 1960ern/70ern zurückverfolgen. Diese Zeit war durch eine neue Lebensweise geprägt: Pop, Rebellion, Science-Fiction, die Einführung neuer Medien in der Kunst und temporäre Installationen, während radikale und visionäre Ideen zur Zukunft der Architektur entwickelt wurden. Einige dieser visionären Ideen, die Architektur und Robotik bereits früh miteinander verbanden, kamen von „Archigram", einer in London ansässigen Gruppe von Architekten. Sie erarbeiteten visionäre Ideen, die Architektur in Kollaboration mit Robotern inszenierte, sie bisweilen sogar selbst als Maschine oder Roboter darstellte. Robotik wird hier zum integralen Bestandteil von Architektur, Gebäude werden zu intelligenten, adaptiven Systemen. In den dystopischen Ideen der Postmoderne verbanden sich gigantische Roboter miteinander, um so neue Städte und architektonische Formen zu generieren → 224

Leider wurden die sehr spekulativen Ideen dieser Zeit nie realisiert, da sie in Teilen zu ambitioniert oder einfach aus ökonomischer Sicht unrealistisch waren. Zugegeben sind riesige mobile, roboterhafte Strukturen, versehen mit künstlicher Intelligenz (KI) ein für die Zeit sehr anspruchsvolles Unterfangen. Gleichwohl waren die Visionen und technologischen Utopien der Zeit für die Generierung einer zukunftsorientierten Wahrnehmung, welche erstmals die direkte Beziehung zwischen Architektur und Robotik thematisierte, von großer Bedeutung. Heute wird das Gedankengut von Archigram, dank der lebhaften Comics, Kunstwerke und Zeichnungen, auf vielerlei Weise gelebt und implementiert. Es legte den Grundstein für weitere Ideen, die Robotik und Architektur symbiotisch verbinden. In den folgenden Jahren resultierte daraus die Einführung und branchenweite Anwendung der Konstruktionsautomatisierung zur Optimierung von Fertigungsprozessen und Kosteneffizienz.

Neue Möglichkeiten für die Architektur durch Bauroboter

Der technologische Utopismus war ein Inkubator für eine neue Ära robotischer Entwicklungen in Architektur und Bauausführung. Architektur als Ausdrucksform und Arbeitsfeld, hat sich seit je her entlang technischen Fortschritts und sozialer Bedürfnisse weiterentwickelt und sieht sich nun mit einer völlig neuen, technologischen Dynamik konfrontiert, die vergleichbar mit

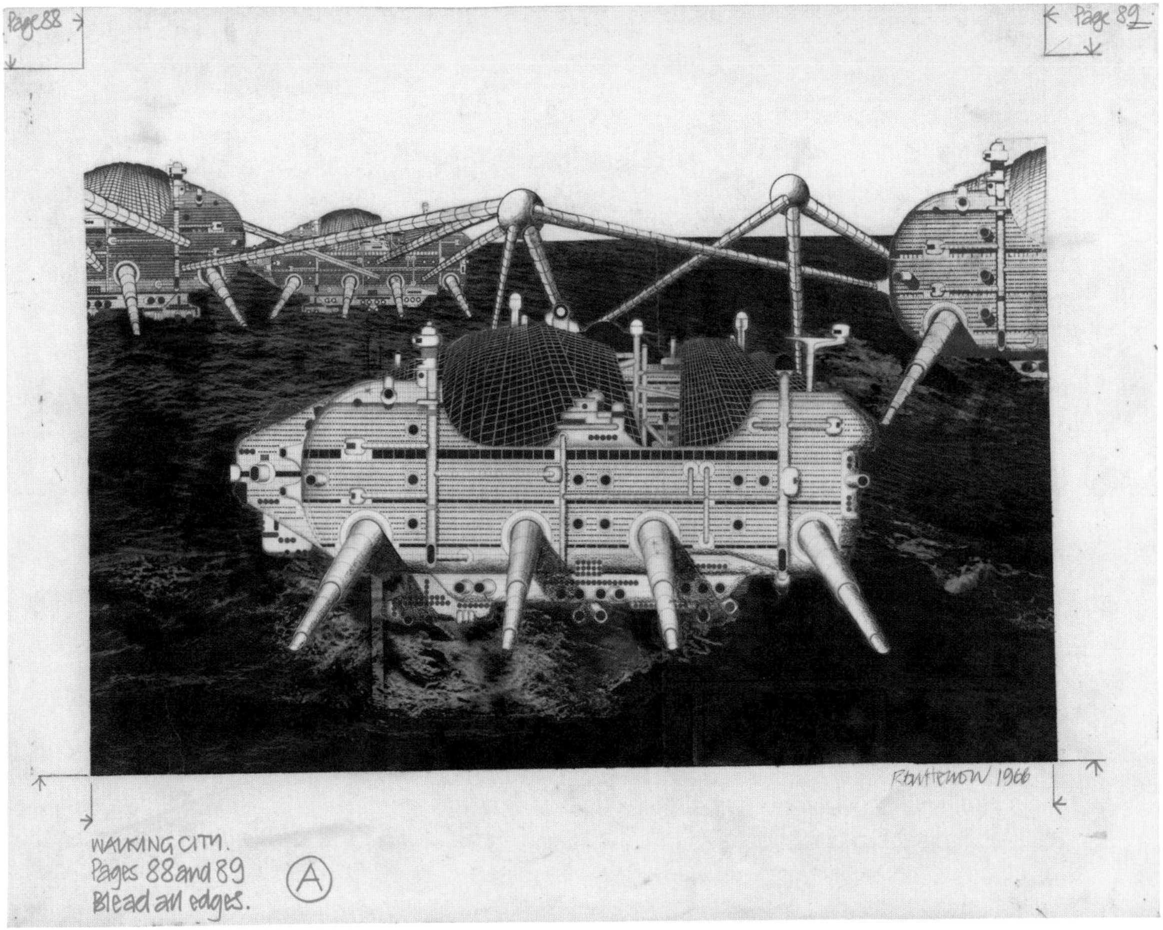
Page 88
Page 89
Ron Herron 1966
WALKING CITY.
Pages 88 and 89
Bleed all edges.
A

224

224
"Walking City on the Ocean, project (Exterior perspective)", Ron Herron, 1966
„Walking City on the Ocean, project (Exterior perspective)", Ron Herron, 1966

Due to the speed and radicality with which their underlying conditions change, architects must sacrifice well-tried concepts in order to formulate new architectural answers, which are driven by technology.

Thereby, new technologies are not something to affirm or be sceptical about, but rather affect the DNA of architecture already today. Architects can and must make use of all modern developments such as the latest visualisation processes, building information modelling (BIM), the Internet of things (IoT), artificial intelligence (AI), big data or robotics. These technologies not only complement sketch pads and drawing boards: they can and must lead to more intelligent designs, constructions and construction processes. For a few hundred years, architects created drawings and would hand them over to the construction site to erect the building based on the information in the drawings. Nevertheless, if architects used the whole scope of digital advancements in the field, especially robotics, that would bring many unimagined advantages.

First, they would need to figure out how to instruct the machines to fulfil the design intent as purely as possible - without losing any information through translation and as seamlessly as possible. Thereby, the programmed information goes straight to the robot, or more precisely the underlying software, and finally to the robot's end effector, which is generally the last component of a robot and responsible for the final execution of the assigned task. The robot understands the digital information and can execute the task while interacting with its physical environment. This seamless workflow without delays or information loss is highly efficient. Moreover, architects can simulate the whole robotic construction process in real time to secure better time management and planning reliability. Thereby, the construction site offers the possibility for robots to execute especially repetitive and physically intense tasks (such as plastering, painting, drilling or the on-site assembly of modular elements etc.) to relieve construction workers.

In this scenario the construction site acts as a test environment with realistic on-site conditions. The on-site investigation can sound out new potential, as well as limitations, and can create a new research basis for further developments. This turns architecture into an extended test laboratory for new construction robots and their realistic application.

Architecture is increasingly becoming a laboratory and experimental field for robotics.

As a result of the above-mentioned further developments, industry is shifting from automation in factories to the direct use of construction robots on the construction site.

dem Aufkommen von Ziegelmauerwerk, Beton oder der Zentralperspektive ist. Aufgrund der Geschwindigkeit und der Radikalität, mit der sich ihre Rahmenbedingungen ändern, müssen Architekten ihre altbewährten Konzepte aufgeben, um neue, von Technik getragene, architektonische Antworten formulieren zu können.

Dabei sind neue Technologien nicht etwas, das es zu bejahen gilt oder das mit Skepsis zu betrachten ist, sondern sie beeinflussen die DNA von Architektur bereits heute. Architekten können und müssen nach Möglichkeit von allen technologischen Entwicklungen Gebrauch machen, wie etwa den neuesten Visualisierungsprozessen, Building Information Modeling (BIM), dem Internet of Things (IoT), künstlicher Intelligenz (KI), Big Data oder der Robotik. Diese Technologien komplementieren nicht nur Skizzenbuch und Reißbrett, sondern können und müssen zu intelligenteren Entwürfen, Konstruktionen und Bauprozessen führen. Über hunderte von Jahren hinweg haben Architekten Zeichnungen erstellt und diese auf die Baustellen weitergereicht, damit, basierend auf den Informationen dieser Zeichnungen, Gebäude errichtet werden konnten. Würden Architekten die volle Bandbreite des digitalen Fortschritts im Fach, insbesondere der Robotik, ausschöpfen, würde das viele ungeahnte Vorteile mit sich bringen.

Zunächst müssten sie jedoch einen Weg finden, die Maschinen nahtlos und ohne Informationsverlust so zu instruieren, dass ihr Entwurf so unverfälscht wie möglich realisiert werden kann. Dabei gehen die programmierten Informationen direkt an den Roboter oder, präziser ausgedrückt, von der Software an den Endeffektor, der die letzte Komponente eines Roboters darstellt und schlussendlich für die Ausführung einer zugeteilten Aufgabe zuständig ist. Der Roboter kann diese Informationen verarbeiten und den Auftrag ausführen. Dieser nahtlose Workflow, ohne Verzögerung oder Informationsverlust, ist hoch effizient. Zudem können Architekten den gesamten robotergestützten Bauprozess in Echtzeit simulieren, um so ein besseres Zeitmanagement und Planungssicherheit zu gewährleisten. Dabei kann der Roboter auf der Baustelle insbesondere repetitive und physisch fordernde Aufgaben (bspw. Verputzen, Anstreichen, Bohren oder die Montage modularer Fassadenelemente) ausführen und dadurch Bauarbeiter entlasten.

In diesem Szenario fungiert die Baustelle als Testumgebung mit realistischen Vor-Ort-Bedingungen. Die Evaluierung vor Ort kann neue Potentiale, aber auch Limitierungen aufzeigen und durch die Rückführung der digitalen Informationen eine Grundlage für Weiterentwicklungen schaffen. Damit wird die Architektur zu einem erweiterten Testlabor für neue Bauroboter und ihre realitätsnahe Anwendung.

Architektur wird zunehmend zum Labor und Versuchsfeld für Robotik.

Die Industrie wandelt sich vor diesem Hintergrund von der Automation in Fabriken hin zur direkten Anwendung von Robotern auf der Baustelle.

From research to practice

For over a decade, the research and development work in the field of construction automation and construction robotics has been carried out through the integration of so-called "soft", information-based technology for on-site construction (such as BIM, techniques for disposition and construction process optimization, sensor systems, etc.). Recently, a renewed interest in the development of so-called "hard" physical-mechanical robot systems for the execution of specific tasks on the construction site can be observed. This manifests itself in an increase in academic research activity, joint industry-academia collaboration projects, the emergence of numerous start-ups, and a strong, growing interest in the development of construction robots among large, established organisations.

This interest is derived from new future scenarios which can nowadays be imagined due to the advancements in the construction industry and the field of construction robotics. Robots will help build and possibly even inhabit our world. The introduction of construction robots for executing repetitive tasks such as drilling or painting, drones for on-site inspections or further measurements, exoskeletons for lifting heavy loads, concrete 3D-printing of an entire building shell, or AI to make complex building adaptations, will make architecture an innovation platform for robotics.

Robots are already being used on-site. The issue is not whether robotics will play a role in the architecture of the future, but how to overcome existing innovation obstacles and occurring problems in the construction process, as well as the planning process in the architecture office.

These problems occur in particular when integrating robots into the existing construction process, because current development activities face significant uncertainties, particularly in terms of the definition and management of system requirements, which are primarily based on vague assumptions about the future. Overall, we are talking about a large and rigid process that would require change but is difficult due to the high number of stakeholders and various interrelated processes. Nevertheless, to make an implementation of robots in the construction industry and architecture possible, it is necessary to create a process-orientated approach, which embeds the system in (technically and economically formed) social movements. Thus importantly: "to explore how construction robots can successfully be implemented and unlock their potential for large-scale applications, a broader analytical perspective that considers both technical and non-technical issues and their interplay is required,"(Pan et al., 2020).

Von der Forschung zur Praxis

Die Forschungs- und Entwicklungsarbeit auf dem Gebiet der Bauautomatisierung und Baurobotik, wurde mehr als ein Jahrzehnt durch die Integration sogenannter „softer", informationsbasierter Technologie für Vor-Ort-Baumaßnahmen (wie etwa BIM, Techniken für die Dispositions- und Bauprozessoptimierung, Sensorsysteme etc.) dominiert. In letzter Zeit ist jedoch ein erneutes Interesse an der Entwicklung sogenannter „harter", physisch-mechanischer Robotersysteme für die Ausführung spezifischer Arbeiten auf der Baustelle zu beobachten. Dies manifestiert sich in einer Zunahme akademischer Forschungsaktivität, an Kooperationsprojekten zwischen Hochschulen und der Industrie, dem Aufkommen zahlreicher Start-Ups und dem stark wachsenden Interesse an der Entwicklung von Baurobotern durch große, etablierte Organisationen.

Dieses Interesse leitet sich aus neuen Zukunftsszenarien ab, die heute aufgrund der Fortschritte in der Bauindustrie und im Bereich der Baurobotik vorstellbar sind. Roboter werden unsere Welt mit bauen und sie möglicherweise irgendwann sogar besiedeln. Der Einsatz von Baurobotern zur Ausführung repetitiver Aufgaben, wie beispielsweise das Bohren von Löchern (TGA), das Streichen einer Wand (beim Innenausbau), Inspektionen durch Drohnen (Vermessungen und Inspektion), das Heben schwerer Lasten durch die Unterstützung von Exoskeletten, der 3D-Betondruck eines gesamten Rohbaus, oder aber KI-Systeme für komplexe Gebäudeadaptionen werden die Architektur zu einer Innovationsplattform für die Robotik machen.

Roboter kommen bereits heute auf der Baustelle zum Einsatz. Es ist somit keine Frage, ob Roboter eine Rolle in der Architektur der Zukunft spielen werden, sondern wie bestehende Innovationshemmnisse und aufkommende Probleme im Bauprozess, sowie im Planungsprozess im Architekturbüro überwunden werden können.

Diese Probleme entstehen insbesondere dann, wenn Roboter in bestehende Bauprozesse eingebunden werden sollen, da sie mit Unklarheiten hinsichtlich der Definition und des Managements von Systemanforderungen konfrontiert sind, welche in der Regel nur auf vagen Zukunftsannahmen beruhen. Insgesamt sprechen wir somit von einem großen und starren Prozess, der zwar einer Veränderung bedürfte, jedoch aufgrund der hohen Anzahl an Stakeholdern und verschiedenen ineinandergreifenden Prozessen schwierig ist. Doch um die Implementierung von Baurobotern zu ermöglichen, bedarf es eines prozessorientierten Ansatzes, der den Bauprozess in sowohl technisch und ökonomisch als auch sozial geformte Bahnen einbettet. Es zeigt sich daher, dass „um zu untersuchen, wie Bauroboter erfolgreich eingeführt und ihr Potential für größere Anwendungen ausgeschöpft werden können, es einer breiten, analytischen Sichtweise bedarf, die sowohl technische als auch nicht-technische Fragen und deren Zusammenspiel betrachtet" (Pan et al., 2020).

253

Construction robot examples

Today's construction robots offer a wide range of use cases. The following text deals with four different robot systems and describes their different applications. Furthermore, the projects showcase how the construction site is being simultaneously used as a research lab/platform to further develop robotic systems (e.g. the adaption of end effectors or even the programming, due to on-site investigations).

The first project is called "HEPHAESTUS"[1] and is a cable-driven panel installation robot. → 225 It is used for the automated positioning and on-site assembly of façade panels via a cable-driven system, which allows the robot to flexibly reach the entire façade in order to assemble the modules. The project highlights how labour-intense construction work and physically exhausting, repetitive tasks on the construction site (related to logistics and installation) can be executed by a robot in a very precise, as well as cost-efficient manner. With this technology the architect can plan, organise and above all execute projects in less time and with higher precision using various sensors, thereby guaranteeing planning reliability. Moreover, on-site testing was an integral part of the research and is binding for the adequate and thus realistic implementation of the design hypothesis.

The "CIC"[2] → 226 is a multifunctional façade and exterior finishing robot for the Construction Industry Council (CIC) in Hong Kong. The proposed use cases were exterior painting, concrete wall-grinding and water-tightness inspection. These use cases can be executed through a linear axis hoisting system, which is attached to the building and works as the robotic platform. Thereby, the robot facilitates the setup of a manufacturing system for the robot. The end effector can reach most of the façade surface and be exchanged for further use cases. This multifunctional modular façade-processing robot was primarily used for finishing work in high-rise housing in Hong Kong and represents how various exterior finishing tasks can be executed by a robot. The project also included a 1:2 semi-functional prototype of the multifunctional façade-processing robot, which was built and tested in a laboratory as a proof of concept (with a laser beam instead of paint for the façade as a use case).

Whereas the first two projects focus more on exterior finishing tasks/use cases, the following projects concentrate on constructing the exterior building shell using different construction methods.

The third project is a robot focussing on 3D printing. Thereby, 3D printing is an additive manufacturing process that is constantly being developed and already used in various work areas, such as the manufacture of dentures or car parts. The 3D printing is characterised

Beispiele für Bauroboter

Die Bauroboter von heute decken ein weites Spektrum von Anwendungsfällen ab. Der folgende Text geht auf vier verschiedene Robotersysteme ein und beschreibt deren unterschiedliche Anwendungsfälle. Darüber hinaus veranschaulichen die Projekte wie die Baustelle simultan als Forschungsplattform genutzt wird, um Robotersysteme weiterzuentwickeln (bspw. bei der Adaption von Endeffektoren oder auch der Programmierung, aufgrund der Vor-Ort Untersuchungen).

Das erste Projekt trägt den Namen „HEPHAESTUS"[1] und ist ein seilzuggeführter Roboter für die Installation von Fassadenelementen → 225 Er wird für die automatisierte Positionierung und Vor-Ort-Montage von Fassadenpaneelen über ein Seilzugsystem eingesetzt, welches dem Roboter erlaubt flexibel die gesamte Fassade zu erreichen, um die Module zusammenfügen zu können. Das Projekt verdeutlicht, wie arbeitsintensive Bauarbeiten und körperlich anstrengende, repetitive Aufgaben auf der Baustelle (bezogen auf Logistik und Installation) durch einen Roboter auf sehr präzise und kosteneffiziente Art und Weise ausgeführt werden können. Mittels dieser Technologie kann der Architekt in kürzerer Zeit Projekte planen, organisieren und sie vor allem mit größerer Präzision durch den Einsatz diverser Sensoren ausführen und dadurch Planungssicherheit gewährleisten.

Der „CIC"[2] 226 ist ein multifunktionaler Fassaden- und Exterieur-Finishing-Roboter für das Construction Industry Council (CIC) in Hong Kong. Die beabsichtigten Anwendungsfälle waren das Streichen, Schleifen von Betonwänden und die Wasserdichtigkeitskontrolle. Diese Anwendungsfälle können über ein Linearachsenhubsystem ausgeführt werden, welches am Gebäude befestigt ist und als Roboterplattform fungiert. Der Endeffektor kann den größten Teil der Fassade erreichen und für weitere Verwendungszwecke ausgetauscht werden. Dieser multifunktionale Roboter wurde primär für Fertigungsarbeiten im Wohnhochhausbau in Hong Kong eingesetzt und veranschaulicht, wie ein Roboter diverse Exterieur-Finishing Aufgaben (Oberflächenveredelungen) übernehmen kann. Das Projekt umfasste ebenfalls ein Prototyp im Maßstab 1:2, der im Labor als Machbarkeitsnachweis gebaut und getestet wurde (mit einem Laserstrahl anstatt Farbe für eine Fassade als Anwendungsfall für das Streichen einer Fassade).

Während die ersten beiden Roboter eher auf Anwendungsfälle im Bereich des Exterieur-Finishings der Fassade fokussiert waren, liegt der Schwerpunkt der folgenden Projekte auf der Konstruktion des Rohbaus unter Anwendung verschiedener Konstruktionsverfahren.

Das dritte Projekt ist ein Roboter, welcher sich auf den 3D-Druck fokussiert. Der 3D-Druck ist ein additives Herstellungsverfahren, welches stetig weiterentwickelt und bereits in diversen Bereichen eingesetzt wird, wie beispielsweise bei der Herstellung von

225
Development of a
cable-driven panel
installation robot
in the project
HEPHAESTUS: This
project received
funding from the
European Union's
H2020 Programme
(H2020 / 2014-2020)
under Grant Agree-
ment Number 732513
Entwicklung eines
Seilzugroboters
zur Installation von
Fassadenelementen
im Projekt
HEPHAESTUS:
Dieses Projekt
wurde durch das
Programm H2020
der Europäischen
Union (H2020 / 2014-
2020) unter der
Grant Agreement
Nummer 732513
finanziell gefördert

226
Development of a
façade-processing
robot for CIC
Entwicklung eines
Fassadenbaurobo-
ters für das CIC

227

227
Concrete 3D printing robot from PERI and Cobot
Beton-3D-Druck-Roboter von PERI und Cobot

228
Hadrian X robotic blocklaying machine / system robot from FBR
Hadrian X Maurerroboter von FBR

228

by the application of different materials in layers – here concrete. →227 The concrete can even be coloured individually by adding appropriate colour granulate, allowing even greater customization of the building-shell material. Moreover, a precise pre-simulation of the concrete printing process on a PC can avoid the corresponding waste of concrete, while new structural shapes can be used that apply less material and are thereby more sustainable. In addition, the insulation material can also be poured into openings provided in the concrete, while apertures for sockets and other installations can be considered in the printing process. In addition, while using concrete 3D printing, a new variety of shapes of convex and concave geometries can be created, not only expanding the designer's freedom, but also reducing material usage. The robot (see Fig. 4) was produced by PERI and Cobot for the aforementioned concrete 3D printing method to create the first 3D printed house in Germany, as well as the largest 3D printed residential building in Europe in 2020. The portal printer system enables the robot to reach every point on the processing surface by moving the print head moves over three axes on a permanently installed metal frame.

The last project is the so called "Hadrian X" robot →228 from Fastbrick Robotics (FBR) and is the first mobile robotic block-/bricklaying machine/system. The robot is capable of constructing the exterior building shell consisting of blocks (e.g. bricks) in an additive manufacturing process in the outdoor environment. Compared to conventional construction methods, the robot reduces waste material and improves planning reliability as well as the individual safety of the construction workers. The data for the procedure is thereby derived from 3D-CAD-models and converted into specific positions by the software, which ensures an accurate positioning. Moreover, the underlying software converts 3D models (e.g. walls) into specific positions, which guarantees accurate block positioning. In addition, the robot uses modular-designed blocks with cores to enable an easy installation of several services within the building shell (Hadrian X® | Outdoor Construction & Bricklaying Robot from FBR, n.d.).

Conclusion

Even though the field of robotics in relation to architecture is still in its early stages, the examples show it has already made significant changes to the way construction projects are planned, executed and maintained today. Things that seemed like science fiction or technological utopianism only a few decades ago are now entirely within the realm of possibility. Robotics will undoubtedly play a major role in the

Zahnersatz oder Autoteilen. Das Verfahren wird durch den schichtweisen Auftrag verschiedener Materialien – hier Beton – charakterisiert. →227 Der Beton kann durch die Beigabe geeigneter Farbgranulate individuell eingefärbt werden und somit neue gestalterische Möglichkeiten generieren. Des Weiteren kann eine Vorab-Simulation des Druckprozesses am PC einen optimalen Materialeinsatz gewährleisten, während neue, materialsparende und somit nachhaltigere Konstruktionen angewendet werden können. Zusätzlich kann das Dämmmaterial direkt in dafür vorgesehene Aussparungen im Beton integriert werden. Dabei können Öffnungen für Steckdosen und andere Anschlüsse im Druckprozess berücksichtigt werden. Bei der Verwendung von Beton-3D-Druck kann außerdem eine Vielzahl an Formen konvexer und konkaver Geometrien erstellt werden, wodurch nicht nur die Gestaltungsfreiheit des Architekten gestärkt wird, sondern der Materialverbrauch außerdem reduziert werden kann. Beispielhaft für eine entsprechende Anwendung ist der in Abbildung 4 gezeigte Beton-3D-Druck-Roboter von PERI und Cobot. In dem gezeigten Projekt ist das erste 3D-gedruckte Haus in Deutschland in der Entstehung zu sehen, welche außerdem das im Jahr 2020 größte 3D-gedruckte Wohnhaus Europas war. Das Portaldrucker-System kann jeden Punkt der Bearbeitungsfläche erreichen, indem sich der Druckkopf über drei Achsen auf einem fest installierten Metallrahmen bewegt.

Der sogenannte „Hadrian X" Roboter →228 von „Fastbrick Robotics" (FBR), ist der erste mobile Roboter, für Maurer-, Verlege- und Ziegelarbeiten. Der Roboter ist in der Lage eine aus Blöcken (bspw. Ziegeln) bestehende äußere Gebäudehülle in einem additiven Herstellungsverfahren im Freien zu errichten. Durch den Roboter wird im Vergleich zu herkömmlichen Konstruktionsmethoden, eine Materialverschwendung ausgeschlossen und die Planungssicherheit, als auch individuelle Sicherheit der Bauarbeiter verbessert. Die Daten für das Verfahren stammen von 3D-CAD-Modellen, welche durch eine Software in spezifische Positionen umgerechnet werden, was eine akkurate Positionierung gewährleistet. Zusätzlich verwendet der Roboter modular aufgebaute Blöcke mit Einsätzen, die eine unkomplizierte Installation diverser Haustechnik in die Gebäudehülle ermöglichen (Hadrian X® | Outdoor Construction & Bricklaying Robot from FBR, o.J.).

Fazit

Obwohl der Bereich der Robotik im Vergleich zur Architektur noch in den Kinderschuhen steckt, zeigen die Projektbeispiele, dass er schon signifikante Veränderungen an der heutigen Art der Projektplanung, -ausführung und -betreuung verursacht hat. Was vor wenigen Jahrzehnten noch wie Science-Fiction klang, oder sich nach technischem Utopismus anhörte, befindet sich nun im Bereich des Möglichen. Die Robotik wird unweigerlich eine

way the construction industry and architecture develop in the coming years, because these flexible, automated systems will help solve many issues and comprehensively optimise workflows across the board. The intersection of architecture and robotics represents an ideal research ground with mutual benefits and future development possibilities. Moreover, there will be a tipping point where it is almost impossible to compete with robots from an efficiency perspective. Decades of research and teaching have laid the foundation for numerous careers, dissertations, start-ups, products, and spin-offs that drive today's growing industrial activity in the sector today.

bedeutende Rolle in der Art und Weise spielen, wie sich Bauindustrie und Architektur in den kommenden Jahren entwickeln werden, denn diese flexiblen, automatisierten Systeme werden bei der Lösung vieler Probleme helfen und Arbeitsabläufe umfassend optimieren. Die Schnittstelle von Architektur und Robotik stellt dabei ein ideales Forschungsgebiet von beiderseitigem Nutzen und zukünftigen Entwicklungsmöglichkeiten dar. Darüber hinaus wird es in Zukunft zu einem Wendepunkt kommen, ab dem es, von einem Effizienzgesichtspunkt aus, fast nicht mehr möglich sein wird mit Robotern zu konkurrieren. Jahrzehnte der Forschung und Lehre haben die Grundlagen für eine Vielzahl von Karrieren, Dissertationen, Start-Ups, Produkten und Spin-Offs gelegt, die heute die treibenden Kräfte der wachsenden industriellen Aktivität im Sektor darstellen.

1
Development of a cable-driven panel installation robot in the project HEPHAESTUS: This project received funding from the European Union's H2020 Programme (H2020/2014-2020) under Grant Agreement Number 732513

2
Development of a façade-processing robot for CIC. This project was commissioned by the Construction Industry Council Hong Kong.

References:
M. Pan, T. Linner, W. Pan, H.-m. Cheng, T. Bock, "Influencing factors of thefuture utilisation of construction robots for buildings: A Hong Kong perspective", Journal of Building Engineering (2020), doi: https://doi.org/10.1016/j.jobe.2020.101220.

Hadrian X® | "Outdoor Construction & Bricklaying Robot from FBR", (n.d.). Accessed on October 10, 2021, at https://www.fbr.com.au/view/hadrian-x.

1
Entwicklung eines Seilzugroboters zur Paneelinstallation im Projekt HEPHAESTUS: Dieses Projekt wurde durch das Programm H2020 der Europäischen Union (H2020/2014-2020) unter der Grant Agreement Nummer 732513 finanziell gefördert.

2
Entwicklung eines Fassadenbauroboters für den CIC. Dieses Projekt wurde vom Construction Industry Council Hong Kong in Auftrag gegeben.

Quellen:
M. Pan, T. Linner, W. Pan, H.-m. Cheng, T. Bock, "Influencing factors of thefuture utilisation of construction robots for buildings: A Hong Kong perspective", Journal of Building Engineering (2020), doi: https://doi.org/10.1016/j.jobe.2020.101220.

Hadrian X® | "Outdoor Construction & Bricklaying Robot from FBR", (n.d.). Retrieved October 10, 2021, at https://www.fbr.com.au/view/hadrian-x.

`229`

Designing the future together

For many decades, the work of countless researchers remained almost entirely overlooked by the general public, despite their essential contribution to social wellbeing. Thus, the typology of research buildings was also characterised by isolation and concealment, shielded off behind high walls and fences. In recent years however, this perception has experienced a fundamental transformation, especially during the Covid-19 pandemic, as their protagonists have become heroes and pioneers in the struggle to overcome the virus. Thus typologies are also gradually changing, opening buildings up to society and affording the discipline a higher profile as a key element of social progress. This book documents this transformation from typological, architectural, functional and operative perspectives, while also presenting potential for future developments.

The task would have been impossible without the articles contributed by our guest authors, to whom I am extremely grateful.

Very special thanks to Stefanie Matthys, whose tireless efforts have ensured the production of this volume, as well as Stefanie Attenberger, Marc Schmailzl and Michael Wolfer for compiling and editing the book's many images, plans and graphics. Lisa Zech and Agnes Essig have given the volume its unique graphic identity. Benjamin Liebelt has translated the German texts into correct English, while Friederike Christoph's copy editing has ironed out any errors. Our sincere thanks to them all.

Finally, special thanks go to all the protagonists who have accompanied us on our journey to develop identity-enhancing laboratory buildings, allowing the architecture to highlight the field's key social role. We dedicate this book to you.

Prof. Hans Nickl, January 2022

Gemeinsam Zukunft gestalten

Die Tätigkeit unzähliger Forscherinnen und Forscher, trotz ihres essenziellen Beitrags zum Wohlergehen der Gesellschaft, erfolgte jahrzehntelang fast unbemerkt von einer breiteren Öffentlichkeit. Somit war auch die Typologie der Forschungsbauten eine der Abschottung und der Verborgenheit, geschützt durch hohe Mauern und Zäune. Diese Wahrnehmung erfuhr jedoch einen fundamentalen Wandel in den letzten Jahren und Ihre Protagonisten, vor allem auch in Zeiten einer Covid-19 Pandemie, wurden zu Helden und Vorreitern bei der Bekämpfung des Virus. Damit erfuhr auch die Typologie einen grundlegenden Wandel mit behutsamen Schritten in Richtung einer Öffnung der Bauwerke gegenüber der Gesellschaft und somit einer bewussteren Wahrnehmung des Metiers als einen festen Bestandteil des gesellschaftlichen Fortschritts.
Das hier vorliegende Buch begleitet diesen Wandel aus typologischen, architektonischen, funktionalen und betrieblichen Blickwinkeln und zeigt Potenziale für eine zukünftige Entwicklung auf.

Dies wäre jedoch nicht möglich gewesen ohne die Beiträge unserer Gastautoren, für die ich mich an dieser Stelle noch einmal ganz herzlich bedanken möchte.

Ein ganz besonderer Dank gebührt auch Stefanie Matthys, deren unermüdliche Arbeit dieses Buch überhaupt erst möglich gemacht hat, sowie für Stefanie Attenberger, Marc Schmailzl und Michael Wolfer für die Zusammenstellung und Bearbeitung der vielen Bilddaten, Pläne und Grafiken. Lisa Zech und Agnes Essig haben dem Werk seine unverwechselbare grafische Identität gegeben, Benjamin Liebelt verdanken wir es, die deutschen Texte in korrektem Englisch vorzufinden und Friederike Christoph, dass wir sie fehlerbefreit lesen dürfen. Auch ihnen ein herzliches Dankeschön.

Ein besonderer Dank gilt jedoch auch all den Protagonisten, die uns auf der Reise hin zu identitätsstiftenden Laborbauten, die ihre wichtige gesellschaftliche Rolle durch eine architektonische Ausprägung hervorheben, begleitet haben. Ihnen gilt die Widmung dieses Buches.

Prof. Hans Nickl im Januar 2022

Editors

Hans Nickl, Prof.
Studied Architecture at the Technische Universität München. In 1979, founded his own architectural office. In 1989, co-founded Nickl & Partner together with his wife Prof. Christine Nickl-Weller. In 1992, appointed Professor of Structural Design at Erfurt University of Applied Sciences. From 2004 to 2017, taught as a guest at the Technische Universität Berlin in the field of "Hospital Design and Healthcare Buildings".

Christine Nickl-Weller, Prof.
Studied Architecture at the Technische Universität München. In 1989, co-founded the architectural office Nickl & Partner in Munich. Conceived and constructed buildings in the healthcare, research and teaching sectors, both in Germany and abroad, as well as development and master plans. In 2008, became CEO of the corporation. In 2019, became Chairwoman of the Supervisory Board. From 2004 to 2017, Professor of "Hospital Design and Healthcare Buildings" at the Technische Universität Berlin.

Christine Nickl-Weller and Hans Nickl have published numerous specialist articles in publications and professional journals.

Herausgeber

Hans Nickl, Prof.
studierte Architektur an der Technischen Universität München. 1979 gründete er ein eigenes Architekturbüro und 1989 zusammen mit seiner Frau, Prof. Christine Nickl-Weller, die Architektengemeinschaft Nickl & Partner. Hans Nickl wurde 1992 auf die Professur für das Lehrgebiet „Konstruktives Entwerfen" an die FH Erfurt berufen und lehrte von 2004 bis 2017 als Gast am Fachgebiet „Entwerfen von Krankenhäusern und Bauten des Gesundheitswesens" an der Technischen Universität Berlin.

Christine Nickl-Weller, Prof.
studierte Architektur an der Technischen Universität München und trat 1989 in die Architektengemeinschaft Nickl & Partner in München ein. Sie konzipiert und realisiert Bauten der Gesundheit, der Forschung und der Lehre im In- und Ausland sowie Entwicklungs- und Masterpläne. 2008 übernahm sie den Vorstandsvorsitz der Aktiengesellschaft, 2019 wurde sie Aufsichtsratsvorsitzende. Von 2004 bis 2017 hatte sie die Professur für das Fachgebiet „Entwerfen von Krankenhäusern und Bauten des Gesundheitswesens" an der Technischen Universität Berlin inne.

Zur Thematik haben Christine Nickl-Weller und Hans Nickl zahlreiche Fachbeiträge in Publikationen und Fachzeitschriften veröffentlicht.

List of authors

Erwin K. Bauer
Certified farmer, graphic designer and font designer. As the founder and Managing Director of buero bauer, Gesellschaft für Orientierung und Identität mbH, manages projects with strategic expertise. He presents the office's diverse competencies in lectures, teaches at the University of Applied Arts Vienna, and works as a juror, curator and publisher.

Stefan Behnisch, Prof. Hon. FAIA
Born in Stuttgart in 1957, studied Philosophy, Economics and Architecture. Founded his own office in 1989, renamed Behnisch Architekten in 2005. Opened additional offices in Los Angeles (1999), Boston (2006) and Munich (2008). Carried out pioneering projects in the field of sustainable building in Europe and the USA. Has taught at various universities in Europe and the USA. Winner of the 2007 "Global Award for Sustainable Architecture" and the 2013 "Energy Performance + Architecture Award".

Lucio Blandini, Prof. Dr.-Ing.
Studied Construction Engineering at the Universities of Catania and Bologna, followed by a doctorate on glass shell load-bearing systems at the Institute for Lightweight Structures and Conceptual Design (ILEK), University of Stuttgart. After completing his Master in Architecture at the University of Pennsylvania Philadelphia and the Architectural Association in London, he became a Project Manager at Werner Sobek AG, appointed Authorised Officer in 2012, and Partner and Board Member in 2018. Since April 2020, Full Professor and Director of the ILEK. His most important projects at Werner Sobek include the Ferrari Museum in Modena, the Etihad Museum in Dubai, the House of European History in Brussels and Terminal 2 at Kuwait International Airport.

Thomas Bock, Prof. Dr. Ing. / Univ. Tokio
Is a professor of the Chair of Building Realization and Robotics at Technical University of Munich (TUM). He is a member of several boards of directors of international associations and of several international academies in Europe, America, and Asia. He serves on several editorial boards, heads various working commissions and groups of international research organizations and has authored and co-authored books from the Cambridge Handbooks in Construction Robotics series and more than 500 articles.

Autorenverzeichnis

Erwin K. Bauer
ist ausgebildeter Landwirt, Grafikdesigner & Schriftgestalter. Als Gründer und Geschäftsführer von buero bauer, Gesellschaft für Orientierung und Identität mbH, leitet er Projekte mit strategischer Expertise. Er präsentiert die vielseitigen Kompetenzen des Büros in Vorträgen, lehrt an der Universität für angewandte Kunst in Wien, juriert, kuratiert und publiziert.

Stefan Behnisch, Prof. Hon. FAIA
geboren 1957 in Stuttgart, studierte Philosophie, Volkswirtschaft und Architektur. 1989 gründete er sein eigenes Büro, das seit 2005 als Behnisch Architekten firmiert. Weitere Standorte in Los Angeles (1999), Boston (2006) und München (2008) folgten. Wegweisende Projekte im Bereich nachhaltigen Bauens wurden in Europa und den USA realisiert. Stefan Behnisch lehrte an verschiedenen Hochschulen in Europa und den USA. 2007 wurde er mit dem „Global Award for Sustainable Architecture", 2013 mit dem „Energy Performance + Architecture Award" ausgezeichnet.

Lucio Blandini, Prof. Dr.-Ing.
studierte an den Universitäten von Catania und Bologna konstruktiven Ingenieurbau, bevor er am Institut für Leichtbau Entwerfen und Konstruieren (ILEK) der Universität Stuttgart über Schalentragwerke aus Glas promovierte. Nach einem Master-Studium der Architektur an der University of Pennsylvania Philadelphia und an der Architectural Association in London trat er eine Stelle als Projektleiter bei der Werner Sobek AG an. Seit 2012 ist er Prokurist, seit 2018 auch Partner und Vorstand des Unternehmens. Seit April 2020 ist er als ordentlicher Professor für die Leitung des ILEK verantwortlich. Zu seinen wichtigsten Projekten bei Werner Sobek zählen das Ferrari-Museum in Modena, das Etihad Museum in Dubai, das Haus der Europäischen Geschichte in Brüssel und das Terminal 2 des Kuwait International Airport.

Thomas Bock, Prof. Dr. Ing. / Univ. Tokio
ist Professor am Lehrstuhl für Baurealisierung und Baurobotik an der Technischen Universität München (TUM). Er ist Mitglied mehrerer Verwaltungsräte internationaler Verbände und mehrerer internationaler Akademien in Europa, Amerika und Asien. Er ist Mitglied mehrerer Editorial Boards, leitet verschiedene Arbeitskommissionen und Gruppen internationaler Forschungsorganisationen und ist Autor und Co-Autor von Büchern der Cambridge Handbooks in Construction Robotics-Reihe und von mehr als 500 Artikeln.

Stefan Bötel

Graduated in Architecture at the TU Darmstadt and subsequently worked in various architectural offices in Hanover and Munich, focusing on highly installed technical buildings. Since 2007, employed at Nickl & Partner Architekten as Head of the Research and Educational Buildings Division. His projects include the Institute for Stroke and Dementia Research in Munich, the Comprehensive Heart Failure Center Wuerzburg and the Institute of Process Innovation in Bayreuth. He is currently responsible for the new construction of the Centre for Digitally Networked Production in Aachen (CdvP).

Brigitte Grass, Prof. Dr.

Studied Business Administration and Business Education at the University of Cologne. Worked as a Research Associate and completed her doctorate. Subsequently employed as a Consultant at the Boston Consulting Group in Düsseldorf. Has over 35 years' experience in higher education, teaching at the FH Köln and elsewhere. Founding Dean of the Hochschule Bonn-Rhein-Sieg, from 2009 to 2019, President of the Hochschule Düsseldorf. She remains a Committee Member of an environmental foundation and is on the Supervisory Board of several companies. She was a foil fencer at the Olympic Games in Munich and Montreal.

Christoph Heinekamp, Dr.

After his doctorate in Chemistry, became a professional researcher in field of medicine. In his capacity as User Coordinator, he supervised the development of Clinical Chemistry at the University Hospital Regensburg. In 1992, he began working on laboratory planning and has been CEO of dr. heinekamp Labor- und Institutsplanung since 1996. As a laboratory planner, he has completed pioneering projects for public and private contractors. Sustainable planning for society has always been the guiding principle for his planning tasks.

Stefan Hell, Prof. Dr. Dr. h.c. mult.

Stefan Hell is a Director at both the Max Planck Institute for Medical Research in Heidelberg and the Max Planck Institute for Multidisciplinary Sciences in Göttingen. Hell is credited with having conceived, validated and applied the first viable concept for overcoming Abbe's diffraction-limited resolution barrier in a light-focusing fluorescence microscope, thereby founding the research field of optical nanoscopy. For this accomplishment he has received numerous awards, including the 2014 Kavli Prize in Nanoscience and the Nobel Prize in Chemistry.

Stefan Bötel

schloss sein Architekturstudium an der TU Darmstadt ab und arbeitete anschließend in verschiedenen Architekturbüros in Hannover und München mit dem Schwerpunkt technisch hochinstallierter Gebäude. Seit 2007 ist er für Nickl & Partner Architekten als Geschäftsleiter im Bereich Forschungs- und Lehrgebäude tätig. Zu seinen Projekten zählen u.a. das Institut für Schlaganfall- und Demenzforschung in München, das Deutsche Zentrum für Herzinsuffizienz in Würzburg sowie das Institut für Prozessinnovation der Fraunhofergesellschaft in Bayreuth. Derzeit ist er für den Neubau des Zentrums für digital vernetzte Produktion in Aachen (CdvP) verantwortlich.

Brigitte Grass, Prof. Dr.

hat an der Universität zu Köln Betriebswirtschaftslehre und Wirtschaftspädagogik studiert. Sie war als wissenschaftliche Mitarbeiterin tätig und hat promoviert. Danach stieg sie als Consultant bei der Boston Consulting Group in Düsseldorf ein. Sie verfügt über eine mehr als 35jährige Erfahrung im Hochschulwesen, lehrte u.a. an der FH Köln, war Gründungsdekan an der Hochschule Bonn-Rhein-Sieg und von 2009 bis 2019 Präsidentin der Hochschule Düsseldorf. Sie ist weiterhin im Vorstand einer Umweltstiftung und in Aufsichtsgremien mehrerer Gesellschaften. Sie war Olympiateilnehmerin in München und Montreal im Damenflorett.

Christoph Heinekamp, Dr.

hat nach der Promotion in der Chemie in der medizinischen Forschung gearbeitet. Als Nutzerkoordinator hat er den Aufbau der Klinischen Chemie am Universitätsklinikum Regensburg begleitet. 1992 ist er in die Laborplanung gewechselt und leitet seit 1996 die dr. heinekamp Labor- und Institutsplanung. Als Laborplaner hat er für öffentliche und private Auftraggeber zukunftweisende Projekte realisiert. Die nachhaltige Planung für die Menschen war die Richtschnur für alle seine Planungsaufgaben.

Stefan Hell, Prof. Dr. Dr. h.c. mult.

ist Direktor am Max-Planck-Institut für medizinische Forschung in Heidelberg und am Max-Planck-Institut für Multidisziplinäre Naturwissenschaften in Göttingen. Hell beschrieb und setzte als Erster ein realistisches Konzept zur Überwindung der Abbe'schen beugungsbegrenzten Auflösungsgrenze in einem lichtfokussierenden Fluoreszenzmikroskop um, und begründete damit das Forschungsfeld der optischen Nanoskopie. Für diese Leistung erhielt er zahlreiche Auszeichnungen, darunter 2014 den Kavli-Preis für Nanowissenschaften und den Nobelpreis für Chemie.

Katharina Hölzl

Information Designer, graduating at the Hochschule der Medien Stuttgart and the FH Joanneum University of Applied Sciences, Graz. At buero bauer, Gesellschaft für Orientierung und Identität mbH, works on exhibition design and orientation planning, presents lectures, and networks the office at events, during workshops and in teaching.

Kepa Iturralde, Dr. Ing.

Is a research associate at the Chair of Building Realization and Robotics at Technical University of Munich (TUM). He is focused on introducing prefabricated modules and developing robotic, automation and digital manufacturing technology into building renovation.

Stefanie Kliemt, Dr.

Studied Applied Science at the TU Bergakademie Freiberg. From 2010 to 2014, Research Associate at the Helmholtz Centre for Environmental Research in Leipzig. In 2015, employed as a Research Assistant at the Center of Molecular Bioengineering TU Dresden; development and direction of the technology platform "Molecular Analysis". In 2018, doctorate in Biochemistry: "Qualitative and quantitative analysis of mediator proteins in bone wound healing processes". Since 2016, Project Engineer and since 2018 Authorised Officer at IPN Laborprojekt GmbH.

Anouk Kuitenbrouwer, Partner KCAP

Architect and urban designer, joined KCAP in 2006 and became partner in 2018. Working on a large range of architecture and urban planning projects in Switzerland, Germany and across Europe, and since 2016 also in South East Asia, Anouk has gained profound experience and has significantly contributed to the development of KCAP's Swiss office. Her expertise is the guiding of multidisciplinary design teams in the fields of urban transformations, station area developments, urban developments at airports, innovation districts and strategic masterplanning. Research is integral of Anouk's work and she is frequently invited for teaching assignments and as an expert for knowledge workshops, conferences and juries.

Thomas Linner, Dr.-Ing.

is a senior scientist and lecturer in building realization and robotics at Technical University of Munich (TUM), and a Guest Associate Professor at the Department of System Design Engineering at Keio University, Japan. Thomas Linner serves as Vice President of the International Association for Automation and Robotics in Construction (IAARC).

Katharina Hölzl

ist Informationsdesignerin mit Abschluss an der Hochschule der Medien Stuttgart und dem FH Joanneum Graz. Sie beschäftigt sich im buero bauer, Gesellschaft für Orientierung und Identität mbH, mit Ausstellungsdesign und Orientierungsplanung, hält Vorträge und vernetzt das Büro auf Veranstaltungen, in Workshops & in Lehrtätigkeit.

Kepa Iturralde, Dr. Ing.

Kepa Iturralde ist wissenschaftlicher Mitarbeiter am Lehrstuhl für Baurealisierung und Baurobotik Robotik an der Technischen Universität München (TUM). Sein Fokus liegt auf der Einführung von vorgefertigten Modulen und der Entwicklung von Roboter-, Automatisierungs- und digitaler Fertigungstechnologie in der Gebäudesanierung.

Stefanie Kliemt, Dr.

studierte Angewandte Naturwissenschaft an der TU Bergakademie Freiberg. Von 2010 bis 2014 Wissenschaftliche Mitarbeiterin am Helmholtz-Zentrum für Umweltforschung Leipzig. 2015 Research Assistent am Zentrum für Innovationskompetenz B-Cube der TU Dresden; Aufbau und Leitung der Technologieplattform "Molecular Analysis". 2018 Promotion im Fachgebiet Biochemie „Qualitative and quantitative analysis of mediator proteins in bone wound healing processes". Seit 2016 Projektingenieur und seit 2018 Prokuristin der IPN Laborprojekt GmbH.

Anouk Kuitenbrouwer, Partner KCAP

Architektin und Stadtplanerin, arbeitet seit 2006 bei KCAP und ist seit 2018 Partner. Sie hat durch Ihre Arbeit an einer grossen Anzahl von Architektur- und Stadtplanungsprojekten in der Schweiz, in Europa und seit 2016 in Südostasien, weitreichende Erfahrungen aufgebaut sowie maßgeblich zum Aufbau des Schweizer Büros von KCAP beigetragen. Ihre Expertise ist die Leitung multi-disziplinärer Entwurfsteams mit Fokus auf städtebauliche Transformationsprojekte, Bahnhofsarealentwicklungen, Stadtentwicklungen an Flughäfen, Innovationsquartiere und strategische Masterplanungen. Forschung ist ein wesentlicher Bestandteil ihrer Arbeit und sie wird regelmässig zu Lehraufträgen und als Expertin zu Workshops, Konferenzen und Jurys eingeladen.

Thomas Linner, Dr.-Ing.

ist Senior Wissenschaftler und Dozent für Baurealisierung und Baurobotik an der Technischen Universität München (TUM) und Gastprofessor am Department of System Design Engineering der Keio University, Japan. Thomas Linner ist Vizepräsident der International Association for Automation and Robotics in Construction (IAARC). Im November 2019 erhielt er den CEN-CENELEC Standards + Innovation Award 2019, im Januar 2021 wurde er vom DIN in dessen Präsidium berufen. Dr. Linner ist Geschäftsführer der CREDO Robotics GmbH.

In November 2019, he received the CEN-CENELEC Standards + Innovation Award 2019, and in January 2021 he was appointed by DIN to its presidential committee. Dr. Linner is the managing director of CREDO Robotics GmbH.

Séverine Marguin, Dr.

Sociologist, Research Associate (postdoc) and Director of the method lab in special research field 1265 "Re-Figuration of Spaces" at the Technische Universität Berlin. Since her doctorate on artist collectives in Paris and Berlin, she has worked in the excellence cluster Bild Wissen Gestaltung, an interdisciplinary lab at the Humboldt-Universität zu Berlin in the research project ArchitekturenExperimente. Her current work focuses on spatial and architectural research, science studies, and experimental and visual methods.

Stefanie Matthys

Studied Architecture at the RWTH Aachen. She worked in Paris at Odile Decq and Brunet Saunier Architecture, before becoming a Research Associate in 2009 at the Technische Universität Berlin, Chair of "Designing Hospitals and Healthcare Buildings". In 2014, she joined Nickl & Partner Architekten AG, becoming the Managing Director of the European Network Architecture for Health in 2017.

Magnus Nickl

Graduated in Architecture at the ETH Zurich. During his three-year research period in Singapore, he managed urban development projects in Singapore, Malaysia and Indonesia. In early 2019, he joined the Board of Nickl & Partner Architekten AG. He is also Managing Director of Nickl & Partner Architects Asia LTD and Nickl & Partner Architekten Schweiz AG, where he is supervising construction of the new D-BSSE laboratory building. A further focus of his work lies in the development of mobile and modular buildings in the health sector.

Jörg Rainer Noennig, Prof. Dr.-Ing.

Professor of Digital City Science at the Hafencity Universität Hamburg and Director of the WISSENSARCHITEKTUR Laboratory of Knowledge Architecture at the TU Dresden. 1998 to 2001, practicing architect in Tokyo, employed at Arata Isozaki & Associates, among others. From 2001, Research Associate at the TU Dresden, where he was appointed Junior Professor of Knowledge Architecture in 2009. Has taught at various international universities and authored numerous publications. He and his teams have received various prizes and awards, including the Ralf Dahrendorf Prize for Research in the European Research Area (2021).

Séverine Marguin, Dr.

ist Soziologin. Sie ist wissenschaftliche Mitarbeiterin (Postdoc) und Leiterin des Methodenlabs im Sonderforschungsbereich 1265 "Re-Figuration von Räumen" der Technischen Universität Berlin. Nach ihrer Promotion über Künstlerkollektive in Paris und Berlin arbeitete sie am Exzellenzcluster Bild Wissen Gestaltung, ein interdisziplinäres Labor der Humboldt-Universität zu Berlin im Forschungsprojekt ArchitekturenExperimente. Ihre aktuellen Arbeitsschwerpunkte sind Raum- und Architekturforschung, Wissenschaftsforschung, experimentelle und visuelle Methoden.

Stefanie Matthys

studierte Architektur an der RWTH Aachen. Sie arbeitete in Paris bei Odile Decq und Brunet Saunier Architecture, bevor sie 2009 wissenschaftliche Mitarbeiterin an der Technischen Universität Berlin im Fachgebiet „Entwerfen von Krankenhäusern und Bauten des Gesundheitswesens" wurde. 2014 trat sie in die Nickl & Partner Architekten AG ein und übernahm 2017 die Geschäftsführung des European Network Architecture for Health.

Magnus Nickl

schloss sein Architekturstudium an der Eidgenössischen Technischen Hochschule (ETH) Zürich ab. Während eines dreijährigen Forschungsaufenthaltes in Singapur führte er städtische Entwicklungsprojekte in Singapur, Malaysia und Indonesien durch. Anfang 2019 trat er als Vorstand in die Nickl & Partner Architekten AG ein. Er ist zudem Geschäftsführer der Nickl & Partner Architects Asia LTD und der Nickl & Partner Architekten Schweiz AG. Dort beaufsichtigte er den Neubau des Forschungs- und Laborgebäudes D-BSSE. Ein weiterer Schwerpunkt seiner Arbeit liegt in der Entwicklung mobiler und modularer Gesundheitsbauten.

Jörg Rainer Noennig, Prof. Dr.-Ing.

ist Professor für Digital City Science an der Hafencity Universität Hamburg und Leiter des WISSENSARCHITEKTUR Laboratory of Knowledge Architecture an der TU Dresden. Zwischen 1998 und 2001 praktizierte er als Architekt in Tokio, unter anderem bei Arata Isozaki & Associates. Ab 2001 war er wissenschaftlicher Mitarbeiter an der TU Dresden, wo er 2009 zum Junior Professor für Wissensarchitektur ernannt wurde. Er lehrte an verschiedenen internationalen Universitäten und ist Autor zahlreicher wissenschaftlicher Arbeiten. Jörg Rainer Noennig und seine Teams erhielten verschiedene Preise und Auszeichnungen, unter anderem den Ralf-Dahrendorf-Preis für Forschung im Europäischen Forschungsraum (2021).

Peter Pfab, Prof.

Studied Architecture at the Technische Universität München and initially employed at the architectural office Franz Kießling. In 1981, employed at the Bavarian State Building Administration, remaining there in various positions until 2017, most recently as Under Secretary. From 1990 to 2017, responsible for university and research buildings in Bavaria. Initially Lecturer and later Honorary Professor of University and Research Construction at the Technische Universität München. Lecturer, expert jury member and, since 2017, consultant.

Susanne Pohl

Studied Chemical Engineering and Environmental Technology at the Fachhochschule für Technik und Wirtschaft in Dresden. Since 2003, Planning Engineer for laboratory systems at IPN Laborprojekt GmbH Dresden, where she became its Authorised Officer in 2004, Managing Director in 2007 and sole Partner in 2008. In 2015, qualification as Expert for Sustainable Building in accordance with the BNB. Expert consulting (assessment of requirements, feasibility studies), planning and construction of research buildings, as well as the refurbishment and conversion of laboratory buildings throughout Germany.

Henrike Rabe

Architect and Building Manager at Berliner Immobilienmanagement GmbH. Studied Architecture in Berlin and Toulouse. Planner at Brisac Gonzalez (London) and Kazuhiro Kojima + Kazuko Akamatsu / CAt (Tokyo), planning libraries, universities, schools and museums. Research on the spaces and practices of science in an interdisciplinary lab at the HU Berlin (2012–2018), the excellence cluster Bild Wissen Gestaltung.

Marc Schmailzl

Research associate and PhD candidate at the Chair of Building Realization and Robotics at Technical University of Munich (TUM). He holds a Master of Architecture degree from the Technical University of Munich (with an exchange year at the Tongji University of Shanghai). Previously worked for several architecture offices and has expertise in the fields of architecture, graphic design, informatics, and robotics.

Friedrich Schmidgall

Interaction designer, heads the Open Lab and acts as a consultant for interdisciplinarity at the Einstein Center Digital Future at the Technical University Berlin. Studied Industrial

Peter Pfab, Prof.

studierte Architektur an der Technischen Universität München und arbeitete zunächst im Architekturbüro Franz Kießling. 1981 trat er in die Staatsbauverwaltung Bayern ein und war dort bis 2017 in verschiedenen Positionen, zuletzt als Ministerialrat, tätig. Von 1990 bis 2017 verantwortete er den Hochschul- und Forschungsbau in Bayern. An der Technischen Universität München war er zunächst Lehrbeauftragter, später Honorarprofessor für Hochschul- und Forschungsbau. Peter Pfab engagiert sich als Vortragender und Fachpreisrichter und ist seit 2017 beratend tätig.

Susanne Pohl

studierte Chemieingenieurwesen und Umwelttechnik an der Fachhochschule für Technik und Wirtschaft in Dresden. Seit 2003 Planungsingenieur für Labortechnische Anlagen bei der IPN Laborprojekt GmbH Dresden. 2004 wurde sie Prokuristin, 2007 Geschäftsführerin und seit 2008 alleinige Gesellschafterin des Unternehmens. 2015 Qualifizierung zur Sachverständigen für Nachhaltiges Bauen nach BNB. Fachliche Beratung (Bedarfsermittlung und Machbarkeitsstudien), Planung und Errichtung von Forschungsneubauten sowie Sanierungen und Umbauten von Laborgebäuden bundesweit.

Henrike Rabe

ist Architektin und Baumanagerin bei der Berliner Immobilienmanagement GmbH. Sie hat in Berlin und Toulouse Architektur studiert und bei Brisac Gonzalez (London) und bei Kazuhiro Kojima + Kazuko Akamatsu/ CAt (Tokio) u.a. Bibliotheken, Universitäten, Schulen und Museen geplant. Am Exzellenzcluster Bild Wissen Gestaltung, ein interdisziplinäres Labor (2012–2018) der HU Berlin, hat sie empirisch und historisch zu den Räumen und Praktiken des Wissens geforscht.

Marc Schmailzl

Marc Schmailzl ist wissenschaftlicher Mitarbeiter und Doktorand am Lehrstuhl für Baurealisierung und Baurobotik an der Technischen Universität München (TUM). Er hat einen Master in Architektur von der Technischen Universität München (mit einem Austauschjahr an der Tongji University in Shanghai). Zuvor war er für mehrere Architekturbüros tätig und verfügt über Expertise in den Bereichen Architektur, Grafikdesign, Informatik und Robotik.

Friedrich Schmidgall

ist Interaction Designer und Leiter des Open Lab sowie Berater für Interdisziplinarität am Einstein Center Digital Future der Technischen Universität Berlin. Er studierte Industriedesign in Saarbrücken und Interaction Design an der Weißensee Kunsthochschule Berlin. Innerhalb des Projekts ArchitecturesExperiments des Exzellenzclusters Image Knowledge Gestaltung der Humboldt-Universität in Berlin erforschte er den Einfluss physischer und digitaler Konfigurationen auf interdisziplinäre Arbeit.

Design in Saarbrücken and Interaction Design at Weißensee Kunsthochschule Berlin. Explored the influence of physical and digital spatial configurations on interdisciplinary work within the project ArchitecturesExperiments at the Cluster of Excellence Image Knowledge Gestaltung of the Humboldt-Universität in Berlin. Co-founder of ARCHIEXP, a studio for interdisciplinary spatial research and design.

Lukas Semmler

After completing his training as a carpenter, studied Architecture at the Fachhochschule Brugg-Windisch. Several years' professional experience in structural engineering. In 1996, at the age of 31, became a Laboratory Planner at F. Hoffmann-La Roche AG in Basel. During the subsequent 25 years at Roche, he shaped its field of laboratories in numerous projects, developing the "Roche Laboratory Guidelines" and "Defined Flexibility", as well as new planning strategies such as "Planning by Omitting".

Werner Sobek, Prof. Dr. Dr. E.h. Dr. h.c.

Architect and consulting engineer. Professor at the Institute for Lightweight Structures and Conceptual Design (ILEK) of the University of Stuttgart. From 2017 to 2020 Chairman of the DFG Collaborative Research Centre SFB 1244 on "Adaptive Building Skins and Structures". Werner Sobek initiated and headed several non-profit initiatives such as the aed e.V.

Florian Starz

Trained as an audio engineer, before studying Metal Construction at the Berufsakademie Mosbach Metallbau. Since 2007, Project Manager at Werner Sobek in the field of façade planning. Since 2020, Team Leader in the Façade Division. His fields of expertise include green façades and finely-structured metal structures.

Andreas Traube

Studied Mechanical Engineering at the University of Stuttgart and began his professional career at Fraunhofer IPA, quickly focusing on laboratory automation. Since 2012, Head of the interdisciplinary Department of Laboratory Automation and Biomanufacturing Engineering. As one of the inventors of the I-DOT technology, he co-founded Dispendix in 2016. His focuses of expertise lie in flexible modular automation and digitising systems with adapted processes for efficient, sustainable laboratories.

Lukas Semmler

studierte nach dem Abschluss der Schreinerausbildung Architektur an der Fachhochschule Brugg-Windisch. Nach einigen Jahren Berufserfahrung im Hochbau durfte er 1996 als 31-Jähriger in die Laborplanung bei der F. Hoffmann-La Roche AG in Basel einsteigen. In den nun 25 Jahren bei Roche konnte er die Entwicklung des Laborfachbereiches mit zahlreichen Projekten, der „Laborrichtlinie Roche" und „Definierter Flexibilität" mitgestalten und neue Planungswege wie „Planung durch Weglassen" entwickeln.

Werner Sobek, Prof. Dr. Dr. E.h. Dr. h.c.

ist Architekt und beratender Ingenieur. Er ist Professor am Institut für Leichtbau Entwerfen und Konstruieren (ILEK) der Universität Stuttgart und Initiator des Sonderforschungsbereichs SFB 1244 über „Adaptive Hüllen und Strukturen für die gebaute Umwelt von morgen". Werner Sobek ist darüber hinaus Gründer und Ehrenpräsident mehrerer gemeinnütziger Initiativen wie z.B. dem aed e.V. 2022 wurde er von der Zeitschrift Cicero als einziger Architekt und Ingenieur in die Liste der 500 wichtigsten deutschsprachigen Intellektuellen aufgenommen.

Florian Starz

Nach einer Ausbildung zum Audio Engineer studierte Florian Starz an der Berufsakademie Mosbach Metallbau. Seit 2007 ist er bei Werner Sobek als Projektleiter im Bereich der Fassadenplanung tätig. Seit 2020 ist Florian Starz auch Teamleiter im Bereich Fassade. Zu seinen Spezialgebieten gehören begrünte Fassaden und filigrane Metallkonstruktionen.

Andreas Traube

Andreas Traube studierte Maschinenbau an der Universität Stuttgart und begann seine Fachkarriere ab 2005 am Fraunhofer IPA und fand dort den frühen Einstieg in die Laborautomatisierung. Dort leitet er seit 2012 die interdisziplinäre Abteilung für Laborautomatisierung und Bioproduktionstechnik. Als einer der Erfinder die I-DOT-Technologie war er 2016 Mitgründer der Dispendix. Fachliche Schwerpunkte sind flexible modulare Automatisierungs- und Digitalisierungstechnik mit angepassten Prozessabläufen für effiziente und nachhaltige Labors.

087
Deutsches Zentrum für Neurodegenerative Erkrankungen in Bonn, wulf architekten gmbh, interior view | photography by Steffen Vogt, courtesy of wulf architekten gmbh

088–093
Laboratory / research building Roche | © Roche: Analytikgebäude, Projektleitung Sabine Grozinger / Roche

094–099
Planung durch Weglassen, Lukas Semmler | Visualisierung © Bruno Ruch / MAS Digitales Bauen FHNW

100
Laboratory / research building Roche | © Roche: Analytikgebäude, Projektleitung Sabine Grozinger / Roche

101–102
Terence Donelly Centre for Cellular and Biomolecular Research, Behnisch Architekten, exterior view | photography by Tom Arban, courtesy of Behnisch Architekten

103
Terence Donelly Centre for Cellular and Biomolecular Research, Behnisch Architekten, section | © Behnisch Architekten

104
Terence Donelly Centre for Cellular and Biomolecular Research, Behnisch Architekten, conservatory | photography by Tom Arban, courtesy of Behnisch Architekten

105–108
Harvard University Science and Engineering Complex, Behnisch Architekten, drawings | © Behnisch Architekten

109
Harvard University Science and Engineering Complex, Behnisch Architekten, section laboratory | photography by Brad Feinknopf, courtesy of Behnisch Architekten

110–112
Max-Planck-Institut für medizinische Forschung, Behnisch Architekten, drawings | © Behnisch Architekten

113
Max-Planck-Institut für medizinische Forschung, Behnisch Architekten, competition presentation | © Behnisch Architekten

118
Zentrum für Virtuelles Engineering ZVE, Fraunhofer-Institut, UNStudio | photography by Christian Richters, courtesy of UNStudio

119
Novartis research building, David Chipperfield Architects | photography by Ute Zscharnt, for David Chipperfield Architects

120
Tangen Polytechnic, 3XN | photography by Adam Mørk, courtesy of 3XN

122
Genzyme Center, Behnisch Architekten | photography by Anton Grassl, courtesy of Behnisch Architekten

123
BSS research building, Nickl & Partner Architekten | © Achim Birnbaum

124
ISMO Institut des Sciences Moléculaires d'Orsay, KAAN Architecten | photography by Fernando Guerra FG+SG, courtesy of KAAN Architecten

127
Experimental zone I © Fabian Scholz

128–131
Cartography of interactions, experimental settings I © Dimitra Megas and © Fabian Scholz

132
Connectivity analyses, experimental setting 16 I © Theodora Georgopoulou and © Henrike Rabe

133
ISMO, KAAN Architecten | photography by Fernando Guerra FG+SG, courtesy of KAAN Architecten

134
Masdar Institute, Foster + Partners Design Team, façade exterior view | photography by Nigel Young / Foster + Partners

135
Masdar Institute, Foster + Partners Design Team, façade detail exterior view | photography by Roland Halbe, courtesy of Foster + Partners

136
Masdar Institute, Foster + Partners Design Team, façade detail exterior view | photography by Nigel Young / Foster + Partners

137
HUB de l'énergie Amiens, Nickl & Partner Architekten | © Philippe Ruault

138
IBS² Grenoble, Nickl & Partner Architekten | photography by Ivan Lukasevic

141–142
Institut Imagine, Atelier Jean Nouvel & Valero Gadan Architectes | photography by Patrick H. Muller, courtesy of Ateliers Jean Nouvel & Valero Gadan Architectes

143–145
Center for Stroke and Dementia Research, Nickl & Partner Architekten | © Stefan Müller-Naumann

148
CIB – Biomedical Research Centre, Vaillo Irigaray, façade exterior view | photography by Rubén Perez Bescós, courtesy of Vaillo Irigaray

149
CIB – Biomedical Research Centre, Vaillo Irigaray, façade section | Ed. Nickl & Partner Architekten, © Vaillo Irigaray

150
CIB – Biomedical Research Centre, Vaillo Irigaray, detail façade exterior view | photography by Rubén Perez Bescós, courtesy of Vaillo Irigaray

155
Institute for Microbiology and Virology, Tübingen, Nickl & Partner Architekten | © Stefan Müller-Naumann

156–157
AGORA Pôle de Recherche sur le Cancer, Behnisch Architekten | photography by David Matthiessen, courtesy of Behnisch Architekten

158
Institut des Sciences Moléculaires d'Orsay, KAAN Architecten | photography by Fernando Guerra FG+SG, courtesy of KAAN Architecten

159
Laboratories for the Faculty of Mechanical Engineering | photography by Moshe Gross, courtesy of Zvi Hecker Architects

160
Research Center ICTA-ICP UAB, Harquitectes, dataAE | photography by Adrià Goula

163
Institute for Physics, Humbolt Universität Berlin, Augustin Frank Architekten | photography by Simon Menges

164
ZSW – Zentrum für Sonnenenergie- und Wasserstoff-Forschung Baden-Württemberg | photography by Jens Willebrand, courtesy of Henning Larsen

165
Textile skin | Ed. LZ Studio, © ILEK

166
Unser Neues Haus 2.0 | photography by Wolfgang Thaler, courtesy of Werner Sobek and Chaix & Morel

167
Kö-Bogen II, exterior view | photography by HGEsch, courtesy of ingenhoven architects and Werner Sobeck

169
Al Wasl Tower, exterior visualisation | © Methanoia and © UNStudio and © Werner Sobeck

170
Al Wasl Tower, façade visualisation | © UNStudio and © Werner Sobeck

171
Adaptive Demonstrator Tower at the University of Stuttgart (ILEK) | photography by René Müller, courtesy of Werner Sobeck

172
Textile skin | © ILEK

180–181
Center for Stroke and Dementia Research, Nickl & Partner Architekten | © Stefan Müller-Naumann

188
Control system, GMP lab, BSS research building | @ Nickl & Partner Architekten

189–190
Security zone, GMP lab, BSS research building, Nickl & Partner Architekten | © Achim Birnbaum

194–196
HIT Heidelberg, Nickl & Partner Architekten | © Johannes Vogt

202
Hotel-like test subject area, CRC Hanover, Nickl & Partner Architekten | © Stefan Müller-Naumann

203
Aquaria at the animal testing centre | © Stefan Müller-Naumann

204–209
Intuitive signages | © buero bauer

211
HCU Digital City Science | photography by Julia Sievert

212–214
The cognitive cockpit | © Prof. Dr.-Ing. Jörg Rainer Noennig

215–217
Translated Geometries, Institute for Advanced Architecture of Catalonia | © Research team: Efilena Baseta, Ece Tankal, Ramin Shambayati

218–223
Laboratories of the future | © Fraunhofer IPA

224
The Walking City on the Ocean, exterior perspective, Ron Herron | © Ron Herron and © New York, Museum of Modern Art (MoMA), Cut-and-pasted printed and photographic papers and graphite, covered with polymer sheet, 11 1/2 × 17' (29.2 × 43.2 cm), Gift of The Howard Gilman Foundation, Acc. n.: 1203.2000, © 2021, Digital image, The Museum of Modern Art, New York / Scala, Florence

225
Development of a cable-driven panel installation robot | © Project HEPHAESTUS, received funding from the European Union's H2020 Programme (H2020 2014-2020) under Grant Agreement Number 7325137

226
Development of a façade-processing robot | © Project for the CIC, commissioned by the Construction Industry Council Hong Kong

227
Gantry concrete 3D-printer | © PERI, Weissenhorn, Germany

228
Hadrian X, bricklaying robot | © Copyright 2021 FBR Limited

229
Sketch, future perspective | © Prof. Dr.-Ing. Thomas Bock Editors

230
Christine and Hans Nickl | © Andreas Nestle

Imprint

The Deutsche Nationalbibliothek lists this publication in the Deutsche Nationalbibliografie; detailed bibliographic data are available on the Internet at http://dnb.dnb.de

ISBN 978-3-03768-258-6
© 2022 by Braun Publishing AG
www.braun-publishing.ch

1st edition 2022

Coordination & content editing | Stefanie Matthys
Drawings, processing of drawings &
coordination of images | Marc Schmailzl
Graphics (unless otherwise indicated) | Stefanie Attenberger
Co-processing of drawings | Michael Wolfer
Graphic concept & layout | www.studio-lz.de
Agnes Essig, Lisa Zech
German to English translation | Benjamin Liebelt
English to German translation (Ch. 1.1, 5.1, 5.5) | Jens Wicher
Proofreading | Friederike Christoph